The Reflective Age

The Reflective Age

Nostalgia at the End of History

Zachary Griffith

RUTGERS UNIVERSITY PRESS
NEW BRUNSWICK, CAMDEN, AND NEWARK, NEW JERSEY
LONDON AND OXFORD

Rutgers University Press is a department of Rutgers, The State University of New Jersey, one of the leading public research universities in the nation. By publishing worldwide, it furthers the University's mission of dedication to excellence in teaching, scholarship, research, and clinical care.

978-1-9788-4379-0 (cloth)
978-1-9788-4378-3 (paper)
978-1-9788-4380-6 (epub)

Cataloging-in-publication data is available from the Library of Congress.
LCCN 2025012711

A British Cataloging-in-Publication record for this book is available from the British Library.

∞ The paper used in this publication meets the requirements of the American National Standard for Information Sciences—Permanence of Paper for Printed Library Materials, ANSI Z39.48-1992.

rutgersuniversitypress.org

For Cheyenne and Zoe

Contents

Introduction 1

1 *Ready Player One*, Nostalgia, and Recognition 22

2 *Stranger Things*, Nostalgia, and Aesthetics 56

3 *Twin Peaks: The Return*, Nostalgia, and Fantasies of Repetition 80

4 *Hillbilly Elegy*, Nostalgia, and Right-Wing Melodrama 104

Conclusion: Nostalgia *After* the End of History? 147

Acknowledgments 153
Notes 155
Works Cited 163
Index 171

The Reflective Age

Introduction

In the title track of Arcade Fire's 2013 album *Reflektor*, singer Win Butler narrates being caught within what can be described as a surreal hall of mirrors, a place characterized by disorientation and misdirection, situated within what he calls "the reflective age." He finds himself "trapped," he tells us in the opening line, "in a prison, a prism of light" and details a search for a way to enter an unknown but desired space through a "connector," only to realize in the chorus that the path forward was simply a "reflektor": "I thought I found a way to enter / but it was just a reflektor / I thought I found the connector / but it was just a reflektor." Unable to make it out by the close of the song, Butler (echoing Jean Baudrillard) descends into a state of frenzy, repeating "just a reflection of a reflection of a reflection of a reflection." The outro interpolates this line with the phrase "thought you would bring me to the resurrector, turns out it was just a reflektor."

The conditions Butler describes serve as a cogent meditation on the nature of twenty-first-century American culture, particularly its ever-increasing obsession with the past. While in other parts of the song, Butler's attention turns inward as he considers the growing disconnect between himself and his wife (bandmate Régine Chassagne), "Reflektor" nonetheless provides a useful heuristic for interrogating the textures of what Simon Reynolds has termed "retromania," and the song's characterization of the present as "the reflective age" provides the central framing for this book.

The most noteworthy element of this period's engagement with the past is the nostalgia boom in media, which largely began with retro and revivalist musical acts in the mid- to late 2000s but went into overdrive in the 2010s and beyond with shows like *Stranger Things* as well as a slew of film and television remakes and reboots that accompanied a broader reincorporation of 1980s, 1990s, and now early-2000s aesthetics into popular style ranging from fashion to graphic design. What we've seen in this period is not simply a resurgence of nostalgic longing, of a desire to go back to the good old days of one's childhood or adolescence, of what we might call experiential nostalgia—that is, nostalgia for one's lived experience (or the perception thereof)—but rather an explosion of what Ryan Lizardi has called mediated nostalgia—nostalgia manifest both for and through media such as film, television, and music. What this ultimately represents is a reordering of the distinction Paul Grainge makes between nostalgic mood (the structure of feeling or affective and experiential discourse) and nostalgic mode (the commodified style or practice manifest in cultural productions) in which the nostalgic mode has come to dominate to such a degree that the mood has become utterly subordinated to it—a matter of style over substance.

"Reflektor" is important here because it helps crystallize several key differences in experiential nostalgia and mediated nostalgia that have developed since the turn of the century, and it serves to illustrate the conditions that help define the period. Critically, analysis of nostalgia is often linked to Walter Benjamin's reading of Paul Klee's *Angelus Novus* as the Angel of History, the backward glancing spectator "at the threshold of past and future" (Boym 29), blown forward by the winds of progress. For Benjamin, the drawing serves as a metaphor for the struggle to comprehend the past as we are hurled blindly into the future. As Svetlana Boym and others have pointed out, however, his reading is a distinctly modernist interpretation of the forces of history and their cultural significance, and we should always remember to historicize Benjamin's insights. To this end, Zygmunt Bauman has argued that, while the image remains powerful, the conditions of modernity that Benjamin found within it no longer adequately reflect the present, and we might conjure a very different reading of Klee's work if we were to reexamine it today: "Were we to look closely at Klee's drawing almost a century after Benjamin put on record his unfathomably profound and indeed incomparable insight . . . what might strike the viewer most is the Angel changing direction—the Angel of History caught in the midst of a U-turn: his face turning from the past to the future, his wings being pushed backwards by the storm blowing this time from the imagined, anticipated and feared in advance Hell of the future towards the Paradise of the past" (*Retrotopia* 2). Bauman's reading is insightful for several reasons, but most notably because it pinpoints a crucial shift in the relationship between past, present, and future from the time of Benjamin's writing. In the years that have followed, Bauman explains, utopian aspirations have been replaced by what he terms "retrotopia": "visions located in the lost/stolen/abandoned but undead past, instead of being tied to the not-yet-unborn and so inexistent future." The major sociopolitical forces of the latter twentieth century in the West, he contends, including especially the "privatization/individualization of the idea of 'progress' and of the pursuit of life's improvements" (*Retrotopia* 5), have led to uncertain and often frightening visions of the future, which served to delegitimize utopian thinking. Its replacement is a backward-glancing cultural narrative, which seeks a return to prior states and structures in order to undo, often unconsciously, the damages of neoliberalism. Bauman's revision, more than anything, represents an important call to reconsider the present's relationship to the past, and rightly recognizes the power of Benjamin's Angel to do so.

Because Bauman's reinterpretation misses the significance of mediated visions of the past in the twenty-first century's cultural landscape, however, his vision of the Angel remains imprecise. In an age dominated by mediated nostalgia, by a retrograde media landscape, and by visions of the past that are always already filtered by the authorizing frame of television and film (in particular), the Angel of History in the twenty-first century isn't captured by the winds of progress, as Benjamin posited over a century ago that it would be, nor is it, as Bauman contends, simply being blown from the horrors of the future toward the paradise of the past. Instead, like Butler in "Reflektor," it is caught in a hall of mirrors: trapped in a prism that, no matter where it looks, refracts its gaze elsewhere. Mediation imprisons the Angel of History so that, as it gazes forward, it is redirected back. A filtered misdirection that refracts the real, rather than reproducing it, replaces Benjamin's unimpeded vision with an inverted and distorted mirror image. The Angel in a hall of mirrors also finds itself unable to escape the image, as the view produced by the mirror is a function of the angle of address—determined, in other words, by the vantage of the present—and therefore its positionality determines what it is able to see. Likewise, the Angel cannot remove itself from the image; it is always present, and its presence always filters, even obscures, what's behind. Without a clear sense of direction and relationality, the Angel in this hall of mirrors is disoriented, often unable to tell front from back, past from future, caught in a perpetual present characterized by disarray, and unable to cleanly determine the path forward that is, at every turn, obscured by a series of misdirections. The images produced in this context cannot truly be called reflection, but are rather a reflektion—a false promise, a mediated and therefore aestheticized (re)production that distorts through its mechanism of production. Disoriented, the Angel is caught in stasis, unable to move forward or backward coherently. This is the popular cultural condition that prevailed in the 2010s.

How did such a predicament arise? As many have pointed out, one way to think about the causes of the retrograde twenty-first century is to situate it within the sociopolitical context of neoliberalism, which went into overdrive in the late twentieth century, producing a radical shift in the way that we think about the future—or, at least, rewrote the terms on which visions of the future attain cogency. Bauman, for instance, has argued that neoliberalism's replacement of ideals of communal social progress with privatization and an emphasis on individuality has led to frightening visions of the future, which have left us unable to imagine that better times lie ahead:

> [Neoliberalism] prompted the pendulums of the public mindset and mentality to perform a u-turn: from investing public hopes of improvement in the uncertain and ever-too-obviously un-trustworthy future, to re-investing them in the vaguely remembered past, valued for its assumed stability and so trustworthiness. With such a U-turn happening the future is transformed from the natural habitat of hopes and rightful expectations into the site of nightmares: horrors of losing your job together with its attached social standing, of having your home together with the rest of life's goods and chattels 'repossessed,' of helplessly watching your children sliding down the well-being-cum-prestige slope and your own laboriously learned and memorized skills stripped of whatever has been left of their market value. The road to future turns looks uncannily as a trail of corruption and degeneration. Perhaps the road back, to the past, won't miss the chance of turning into a trail of cleansing from the damages committed by futures, whenever they turned into a present? (*Retrotopia* 5)

Mark Fisher, too, has written extensively about what he calls "capitalist realism: the widespread sense that not only is capitalism the only viable political and economic system, but also that it is now impossible even to imagine a coherent alternative to it" (*Capitalist Realism* 2), which has subsequently produced an inability to imagine a better future, one that hasn't been ravaged by the neoliberal status quo. This concept describes a phenomenon that is the culmination of a series of developments in the latter half of the twentieth century, synthesizing the response to the conditions that arose out of the shift to post-Fordist economics in the late 1970s, austerity programs in the 1980s, the demise of the Soviet Union in the early 1990s, and the wholesale triumph of neoliberal politics heralded by each. Following these events, capitalist realism, by the mid- to late 2000s, had established itself as the predominant structure of feeling in much of the West. These forces, Fisher later argues in *Ghosts of My Life*, ultimately coalesced to produce "the slow cancellation of the future" (2), referring to the gradual loss of the modern progressive teleology that constructs the future as not just temporally but functionally, formally, and qualitatively different (and better) than the present. Along the same lines, Fredric Jameson once noted that "where everything now submits to the perpetual change of fashion and media image [. . .] nothing can change any longer" (*Seeds of Time* 18), and the result is a paradoxical continuity of instability, a regularity of rapid change that in turn destabilizes the boundary between present and future: a constantly changing present renders the duration of the "present" unclear and also makes the future unpredictable. Within these confines, a turn to the past seems like the only remedy.

As Boym has pointed out, nostalgia regularly appears as a significant cultural force in times of "accelerated rhythms of life and historical upheavals" (xiv), and these circumstances have undeniably defined the conditions of life in America following Reagan's radical reorganization of the economy in the 1980s and the Silicon Valley tech boom of the mid-1990s, both of which continued into the twenty-first century. However, what Fisher, Bauman, and Jameson point to is not purely the accelerated rhythms of life or historical upheaval—though both are undeniably true—but rather those forces combining within the context of a sociopolitical order that has fundamentally altered the way we conceive of the past and the future. In its reluctance to imagine a better future and its turn toward reproducing artifacts of the past, this cultural milieu reflects what Fisher identified as "the suspicion that the end has already come, the thought that it could well be the case that the future harbors only reiteration and re-permutation" (*Capitalist Realism* 3).

Fisher was, of course, not the first to notice these trends. In particular, the idea that the Western world was reaching, or had reached, some kind of terminal state had been discussed in some form or fashion for several decades by 2009—as Fisher himself put it, "This malaise, the feeling that there is nothing new, is itself nothing new" (*Capitalist Realism* 6). This notion finds its critical antecedent expressed most forcefully in Francis Fukuyama's concept of the end of history, first laid out in his 1989 article "The End of History?," and elaborated upon in his best-selling follow-up, *The End of History and The Last Man* in 1992.[1] In the time since, Fukuyama's thesis—that, following the collapse of the Soviet Union, Western liberal democracy had triumphed as the final development in human government—which has been both widely derided and significantly misunderstood,[2] remains profoundly influential. This was not, however, always the case, as Perry Anderson pointed out in 1992: "The most striking feature of the discussion which followed the publication of Fukuyama's essay was the virtual universality of the rejection which it met. For once, most of the Right, Centre and Left were united in their reaction. For different reasons, liberals, conservatives, social democrats, communists all expressed incredulity or abhorrence of Fukuyama's arguments" (284). The subsequent popularization of the phrase "the end of history" was driven not by the fact that it reflected what many were thinking, but by a remarkable prescience (or, as Louis Menand calls it, luck). Fukuyama, as Menand explains, "got out about six months ahead of the curve—his article appearing before the Velvet Revolution, in Czechoslovakia, and before the dismantling of the Berlin Wall, in November 1989. Fukuyama was betting on present trends continuing." In other words, his great success was in the realm of prediction rather than description; he was not, at least initially, describing a widely held belief. The fall of the Berlin Wall and the dissolution of the Soviet Union that followed shortly thereafter imbued Fukuyama's work with a prophetic quality; it seemed as if events had conspired to confirm his thesis. As Anderson put it, "There has rarely been a more striking rebondissement in the fortunes of an idea. Within a year, an arcane philosophical wisdom had become an exoteric image of the age, as Fukuyama's arguments sped around the media of the globe" (281). These developments, in other words, catapulted "the end of history" into public consciousness such that, with the publication of his book three years later, Fukuyama was now responding to a cultural milieu he had helped shape. The tentativeness of "The End of History?" (signaled in the article's title taking the form of a question) was thus replaced by an unmistakable triumphalism in *The End of History and the Last Man* as Fukuyama's thesis had come to reflect the dominant attitude in much of the West. Fukuyama's task in this new context was to provide proof for a vision of the world that had already taken hold—as a blurb from Charles Krauthammer on the back of the 2006 edition put it, "Until now, the triumph of the West was merely a fact. Fukuyama has given it a deep and highly original meaning."

Far from suggesting that the end of history meant that events would cease to occur, as many of his critics suggested, Fukuyama, building on the work of Hegel (and, more importantly, Alexandre Kojève's interpretation of Hegel[3]), instead proposed an end to "history understood as a single, coherent, evolutionary process" (*End of History* xii). Contra Marx, Fukuyama (a neoconservative political scientist once mentored by Allan Bloom) contended that the historical dialectic ended not in communism but in the already established liberal democratic order. In the absence of a viable alternative, and on the basis that it was supposedly free from contradictions and "completely satisfying to its citizens" (*End of History* 139), Fukuyama argued that Western liberal democracy, supported by a free-market capitalist economy, had emerged as the only rational—and thus final—ordering of human society, "the endpoint of mankind's ideological evolution" ("End of History?" 4). We could, he explained, improve our implementation of the system but not the system itself. As Margaret Thatcher famously put it, there was no alternative. Psychically, Fukuyama explained,

> We who live in stable, long-standing liberal democracies face an unusual situation. In our grandparents' time, many reasonable people could foresee a radiant socialist future in which private property and capitalism had been abolished, and in which politics itself was somehow overcome. Today, by contrast, we have trouble imagining a world that is radically better than our own, or a future that isn't essentially democratic and capitalist. Within that framework, of course, many things could be improved: we could house the homeless, guarantee opportunity for minorities and women, improve competitiveness, and create new jobs. . . . We can also imagine future worlds that are significantly worse than what we know, in which national, racial, or religious intolerance makes a comeback, or in which we are overwhelmed by war or environmental collapse. But we cannot picture to ourselves a world that is

> essentially different from the previous one, and at the same time better. Other, *less reflective ages* also thought of themselves as the best, but we arrive at this conclusion exhausted, as it were, from the pursuit of alternatives we felt had to be better than liberal democracy. (*End of History* 46; emphasis added)

"If we are at a point where we cannot imagine," Fukuyama concluded, "a world substantially different from our own, in which there is no apparent or obvious way in which the future will represent a fundamental improvement over our current order, then we must also take into consideration that History itself might be at an end" (51).

Regardless of his success in proving that History ends with liberal democracy,[4] Fukuyama's rendering of the end of history remains important in one key way: Although it drew skepticism from most critics, and recent events (in particular, the lasting impact of religious fundamentalism, the emergence of Donald Trump, the rise of right-wing populism globally, and the Russian invasion of Ukraine) have led Fukuyama to revisit his own diagnosis,[5] the end of history nonetheless expressed an attitude that would come to dominate the West's cultural unconscious in the years that followed. As Slavoj Žižek remarked in 2009, "It is easy to make fun of Fukuyama's notion of the 'End of History,' but most people today are Fukuyamean, accepting liberal-democratic neoliberal capitalism as the finally found formula of the best possible society" (*First as Tragedy* 88). Even in the face of the multitudinous crises before us in the twenty-first century, end-of-history thinking has given shape to the way that much of the world, and particularly the United States, conceived of their solutions. Indeed, though recent developments like Trump's re-election have begun to pose a significant challenge to the liberal democratic order, throughout most of the twenty-first century there was a remarkable consensus about the stability and overall validity of present systems, particularly among the country's political elite. Thus, while many use the moniker more narrowly to refer to the immediate aftermath of the collapse of the Soviet Union and the early part of the 1990s contemporaneous to Fukuayama's diagnosis, the premises that underwrite "the end of history" have remained operative beyond its initial moment of appearance. Indeed, though some might point to 9/11 as a key point of divergence from the posthistorical 1990s, and the early- to mid-2000s certainly saw significant shifts in the political and cultural environment of the United States (including, especially, the enactment of new laws and the emergence of a new kind of resistance to American geopolitical hegemony, both of which changed how the nation conceived of itself), these shifts—or, more specifically, the responses to these shifts—were underwritten by the same principles that Fukuyama initially described. The 2008 financial crisis was another point of potential rupture that, in the end, only served to reinforce the supremacy of the ideology of the end of history. In fact, one could argue that the true nature of the end of history (its resistance to change and preference for the management of decline and rearrangement of suffering—that, is, its dead-end teleology) only became recognizable once the recession and other potentially transformative crises emerged and either went unaddressed or were used to justify further entrenchment in the status quo—only as, in other words, the *ends* of the end of history became apparent. The Financial Crisis and Obama's response to it, in other words, marked the period beyond which stagnation and decline became standard, further highlighting a political regime's unwillingness, or inability, to respond accordingly. Crises occur (and recur), but for much of the twenty-first century the consensus has held that there are no structural, systemic solutions available. Less a period characterized by 1990s euphoric triumphalism, therefore, the end of history should be understood as a period marked by these responses (or lack thereof) to the novelties that arose in the years afterwards.[6]

Subsequently, nothing ever really ends at the end of history. The shifts that do occur have largely come in the form of short-term tweaks (surges vs. drawdowns, tax rate hikes vs. cuts) rather than wholesale alteration. Mainstream political (and, arguably, social) discourse in the posthistorical United States has, until very recently, more often been a debate between theories of management than between truly, structurally, different visions. What emerged, then, is a phenomenon Mike Davis has called a kind of "pathological presentism," in which "all calculations [are made] on the basis of short-term bottom-lines in order to allow the super-rich to consume all the good things of the earth within their lifetimes" ("Thanatos Triumphant"). Major problems, consequently, rarely get solved, just managed differently. "Few periods," as Jameson explained in 2003, "have proved as incapable of framing immediate alternatives for themselves" ("End of Temporality" 704). Even when, as of late, apparent threats to the global liberal democratic consensus emerge (such as Brexit in the UK, nascent fascist movements in the United States and Europe, and Putin's challenges to the postwar status quo[7]—the last of which was featured on the cover of *Time* magazine under the headline "The Return of History"[8]), their character is typically one of regression to an earlier system instead of progression toward something new: devolution rather than evolution. The end of history, then, is a period marked by, at best, a kind of weak incrementalism and, at worst, a desire for complete reversion to a prior form. Even in electoral politics, the debate is rarely over whether we *should* go back but, rather, over what time period we ought to revert to: In 2016, 2020, and 2024, for instance, Trump's "Make America Great Again" campaign promised a return to a mythical past where, as Wendy Brown put it, "families were happy, whole, and heterosexual, when women and minorities knew their place, when neighborhoods were orderly, secure, and homogeneous, when heroin was a black problem and terrorism was not inside the homeland, and when a hegemonic Christianity and whiteness constituted the manifest identity, power, and pride of the nation and the West (5)," while Biden 2020 sought to restore "the soul of the nation" via a return to the conditions of the pre-Trumpian paradise of the Obama era. In 2024, the Harris campaign briefly floated the slogan "We Are Not Going Back" as a rejection of Trumpian nostalgia, but ultimately abandoned this messaging in favor of Bidenesque status quo politics and nostalgia for disappearing bipartisanship that revolved around a very public embrace of polarizing figures from the Bush administration.

Several critics over the past three decades have noted that this sense of repetitiveness has plagued the West since the fall of the Berlin Wall. As early as 1991, Baudrillard claimed that the posthistorical world is not cyclical so much as recyclable; the West, he argued, is defined more than anything by its constant recycling of the leftovers of the twentieth century's major conflicts and ideologies, an endless procession of the reiteration of prior forms. "All the archaic, anachronistic forms," he explains, "are there ready to re-emerge, intact and timeless, like the viruses deep in the body. History has only wrenched itself from cyclical time to fall into the order of the recyclable" (*Illusion of the End* 27). Cyclical time, Baudrillard reminds us, conventionally denotes some kind of progress—or, at least, change—even if it is just a matter of moving from one (novel, albeit repetitive) structure to another. The end of history is, on the contrary, defined by its resistance to change of this sort. Instead, as Bauman argued in *Liquid Modernity*, the posthistorical West is, at least in terms of sociocultural composition, much more fluid, constantly reshaping itself into preestablished molds. Thus, while the larger political shape remains static, and its deleterious effects gradually seep into the social world, the public is left to recompose itself in response to a rapidly decaying sociopolitical landscape. Without a goal on the horizon, and in a "historical situation whose contours it does not know" (Berlant 225), the public turns to the forms of the past.

Paradoxically, as Baudrillard points out, this pattern of infinite recycling, where everything that fades is subject to a return, marks the end of history as a time of endlessness: "There is no end any longer, there will no longer be any end . . . history itself has become interminable. . . . Things are in a state which is literally definitive—neither finished, nor infinite, nor definite, but de-finitive that is, deprived of its end" (*Illusion of the End* 115, 120). Posthistorical occurrences are often marked as much by this lack of finality as anything else, and management of catastrophe, a form of endless deferral, is the predominant mode of operation: Wildfires are extinguished only to return in more devastating proportions; ice caps melt and sea levels rise year on year; a pandemic becomes endemic; a president loses an election, contests the results, immediately runs again, wins, and begins floating the idea of a third term. The end of history resists punctual moments and narrative closure. As Baudrillard explained, "It is as though history were rifling through its own dustbins and looking for redemption in the rubbish" (*Illusion of the End* 26).

Revision is, of course, endemic to both nostalgia and the posthistorical world, and nostalgia operates in cycles, with major upheavals in taste and style resolidifying every twenty or twenty-five years before melting away again, just as sociopolitical forms are continually (re)emerging and fading. Nostalgia prevails at the end of history precisely because of this compatibility. At the same time, nostalgia also occupies a tense position: Large-scale political change is relatively scarce at the end of history, but it also often seems as if things are changing at a greater pace than ever on the level of culture. Nostalgia is part of this trend, as it emphasizes superficial notions of change in the form of cultural shifts (sometimes produced by nostalgia waves themselves). Thus, nostalgia is simultaneously a reaction to the perpetual onslaught of aesthetic change and an effort to produce another aesthetic change through the inauguration of a new (old) regime—an exhausting cycle produced by an increasingly exhausted cultural landscape. The relationship between nostalgia and the end of history is thus more complex than it might first appear: On one hand, the conditions of the end of history provide the catalyst for expressions of nostalgic longing, dictating what is longed for; on the other hand, nostalgic expressions in media also (re)produce the political, social, and cultural values of the posthistorical world. The end of history, in other words, revises conventional nostalgia, remaking the concept in its own image, and nostalgia subsequently appears in forms that perpetuate the system whose conditions initially gave rise to it.

Posthistorical nostalgia thus shapes, and is shaped by, an overwhelmingly mediated culture that emphasizes particular expressions and objects of retrograde fascination. As the following chapters will indicate, the nostalgia industry is a major force in the posthistorical revisionist impulse. Driven by the need to reconfigure itself for present tastes in order to be resold, nostalgia TV, in particular, subjects the past to a process of rehabilitation, as its artifacts are revived and repaired—often a more deliberate and direct procedure than the one I describe in *Stranger Things* (chapter 2) because the act of revision is carried out on the original rather than an homage. *Stranger Things*, and *Ready Player One* (the subject of chapter 1) to an extent, repairs the past through mystification and misdirection, recomposing and reframing its nostalgic attachments under the rubric of aesthetics; revivals and reboots (the subject of chapter 3), on the other hand, rehabilitate the nostalgic objects themselves and, in doing so, the historical pasts they reflect.

What results, then, is a nostalgia that is unlike that which has come before. "Nostalgia" as popularly construed and deployed today has been divorced from its conceptual roots, and is in some ways alienated from the meanings it held throughout much of the twentieth century as well. As a number of scholars have shown, although the term has a fairly long history, it has only recently taken on the character we now associate with it. First coined by Swiss doctor Johannes Hofer in 1688, the term is derived from two Greek concepts: *nostos*, "return home," and *algia*, "longing," representing "a longing for a home that no longer exists or never existed . . . a sentiment of loss and displacement" (Boym xiv). For Hofer, "Nostalgia was said to produce 'erroneous representations' that caused the afflicted to lose touch with the present . . . the nostalgic was possessed by a mania of longing" (Boym 3–4). In its early form, nostalgia was viewed as a curable disease, akin to the common cold (Boym xiv), and seen as a root cause of a number of symptoms such as insomnia, anorexia, melancholic madness, or abjectness (Armbruster 19). This conception grew in popularity throughout the early parts of the eighteenth and nineteenth centuries. Yet, as Linda Austin points out, the term had virtually disappeared by the 1870s, having been invalidated by new research in fields such as bacteriology and cellular pathology (1). As the twentieth century began, and the pace of progress and geographic mobility increased, nostalgia had shifted from being a curable medical illness to an incurable condition of the spirit or psyche (Hutcheon)—what Boym refers to as "not merely an individual sickness but a symptom of our age, a historical emotion" (xvi). The temporal/historical dimension we now associate with the term also became an integral part of the definition at this time, with the ache for home of Hofer's original conception replaced by a longing for a bygone temporality. Nostalgia began as a symptom of spatial displacement at a time when geographic mobility was relatively uncommon and grew into a symptom of progress as the revolutions of modernity, political and technological, changed the pace of life. Michael Pickering and Emily Keightley note that this shift from spatial dislocation to temporal dislocation involved "the sense of feeling oneself a stranger in a new period that compared negatively with an earlier time in which one felt, or imagined, oneself at home" (922). In this process of demedicalization, "nostalgia also began to be seen not just as an individual emotion, but as a collective longing for a happier, singular, more innocent age" (Reynolds xxv). Nostalgia, in this conception of the term, arises largely "in compensation for a loss of faith in progress, and for what is socially and culturally destroyed in the name of progress" (Pickering and Keightley 920).

In the reflective age, however, longing is no longer the primary affect of nostalgia, replaced instead with infatuation and a desire to (re)experience that, thanks to streaming, are much easier to satisfy than in the past—at least on the surface. Two factors have enabled this shift. First, the overwhelming majority of cultural expressions of nostalgia are primarily linked to media rather than, say, personal memory. Though films, television, and music may produce an association with lived experience, that lived experience is often shaped by a mediated frame through which the association is coded and/or accessed. In this way, media actually gives shape to lived experiences even if the text in question produces conventionally nostalgic connections to an individual's memory. Moreover, expressions of nostalgia in the twenty-first century are more often centered on media itself than on the personal experiences captured by it, a development seen most cogently in the overwhelming volume of reboots, long-delayed sequels, and spin-offs that permeate the current TV and film marketplace in place of more conventional backwards-glancing narratives based primarily on common experiences in childhood and adolescence. Music and fashion, too, remain decidedly retrograde in much of their aesthetic posturing. Charli XCX's 2018 hit "1999," whose chorus expresses the singer's wish to "go back to 1999," is, for instance, sonically indistinguishable from the turn-of-the-century pop it reveres, and which forms the foundation of its longing. Its video, significantly, is an entirely mimetic exercise that places the singer within recreations of iconic music videos and films of the late 1990s, interspersed with images of her seated on the floor in a black turtleneck and glasses and holding a colorful iMac. This construction locates her desire not simply to go back to her childhood but to do so framed by the iconography and popular aesthetics of the period. Despite its more traditional nostalgic exclamations ("I just wanna go back / back to 1999 / take a ride through my old neighborhood"), the song reflects the merging of memory and experiential desire with media, stating in the second line of its chorus "I just wanna go back / to 'hit me baby one more time.'" The song, as well as the cultural moment it reflects, thus conflates traditional nostalgic longing and mediated infatuation, resulting in a nostalgia that exceeds merely the combination of longing and loss.

Ironically, the 1980s—the primary object of nostalgic fixation of the majority of the 2010s—represents an interesting example of the shifting nature of nostalgic media. The dominant form of nostalgic narratives in the 1980s in films such as *Stand by Me*, *A Christmas Story*, and *Back to the Future* as well as TV shows such as *The Wonder Years*, is one in which the backward-glancing is baked into the story itself, in the form of either a narrator reflecting on past events or, in the *Back to the Future* series, a character physically traveling to the past from the present. There is, in other words, a recognition of the mnemonic and transportational elements of traditional nostalgia at the core of these narratives. In contrast, in 2010s shows like *Stranger Things*, the reflective or transpositional authorizing frame has been removed, so that returning to the past, instead of functioning as an individual's experience or an act of memory, lacks any explicit narrative motivation. The justification for turning to the past precedes the turn itself, marking this form of nostalgia as prefabricated rather than personal.

The 2010s also saw a rise in what Linda Hutcheon has called "armchair nostalgia" (204)—or, what James Murphy of LCD Soundsystem has more aptly labeled "borrowed nostalgia"—a kind of performative nostalgia manifest not in the individual's past experience but through an infatuation with the products and aesthetics of someone else's life. The late-2010s/early-2020s '90s fashion revival among teens and young adults who lack memories of the '90s testifies to such a trend. For Gen-Z listeners (born between 1997 and 2012), Charli XCX's replication of Spice Girls and TLC music videos in "1999" might produce this ersatz emotional resonance. Borrowed nostalgia is illustrated perhaps most powerfully, however, by a series of items sold by the clothing retailer Urban Outfitters, whose brand targets trendy teen and twentysomething consumers. For a period in the late 2010s, the company sold facsimiles of early 2000s–style mixed CDs, complete with simulated handwritten permanent marker tracklists alongside random assortments of decorative used VHS tapes, providing millennial customers the chance to buy an artifact from their past and digital-native zoomers the chance to "reexperience" a past they never really experienced in the first place. If traditional nostalgia is conventionally animated by loss and a longing for something that is no longer, borrowed nostalgia, on the other hand, represents a paradoxical longing to recover that which one never had—which may never have existed to begin with. This expression of a nostalgia disconnected from experience is yet another instance of the break of what we call "nostalgia" from its linguistic and conceptual origins.

The second factor in the shifting discursive nature of nostalgia is the overwhelming increase in accessibility made possible by streaming services. Today, one can, at the click of a button, immerse themself fully in the 1990s of their childhood, spending a day (or week or month or even year) watching *Friends* and listening to Hanson. The popularity of retro fashion and aesthetics allows people to spend their entire lives surrounded by ephemera of the past. This paradigm, which Lizardi has called our "playlist past" (3), doesn't simply provide audiences with a brief memory of better days; it seeks to fully embed them within it, constructing the past as a location of viable sustained, easily accessible escape—as chapter 1 illustrates, an especially powerful notion in a posthistorical world defined by a lack of alternatives. In this context, nostalgia and the nostalgic media that is its most prominent expression pivot on the possibility of a sustainable escape from the now. It functions not as a temporary reverie but a viable way of interacting with both the past and present, in a world now broadly conceived as a mediated space. The playlist past, then, provides not only a reminder of something lost, but the opportunity to regain it. The question remains, however, that if something can so easily be recovered, is it truly lost? Historically, the basic premise of nostalgia is that it is a longing for something that decidedly cannot be regained; what happens, then, if the object of desire is media(ted) or aesthetic(ized), both of which enable the lost object to be regained at the push of a button? And if one's longing can be abated even partially by the recreation of the original experience—if, in other words, the duration of *longing* is cut *short*—is it still longing in the traditional sense?

Mediated nostalgia therefore calls into question the absence at its conceptual core. Because these lost nostalgic objects are often still accessible, the idea of nostalgia seems paradoxical. If conventional nostalgia relies on the notion that one can't ever go home, what should we make of a nostalgia based upon returning home (or its facsimile)? In such cases, irrecoverable nostalgic loss is converted into an absence that is at least partially resolvable. Yet, when nostalgia is centered on an irrecoverable time period that is defined primarily by its media and aesthetics, the return home afforded by media is ultimately incomplete: While the aesthetics and media that have come to represent the period are easily retrieved, the time period itself remains wholly irrecoverable. There emerges then a substitutional premise for nostalgic media and aesthetics, which function as approximations that appear close but are actually more distant than they initially seem. Those who turn to these texts in search for connection to a lost past, are ultimately left unfulfilled. In the end, the promise of a connector ultimately turns out to be a reflektor.

This development, too, raises an important question: If nostalgia has been distanced from longing and loss, what replaced them as the primary driver of nostalgia? Reflective-age nostalgia verges on a new paradigm, which replaces longing and loss with the pleasures of the style of the era. The past then becomes the site of mediated aesthetic infatuation. Above all else, one is drawn to the '80s not because of how it was but because of how it looked and sounded, such that the difference between past and present is stylistic rather than personal or political. The 1980s in this model is defined more by neon and synthesizers than by Reagan and austerity; the social and political dimensions of the past are subsequently flattened in favor of the superficially depoliticized cultural—the same operation produced by the end of history more broadly.

In many ways, this conception of nostalgia reflects what Jameson identified as an important feature of postmodernism: that the period saw the development of nostalgic media that was based less in explorations of individual memory or prior experience and more in an attachment to the techniques and forms of the past. Specifically, Jameson writes about what he calls "nostalgia films," which are not "passionate expressions of that older longing once called nostalgia," but are, rather, "a depersonalized visual curiosity" (*Postmodernism* xvii). These films, he contends, "project [pastiche] onto a collective and social level . . . approach[ing] the 'past' through stylistic connotation, conveying 'pastness' by the glossy qualities of the image" (19). This tendency comes in the context of a prevailing vision of a postmodernity that, as Anna Kornbluh has succinctly summarized, "revels in mediation . . . activates pastiche . . . embraces the surface and eschews depth . . . [and] inscribes a 'crisis of historicity'" (13). The arguments presented in this book are heavily influenced by Jameson's work, and there are considerable areas of overlap not only in the treatment of nostalgia—particularly, as chapter 2 attests, regarding the role of aesthetics in reconstructions of the past and the related evasion of historical thinking—but also in the description of the broader cultural field. Despite these similarities, however, key differences exist between the postmodern period Jameson so compellingly articulates and the posthistorical world this book describes. This is especially evident in the realm of nostalgia, and the analysis presented in this book is better understood not merely as a repetition of Jameson's ideas but rather as a critical extension that seeks to articulate how those tendencies have continued and, indeed, evolved in response to changing sociocultural conditions over the last forty years. Kornbluh has correctly pointed out that "critics increasingly agree that postmodernism no longer furnishes the logic of the contemporary" (12); though a consensus about its replacement has not yet emerged,[9] *The Reflective Age* illuminates many of the points of rupture and of continuity that characterize this transition. While we may not be fully within the postmodern anymore, neither, these chapters suggest, are we fully beyond it.

One notable point of digression can be found in the role that temporal and aesthetic attachments play in Jameson's discussion of postmodern nostalgia films. In "Postmodernism and Consumer Society," for instance, Jameson's analysis draws on the *Star Wars* trilogy, which, he argues, reinvents the experience of the "Saturday afternoon series of the *Buck Rogers* type—alien villains, true American heroes, heroines in distress, the death ray or the doomsday box, and the cliff-hanger at the end whose miraculous solution was to be witnessed next Saturday afternoon" (116). *Star Wars*, he continues,

> satisfies a deep (might I even say repressed?) longing to experience [Saturday afternoon serials] again: it is a complex object in which on some first level children and adolescents can take the adventures straight, while the adult public is able to gratify a deeper and more properly nostalgic desire to return to that older period and to live its strange old aesthetic artifacts through once again. This film is thus metonymically a historical or nostalgia film: unlike *American Graffiti*, it does not reinvent a picture of the past in its lived totality; rather, by reinventing the feel and shape of characteristic art objects of an older period (the serials), it seeks to reawaken a sense of the past associated with those objects. (116)

Jameson's reading of *Star Wars*' nostalgic appeal is notable because it is founded in the film's *indirect* reference to a historical period, which provides ersatz nostalgic satisfaction for viewers who associate the style with longed-for past experience. It is worth emphasizing, in this light, that in borrowing the Saturday afternoon style, so to speak, the film reproduces a form that is diegetically divorced from the historical context it represents: *Buck Rogers*'s style may be representative of an aesthetic that is linked to a time period, but that style was not deployed in an attempt to represent that period itself—it was a *product* of midcentury America rather than a *depiction of it*. Further, while a certain nostalgia for '50s sci-fi may be present at the core of *Star Wars*, one cannot argue that this is foundational to its narrative purpose or popular reception; though present, nostalgia is far from being the central force in the series' appeal, even if those resonances may exist. These attachments, in other words, are embedded deep within these works. *Body Heat*, another example of the "nostalgia mode" that Jameson cites, is, despite its formal attachments to aesthetics of the past, likewise disconnected from the time period whose aesthetics it apes. Though Jameson is correct to point to the similarity between *Body Heat* and earlier noirs like *Double Indemnity* (*Postmodernism* 20), the film is also unambiguously set in the present, and though, like *Star Wars*, some of its appeal derives from the way that it reproduces these styles in another setting, this "nostalgic" attachment to form is, again, not a primary feature of the film's appeal, nor is it tied to the film's diegetic world. In contrast to these examples, the connection between aesthetic form and historical period is much more direct in the nostalgic media we've seen in the twenty-first century, borne from a merger of traditional temporal nostalgia with the late capitalist emphasis on the reproduction of style Jameson identifies. What results is a nostalgic text that more overtly gestures toward aesthetics in its reproduction of historical periods themselves. *Stranger Things*, for example, reflects a nostalgic attachment to both a form/aesthetic (adventure films, synthesizers, etc.) and a time (the 1980s), but—and this is the crucial difference—with the form figured as the defining feature of its depiction of the time. Unlike *Star Wars* and *Body Heat*, these nostalgic appeals reside on the surface.

Another important distinction is that the tendencies Jameson identified in these nostalgia films were, at the time, part of a novel and significant, yet relatively narrow, trend that has, in the years since, come to dominate much of the media landscape. In one sense, this continuity has resulted from the fact that many of the socioeconomic conditions he described in the 1980s have continued into the twenty-first century, and thus the cultural-aesthetic forms that he identified as a response to those conditions have also persisted. Even as other social, economic, cultural, and aesthetic forms emerged, in other words, we have never moved *fully* beyond the postmodern as Jameson describes it—this stasis is, again, the fundamental premise of the end of history. Yet, even in this broad continuity there are new developments. Most intriguingly in this context, the traits he identified in quintessentially postmodern texts are also now being repeated in contemporary nostalgic texts as they attempt to recreate the postmodern world through reference to its media. The turn toward mediation, parody, and pastiche that Jameson described in the 1980s, therefore, has led to a unique doubling effect in nostalgic media of the 2010s: These novels, films, and television shows are further entrenched in postmodernist artistic logic due to their mimicry of the initial pastiches and parodies that Jameson wrote about—Baudrillardian copies of copies of copies. What makes contemporary nostalgic media distinct from those works identified in *Postmodernism*, in other words, is that we are witnessing the production of aesthetically postmodern copies of aesthetically postmodern "originals." Jamesonian postmodernism emphasized comparatively singular simulacra, while the texts described in this project are multiple: simulacra of simulacra, pastiche of pastiche, mediated copies of a multiplicity of multiply mediated objects without any stable point of origin—endless replication compounding itself endlessly. What we see in this period, then, is not simply a *continuation* of the aesthetic tendencies Jameson articulated, but a *reproductive intensification* of them.

This, in part, results from the stagnant neoliberalism that conditions of the end of history, where cheap repetition of prior forms reigns supreme. Here lies another key distinction: Part of what characterized postmodernism was its novelty, even in its emphasis on aesthetic re-production (which was nonetheless a new cultural practice); part of what characterizes the end of history, on the other hand, is its unoriginality. The end of history can thus be understood as postmodernism (itself anchored to the decline and end of modernity—thus we have another example of end-of-history repetition) on its last legs, drained of the novelties that once energized it. As a practice, postmodernism aestheticized, spectacularized, and otherwise redefined, hollowed, and/or commodified the novelties of modernity; the end of history is what it looks like when postmodernity runs out of gas and has to direct its productive processes at its own refuse—the postmodern commodity recommodified. Thus, in the simplest terms, though many of the tendencies that Jameson identified in the 1980s remain in circulation, they have also escalated and mutated in ways *Postmodernism* did not describe.

Nonetheless, Jameson's foundational claim that postmodernity (and nostalgic media, specifically) produces—or reinforces—a loss of situatedness and historical context, remains useful for understanding the cultural tendencies of the end of history. If reflective-age nostalgia is indeed distanced from loss and longing, as I have argued, and those components have been replaced by a more immediate infatuation with style, then what has also been lost (or at least minimized) in this reformulation is the reflective nature of nostalgia as it has traditionally been conceived. Conventionally, nostalgia has often been construed as producing constructive revelations that increase awareness of placedness, provoking an attentiveness to the passage of time and the nature of existence within an ever-changing landscape—a notion that Boym labeled "reflective nostalgia." For Boym, nostalgia can be subdivided into two categories: the aforementioned individualized, reflective mode, and a more collective restorative one. The latter, she argues, "stresses [the etymological root] nostos [return home] and attempts transhistorical reconstruction of the lost home." This type of nostalgia is largely undertaken by the state through the erection of museums, memorials, and other memory-institutions, and is often used by right-wing political projects that seek to emphasize national memory "based on a single plot of national identity." On the other hand, she explains, reflective nostalgia "thrives in [the etymological root] algia, the longing itself, and delays the homecoming—wistfully, ironically, desperately," and is thus the realm of art and artists. Crucially, she writes, "Restorative nostalgia protects the absolute truth, while reflective nostalgia calls it into doubt" (xviii). Reflective nostalgia is decidedly intellectual in nature, and, as Boym points out, can lead to profound ruminations on the constituent components of nostalgia especially—loss, longing, and the passage of time. Nostalgia also traditionally relies on a lack, the recognition of which serves to critique the present. Absent these components, however, mediated nostalgia in the reflective age is structurally incapable of producing such thought—and, indeed, such an endeavor is functionally antithetical to it.[10] Its engagement is as superficial as the object itself. Reflective-age nostalgia is often based on the aesthetics that appear to define an era, constructed out of a curated selection of artifacts of the pop culture of the time. Built on, and perpetuated by, a quasi-generic formulation of the period, the objects of this nostalgia may or may not correspond to an original (whose existence may also be dubious to begin with). Thus, nostalgia forged in aesthetic reproduction is further distanced from whatever real might have existed. For this reason, nostalgia in the reflective age is ultimately alienating.

"Reflektor" describes a search for a "connector," and historical reflection, broadly, and nostalgia, more specifically, have both long been construed as means of reconnection. There is a consistent emphasis in culture and scholarly work on the power of glancing backward to produce a sense of belonging, community, and continuity. This is particularly the case with the restorative nostalgia produced by state institutions, but it is broadly present in any such act. Turning to the past, in these formulations, provides a link between past and present. The value of such a notion, however, pivots on the qualities of the object that represents "past" and on the construction of "the past" therein. In other words, if the past one turns to in order to connect is, in fact, not reflective of the historical, social, political, or material reality, or is oriented in such a way that those elements are obscured, then where does that connection lead? The result of this paradigm is a nostalgia that is regularly divorced from its critical potential, one that leaves behind (or at least subordinates) the reflective frame that encourages the nostalgiac to consider the passage of time and the changes that have ensued. When highlighted by narrative structure, this raises the critical question: Why was the past so much better? Without this reflective element, which in part serves to anchor nostalgic fantasy in the realm of history, context, and—at least in a sense—the real, we find ourselves adrift, unable to adequately situate past and present, and the pathways between them remain obscured. In this way, nostalgia in the reflective age represents a kind of false promise, one that is derived both from its emphasis on aesthetics and from its simulacral nature: Once again, what appears to be a connector turns out to be a reflektor.

One might ask, in light of this shift in nostalgia's connection to the past, if reflection is actually missing, why we should call it "the reflective age." In fact, this relative absence of reflective nostalgia reveals one of the central characteristics of the reflective age: The conventional traits of nostalgia (reflection, longing, loss) don't appear to be missing at all, as their absence is obscured by misdirection. This project's title is thus ironic because the end of history is increasingly oriented toward the past and increasingly alienated from it. We are inundated with reflections of the past that appear clear but often at best are only refractions, disorientating reflections of a reflection of a reflection of a reflection.

The reflective age is, in sum, a moment defined by a retrograde cultural landscape whose character and omnipresence combine to produce disorientation and an inability to reckon with past, present, or future, driven especially by a nostalgia that leaves behind its historical antecedents and critical functions in favor of an emphasis on aesthetics, style, and the immediate pleasures of infatuation and repetition of the familiar. As Baudrillard remarked, despite the moniker, the posthistorical world is actually a time of endlessness, in which nothing ever really ends and old ideas and artifacts are constantly on the verge of returning. The progressive novelty that characterized much of the twentieth century, in other words, has given way to an era of rampant recycling. As such, visions of the past in the reflective age are pervasive, but they are also unstable, disconnected, and incoherent—despite, paradoxically, often being positioned as a remedy for the same traits in the present. The chapters of this book examine how narratives of the 2010s and early 2020s reflect this shifting relationship to the past, present, and future, illuminating its foundations in the conditions of the end of history. Conventionally defined by a longing for a lost time and/or space, nostalgia at the end of history has taken on new dimensions; each of the texts I discuss illustrates significant aspects of this cultural paradigm, from the hyper-aestheticization of the past and the elevation of reference and recognition in identity formation to the fraught desire to revise and repeat in the face of decline and the growing popularity of nostalgic appeals in contemporary right-wing political melodrama.

Chapter 1 analyzes Ernest Cline's 2011 novel *Ready Player One* and its 2020 sequel *Ready Player Two*, arguing that the novels reveal how the end of history's twin pillars of stagnation and decay, coupled with the notion that there is no alternative to the present system, have encouraged the notion that the past is the only viable refuge from the horrors of the present. At the same time, the period's emphasis on mediated pasts leads nostalgic subjects not only to misrecognize the past into which they wish to flee but also the circumstances that led to this point. Cline's novels also illuminate the depths of the posthistorical elevation of culture over politics—seen in the novels' emphasis on nostalgia induced through references to mediated artifacts alone—as well as its effects on identity formation resulting from the way that neoliberalism indexes identity to patterns of consumption. Recognition, the novels illustrate, is often no longer a political issue connected to one's fundamental rights, but rather a matter of the social capital accorded to the media that define one's life. Politics, in other words, appears to be a dead end, so social life becomes a matter of pure prestige, and being seen and heard, in this context, is a function of the status of one's taste. Together, I argue, these shifts create a barrier to remedying the posthistorical stagnation and decay from which the nostalgiac flees.

Chapter 2 examines the Netflix series *Stranger Things* as the archetype of this paradigm's aesthetic logic, showing how it substitutes hollowed-out allusions to media for a deeper engagement with the historical period it purports to capture. The series, I argue, is functionally akin to an empty container into which audiences can project whatever meanings they wish, as it regularly reduces historical elements to markers of genre or trope that can produce a seemingly endless array of interpretations. In this process of reconstructing the 1980s based on mediated reference, the series also inadvertently reproduces many of the political problems of the period's media, including its regressive racial politics and conservative distrust of government. As a result of these traits, *Stranger Things*' attempts to symbolically confront and conquer the horrors of the past that it hides behind metaphor and trope ultimately fall short, as the show fails to conceive of them as anything other than aesthetic form. A better future, the series suggests, is not possible, and things will only ever get worse—a conclusion that is provoked by its unwillingness to confront these problems beyond the sphere of trope and aesthetics.

Chapter 3 reads *Twin Peaks: The Return*, the 2017 revival of the celebrated 1990s television series, as a commentary on televisual reboots/revivals and the repetitiveness that has plagued twenty-first-century American culture. Politically, the end of history is marked by stagnation, decay, and a preference for management over resolution; culturally, it is defined by an apparent lack of novelty and the constant return of dead styles amid seemingly unending shifts in trends—progressing, in other words, in the circular fashion of a treadmill. The series, I argue, provides a profound critique of the ways in which televisual reboots and revivals seek (and inevitably fail) to symbolically repair the problems of the present by returning to, and revising, the crises of the past. Agent Cooper's failed quest to return to the timeline of the original series and save Laura Palmer, in this light, symbolizes the way that nostalgia and nostalgic media function as cruelly optimistic fantasies that bind individuals to forms that no longer work (and arguably never did) as they seek refuge from, or endeavor to repair, the ravages of the present.

Chapter 4 shifts focus from media and cultural productions to consider the role that nostalgia plays in politics at the end of history. In particular, the chapter shows how nostalgia functions within the American right's increasingly overt appeals to melodramatic narratives of white victimization. Through a discussion of the "deep story" of Tea Party resentments laid out in Arlie Russell Hochschild's *Strangers in Their Own Land*, the chapter begins by examining the centrality of "victimization" and melodramatic framing within the right's political project, identifying how claims of loss, both explicitly and implicitly, form the foundation of the recent populist wave that culminated in the election of Donald Trump in 2016 and 2024. The majority of the chapter analyzes *Hillbilly Elegy*, the 2016 memoir by now–Vice President J. D. Vance, which illuminates the right's attempts to construct, and elicit sympathy for, a coherent, homogeneous "white working class" whose singular suffering is depicted as the result of losses instigated by the end of history's neoliberal economic agenda. In doing so, I show how this framework is supported by nostalgic visions of lost virtue and racial decline. The chapter concludes with analysis of more recent manifestations of right-wing, often forthrightly fascist, nostalgic melodrama found in online spaces. Analyzing so-called retvrn posting, as well as its philosophical underpinnings as expressed in the New Right manifesto *Bronze Age Mindset*, I show how this movement fuses conventional right-wing racial melodrama with reflective-age nostalgic appeals to produce an ideological project whose reaction to the end of history transcends conventional Republican nostalgia for earlier eras of capitalism. The resulting ideology, I show, takes the right's familiar nostalgic melodrama of white victimization and the reflective age's emphasis on ahistorical aesthetics to their logical end.

Together, these chapters illuminate the changing nature of nostalgia at the end of history, highlighting the ways in which the period's sociocultural logic and political conditions have altered how we interact with the past and conceive of our present and future. With its unique combination of post–Cold War triumphalism, neoliberal rationality (including, especially, its championing of the cultural over the social and political), and economic stagnation, the end of history, this book illustrates, should no longer be understood as a political punchline or a case of one author's naive presentism, but rather as a coherent and profoundly significant frame for understanding American culture in the early twenty-first century. Likewise, this book articulates the need for greater recognition of nostalgia's emergence as a central force in contemporary America, and thus its value in understanding the contours of the cultural moment.

CHAPTER 1

Ready Player One, Nostalgia, and Recognition

This is the world out of which *Ready Player One* was conceived: a static state in which a litany of eminently visible crises have emerged, but change has become scarce; a world for which there is no coherent plan, and when problems arise the social and political are seized by a reactive frenzy; a world that, as Adam Curtis has explained, "doesn't tell [us] visions about the future . . . doesn't tell us what this is all for . . . has no story of what's coming tomorrow" ("Units of One"). In its bleak vision of an increasingly stagnant future, gripped by retromania, whose temporal march forward is marked only by a procession of unmitigated decline, Ernest Cline's 2011 bestselling novel *Ready Player One* stages a unique failure of imagination.

The novel follows Wade Watts, a teenager living in an Oklahoma City trailer park in the 2040s, as he makes his way through a pop culture treasure hunt within the OASIS, a massively multiplayer online virtual-reality video game where most of the world's population now spend their time. Five years before the start of the novel, the death of OASIS creator James Halliday inaugurated a contest within the platform, with his estate and sole control over Gregarious Simulation Systems (GSS), the company that runs the OASIS, as the prize. In the ensuing years, the competition, which revolves around solving a series of riddles leading to a hidden Easter Egg, has become a worldwide phenomenon. In addition to millions of competitors worldwide, the hunt has also attracted the interest of IOI, a rival megacorporation intent on winning control of the OASIS in order to further monetize it. After becoming the first player to solve one of Halliday's puzzles, Wade emerges as the world's best hope of keeping the OASIS out of the hands of IOI. Thanks to his superior knowledge of 1980s pop culture, and with the help of a small group of friends, Wade eventually succeeds in finding the egg, winning the competition and taking sole control of the OASIS.

The dystopian future that forms the backdrop of the novel's action is speculative, but only insofar as the widespread effects of climate crisis, poverty, and geopolitical turmoil that it invokes are worse than when the book was written; they are, however, fundamentally the same conflicts we face today. This is to say that, despite being set thirty years after it was written, there is nothing really new in the future of Cline's novel. Even the OASIS is merely an extrapolation of present technologies (instead of restricting participation in the virtual world to visuals alone, as is the case with current tech like the Oculus Rift, haptic sensors and motion-tracked treadmills have replaced controllers, enabling a full range of movement and sensory perception). Indeed, though parts of the world have migrated operations into the OASIS (public school, for instance, is now entirely virtual, with students arriving each morning to simulated classrooms, in a simulated building, on a simulated planet), essentially very little has actually changed.

Culturally, too, Cline's world is inert. There is no new music, film, or television to speak of, no new forms of digital culture or social media trends, no new festivals, holidays, political movements, or even religious cults. Here, in light of the increased visualization of digital/social culture heralded by Instagram, Snapchat, and TikTok, Cline's version of the future, which was released into the world the year after Instagram's founding and several years before the other two were introduced, is simultaneously prophetic and stale. The OASIS is an inherently visual platform, and one of its central functions is the literalization of digital spaces—online schooling in virtual classrooms, the replacement of internet chat rooms (already largely a relic of an earlier Internet age in 2011) with digital rooms filled with pixel walls and furniture. As such, it scales the current trend toward visualization in social media today into an all-encompassing fact of life. Digital "spaces" are no longer metaphorical. Yet it also imagines a world in which the thirty years from its time of publication to the time in which it's set basically produced only two cultural events (the OASISifcation of everything and the Easter Egg hunt–induced nostalgia boom), and both are related to the same product. Interestingly, in a recent case of life imitating art, Facebook, as part of their rebranding as Meta in October 2021, announced the creation of the Metaverse, a virtual reality space within their platform that closely resembles the OASIS. A trailer for the product showcased founder Mark Zuckerberg selecting an avatar and walking viewers through a series of features, including playing poker with friends and watching TikToks. Most notably, the ad positions the Metaverse as a platform for business meetings, inadvertently showcasing the limits of imagination inherent in the end of history (nothing here is new, it's simply the virtualization of what already exists) while also marking how uninnovative Cline's vision of the future really is.

The world, *Ready Player One* tells us, has basically descended into monoculture and mono-modality: Novelty arrives solely within the OASIS (and, even then, only really in the form of new planets and games, which themselves receive only passing reference within the book). This is not to say, however, that Cline's world is devoid of culture; it is, in fact, obsessed with cultural objects—it's just that none of them are new. The competition created by Halliday, a child of the 1980s and a pop culture fanatic, took the form of a series of Easter Egg hunts requiring extensive knowledge of video games, music, and movies from the time in which its creator grew up. As Wade explains, "This led to a global fascination with 1980s pop culture. Fifty years after the decade had ended, the movies, music, games, and fashions of the 1980s were all the rage once again. By 2041, spiked hair and acid-washed jeans were back in style, and covers of hit '80s pop songs by contemporary bands dominated the music charts. People who had actually been teenagers in the 1980s, all now approaching old age, had the strange experience of seeing the fads and fashions of their youth embraced and studied by their grandkids" (8). Cline thus stages a dystopian vision of the future in which the whole of the planet has become fixated on '80s pop culture. The novel is filled to the brim with references to popular movies, music, and games from the era, as Wade and other "gunters" (slang for "egg hunters") have laboriously studied *Anorak's Almanac*, Halliday's published journals named after his OASIS avatar, in search of clues to help them solve the first puzzle. As Wade explains, "The Almanac was over a thousand pages long, but it contained few details about Halliday's personal life or his day-to-day activities. Most of the entries were his stream-of-consciousness observations on various classic videogames, science-fiction and fantasy novels, movies, comic books, and '80s pop culture, mixed with humorous diatribes denouncing everything from organized religion to diet soda" (7). Wade has not only read the *Almanac* dozens of times, but has watched, played, or listened to each of the thousands of artifacts mentioned in the text: "I read every novel by every single one of Halliday's favorite authors," he explains. "And I didn't stop there. . . . If it was one of Halliday's favorites like *WarGames*, *Ghostbusters*, *Real Genius*, *Better off Dead*, or *Revenge of the Nerds*, I rewatched it until I knew every scene by heart. . . . I watched every episode of *The Greatest American Hero*, *Airwolf*, *The A-Team*, *Knight Rider*, *Misfits of Science*, and *The Muppet Show*. . . . He listened to everything. So I did too. Pop, rock, new wave, punk, heavy metal. From the Police to Journey to R.E.M. to the Clash. I tackled it all" (62–63). Wade maintains an encyclopedic knowledge of these items, which he gleefully flaunts at every opportunity, challenging friends and rivals (and readers) with bits of obscure trivia ("Can you name the next three games in the [*Swordquest*] series?"). This proves extremely valuable as he makes his way through the stages of the hunt after being the first to complete the initial challenge five years after it began. In one part, Wade is placed within a simulation of the 1983 film *WarGames* and tasked with role-playing as its protagonist, David Lightman. To win, he must recite, without error, every single line of dialogue spoken by Matthew Broderick's character as the film plays out around him. The same trick is repeated toward the end of the novel, when he must reenact every scene from *Monty Python and the Holy Grail*—a task he relishes: "Reenacting the film wasn't just easy—it was a total blast" (357).

Even outside of the contest itself, the novel is riddled with references to pre-existing media and consumer products (*Entertainment Weekly*'s review called it "the literary-fiction equivalent of VH1's *I Love the 80's*"). Take, for instance, its discussion of the intellectual properties that have been ported into the OASIS:

> GSS had also licensed preexisting virtual worlds from their competitors, so content that had already been created for games like *Everquest* and *World of Warcraft* was ported over to the OASIS, and copies of *Norrath* and *Azeroth* were added to the growing catalog of OASIS planets. Other virtual worlds soon followed suit, from the *Metaverse* to the *Matrix*. The *Firefly* universe was anchored in a sector adjacent to the *Star Wars* galaxy, with a detailed re-creation of the *Star Trek* universe in the sector adjacent to that. Users could now teleport back and forth between their favorite fictional worlds. *Middle Earth. Vulcan. Pern. Arrakis. Magrathea. Disc-World, Mid-World, Riverworld, Ringworld.* Worlds upon worlds." (49; emphasis added)

For Cline, it wasn't enough, apparently, to note that worlds from various movies and games existed in the OASIS; they needed to be catalogued. This is how the novel works: Rather than describing things, Cline typically just says they look like, or *are*, something from a movie, show, or game. Notably, the reader's recognition of these artifacts (or lack thereof) is usually unaddressed—either you know what Arrakis is or you don't. Save for the occasional brief identifier when the reference is particularly central to the plot ("I was inside the first scene of *Monty Python and the Holy Grail*. Another of Halliday's favorite films, and perhaps the most beloved geek film of all time" [355]), the entirety of the novel follows this pattern. Hardly a page goes by without at least one nod to a movie, song, game, or consumer product from the 1980s. As Jonathan Alexander notes, even the Twitch-esque streams that Wade and his friends operate "are filled with pre-existing content, favorite TV shows, anime, or movies, played on endless loops" (529–530): "Art3mis," Wade explains, "also ran her own vidfeed channel, Art3misvision, and I always kept one of my monitors tuned to it. Right now, she was airing her usual Monday evening fare: an episode of Square Pegs. After that would be ElectraWoman and DynaGirl, followed by back-to-back episodes of Isis and Wonder Woman. Her programming lineup hadn't changed in ages. But it didn't matter. She still got killer ratings" (203). Seemingly everything in the novel is anchored to some '80s specificity: Watches are *Swatches*, sunglasses are *Ray-Bans*, VCRs are *Betamaxes*. Media and consumption are inescapable.

To those unfamiliar with Cline's novel, or with Steven Spielberg's 2018 film adaptation, this might sound like the premise for a salient critique of twenty-first-century American culture. *Ready Player One*'s merging of dystopia, simulated reality, and hyperfixation on nostalgia for consumer products seems perfectly designed to offer astute insights into the same backward-glancing nature of the reflective age that this book seeks to describe. And it does—albeit indirectly and inadvertently. This pursuit (such that it exists) is undercut by the fact that Cline is not only *not* seeking to offer such a critique, but his inclusion of these elements is actually a matter of pure homage and celebration. A self-described "full-time geek" (Egan) who traveled between stops on the novel's book tour in a vintage DeLorean complete with a model *Back to the Future* flux capacitor, Cline is as infatuated with '80s pop culture as his character Halliday. The novel's nostalgic fixation on the 1980s largely comes from the fact that its creator (born in 1972) maintains a nostalgic fixation on the 1980s of his adolescence;[1] his characters reference things because he likes them (and, crucially, because he wants his readers to like them too). Further, while the novel's '80s retromania may have been launched by the contest, Cline repeatedly emphasizes the idea that Wade and his friends *really do love this stuff* and aren't just in it for the prize. For Cline, this is not the story of a decaying planet whose abject citizens are locked into a dog-eat-dog contest driven by an unnatural obsession with the pop culture of an era they never experienced; it's a righteous struggle for the soul of the internet between the true fanatics who appropriately revere '80s pop culture and the "poseurs" who are just using the contest to win glory, wealth, or power. The abundant references throughout the novel thus express unbridled enthusiasm rather than social commentary; as Laura Hudson correctly points out, "Ready Player One [is] far too joyously self-absorbed in its referential excesses to step back and examine what they might mean" ("Serious Bill-Paying Skillage").

To the extent that it does present some kind of critical agenda, the novel's focus is instead on the dangers of *excess*, tied directly to its virtual world. Its penultimate chapter concludes with the gamer equivalent of Ferris Bueller's "You just might miss it" quip: "As terrifying and painful as reality can be, it's also the only place where you can find true happiness. Because reality is *real*" (364). *Ready Player One*, put simply, is more concerned with people playing games by themselves at the expense of their social life (despite otherwise championing the community-building that the OASIS provides) than it is with the sociocultural textures of a dying empire (even as it readily invokes them). Its message, exemplified in the aphorism above, is that, while escapism is necessary, people should be careful not to come untethered from those around them. Notably, despite being a form of escapism, nostalgia is not similarly problematized within the novel, and is seemingly exempt from Cline's warning—which makes sense given that nostalgic escapism is arguably the novel's raisin d'être. "Nostalgia," Cline explained in an interview with *Slate* in 2015, "is good. Nostalgia is like video games, or music, or movies. It's a form of escapism," adding, "I wasn't trying to make a judgment call [in the book]" (Brogan). This separation between form and content enables Cline to produce a dying world captivated by bygone styles from half a century earlier (which hardly any of the remaining population experienced the first time around) motivated by a winner-take-all competition that promises its winner untold fame and fortune, while also using this setting not as a source of lament, or even a warning of things to come, but simply as the staging ground for an action-adventure novel whose ultimate moral is that you should log off from time to time.

It's worth emphasizing, in light of all of this, that the novel's dystopian setting is really just a checklist of tropes from the twenty-first-century apocalyptic imagination. Climate change, energy, technology, corporate power, capitalism, poverty, war, famine, disease: All of these forces converge in *Ready Player One*'s vision of the future, but they also remain largely outside of the plot itself, existing mainly as a backdrop for the novel's action. There is, for instance, no attention paid to the environmental impact of powering something as massive as the OASIS. In fact, in a strange twist, the novel actually suggests that the energy crisis helped *foster* the growth of the OASIS: "The ongoing energy crisis contributed greatly to the OASIS's runaway popularity. The skyrocketing cost of oil made airline and automobile travel too expensive for the average citizen, and the OASIS became the only getaway most people could afford" (59). Poverty is also only invoked to offer a backstory for its protagonist who, by the midpoint of the novel, has earned enough money from his progress in the competition to leave behind the Oklahoma City trailer park in which he grew up. This is dystopia as blank form, a genre not only emptied of its original critical function, but subsequently repurposed for unadulterated fun. As an author, this is Cline's MO. James Hibberd correctly points out in a 2020 interview with Cline published in *Entertainment Weekly* that, despite their settings, *Ready Player One* and Cline's 2015 follow-up *Armada* (in which the world, facing a hostile alien invasion, is saved by a guy who's really good at video games) are "far from bleak downers; both serve as wish-fulfillment escapist page-turners centered around high-stakes pop culture-stuffed treasure hunts, a world his fans are rather eager to reenter." Constance Grady's summary of the novel in *Vox* illustrates this incongruity: "The premise [of the novel] is appealingly *silly* and *insubstantial*: It's 2045, and the *dystopian* world has become *unbearable*" (emphasis added). Cline himself echoes the same sentiment toward the end of the *Slate* interview:

> [Jacob Brogan:] *Ready Player One* offers a pretty bleak vision of the future. The world is broken, and there's almost no way to fix it, so all that's left to do is get really good at video games. Do you share the novel's cynicism?
>
> [Cline:] The human condition is by its very nature painful. Becoming aware that you're going to die some day informs the rest of your life. And it's also what gives your life meaning, urgency. Virtual reality would be the ultimate escape, a copy of reality that's the way you want it to be, which makes human beings dodge to some degree, but it's also dangerous, as the

> real world, where our real lives happen, becomes less urgent. But I wasn't trying to write a cautionary tale with *Ready Player One*—I was just trying to write a fun science-fiction action adventure story in the vein of the stories I loved.

To read *Ready Player One* as its author apparently intended requires readers to divorce the novel's dystopian setting from its core meaning in a way that seems antithetical to the very existence of dystopia. This raises the question, why invoke a dying world at all if only to shrug at it and look elsewhere?

To ask readers not only to imagine a hopeless future, but actually to find pleasure in it is, on its face, a strange request. It seems contradictory. And yet, a survey of popular American media of the past two decades (at least) suggests that this kind of dystopian entertainment is exceedingly common. From disaster movies and postapocalyptic fiction to the mid-2000s zombification of all kinds of media, imagining a bleak future has become the standard. To imagine a dystopian future is then to do what everyone else does. One might ask, nonetheless, why dystopia has become so commonplace, and if there's any broader relationship between the novel's setting and its narrative purpose that might clarify this trend. Here, the interview with *Slate* reveals something interesting about the way that Cline conceives of the dystopian imagination. After Brogan pushes back against the author's retreat into intent—"But do you think that dystopias . . . hurt our ability to imagine a better future?"—Cline responds, "I think real life hurts our ability to imagine a better future." In this statement, Cline recognizes a connection between social conditions and fictional dystopian futures, that the social shapes the aesthetic. Dystopian fiction, in other words, is the product of a world that encourages one to imagine a negative future. This is not a new formulation, of course; what is noteworthy, however, is that, in writing *Ready Player One*, Cline responds to these conditions by constructing a world not of *escape*—one in which characters triumph over these challenges to make the world anew—but of *escapism*, where the central motive is distraction. The characters in this novel are not trying to piece together a new society from the rubble or trying to rebel against an oppressive government—in other words, to effect systemic change; they're just trying to find a way to shut it all out and have fun. *Ready Player One* in effect turns its back on the problems of the world, even as it regularly suggests their inevitability.

In this way, the novel is borne of and pivots upon an inability to imagine anything better. At the conclusion of the *Slate* interview, Cline offers only the faintest glimmer of hope (one that, perhaps unsurprisingly, takes the rhetorical form of an '80s action-adventure movie): "Today, the cavalier attitude that a lot of people have about climate change and overpopulation, deforestation and oceans dying off, all of that, is really scary. But also, as human beings, that's when we really shine and kick ass, when our backs are to the wall and our whole species' survival is in question." It's unclear what prior pseudoapocalyptic events Cline is referring to, but he's not alone in adopting this vaguely deterministic, bystander theory of change: *Surely somebody will do something.* In light of these beliefs, it's also unsurprising that the novel repeatedly presses the claim that there is no clear solution to any of the problems facing the world. The disbelief in the possibility of fundamental change is why Wade and his cohort are so focused on saving the OASIS from the evil corporation that wants to gain control of it and overmonetize their only viable form of escape/-ism: Without escapism, they have nothing, and fighting to ensure that such a totalizing form of escapism isn't necessary is evidently out of the question. And, as Cline implies above, it doesn't have the makings of a "fun" novel. Repeatedly, the novel emphasizes the related notion that we are surrounded by systems beyond our control, and that all action outside the OASIS is just "rearranging deck chairs on the Titanic" (201). The goal, really, is to ensure control over the management of the inevitable decline. In this, *Ready Player One* anticipates Adam Curtis's arguments, in his 2016 film *Hypernormalisation*, about the contemporary pattern of constructing alternate realities in an effort to manage the *unmanageable.*

It would be very easy for Cline's novel to push beyond mere management and end with its heroes saving the world from its impending demise or, at the very least, offering a path to salvation. Such an ending would not outwardly compromise the novel's fidelity to its genre, nor contradict its message. One might argue, in fact, that Wade shifting the novel's focus outside the OASIS in this way would actually enhance its message about the value of not abandoning the real world. This is not to say that Cline is obliged to follow this path, but to point out that the lack of contradiction suggests another reason for the novel's focus to remain virtual. If not directly related to artistic cohesion, then perhaps the reason is that Cline simply believes that solving these issues would be a bridge too far, too much of a fantasy, even for a "fun sci-fi action-adventure novel." Perhaps even a novel where a bunch of teenagers outwits the second-most powerful corporation on the planet, with access to unlimited resources, must have its limits. And yet, for a book so thoroughly driven by homage, that depicts a fantasy whose dimensions are shaped by these influences at every turn, it's curious that its big ending doesn't have the same weight. The novel's final battle in the OASIS, between gunters loyal to Wade and IOI's slew of mercenaries, is appropriately grand in scale—bearing all the hallmarks of famously epic scenes like the Battle of Helm's Deep from *Lord of the Rings*—but, in terms of real-world consequences, it barely registers: "The status quo established at the beginning of the narrative," Jonathan Alexander explains, "does not change: the world's primary communications networks will still be in the hands of a billionaire whom the rest of the users will have to trust to keep them safe from more villainous billionaires. The only difference is that a nerd now has control" (529). And even this is just a continuation of the status quo, as, at least at GSS, a nerd was already in control. Wade replacing Halliday ensures that nothing will change—and this is by design: Wade wins the contest by proving that he knows Halliday's favorite things better than anyone on the planet. Poverty, starvation, the energy crisis, climate change, and every other horror of contemporary life the novel invokes also remain completely unaffected. This is not incidental, but actually essential to the world Cline has built: The persistence of these conditions is necessary because Wade's triumph is only given meaning by the continued existence of the crises threatening the world; if the world were made better, the battle for the OASIS would lose its significance—a fitting conclusion in a posthistorical world that, as Baudrillard once pointed out, is more concerned with *preventing* things from happening than producing new events (*Illusion of the End* 17).

The scope of the novel's victory is therefore at odds with the '80s media it reveres, most of which is significantly more ambitious: Luke, Han, and Leia save the galaxy from authoritarianism, David Lightman prevents thermonuclear war, and Indiana Jones prevents the Nazis from attaining immortality, while Wade only manages to secure the future of video games (and only until everything else collapses). Here, the novel's desire for realism (or, at least, *believability*) seems to have come into conflict with its fantasy, producing a contradiction that it must try to reconcile: How do you save a world that can't be saved?

The answer is found in the fact that they do save *a* world. Keeping the OASIS out of the hands of the greedy megacorporation IOI prevents a future in which the problems of the real world leak into the virtual one. Early in the novel, Wade lays out the stakes involved in preventing IOI from gaining control of the OASIS: "They would start charging a monthly fee for access to the simulation. They would plaster advertisements on every visible surface. User anonymity and free speech would become things of the past. The moment IOI took over, the OASIS would cease to be the open-source virtual utopia I'd grown up in. It would become a corporate-run dystopia, an overpriced theme park for wealthy elitists" (33). IOI is presented in contrast to Halliday's *benevolent* megacorporation, GSS—which, as Wade explains in the sequel, has become an "unstoppable megacorporation with a global monopoly on the world's most popular entertainment, education, and communications platform" (29). Thus, as A. O. Scott points out in his review of the film, *Ready Player One* (book and novel) relies on a dichotomy that doesn't exist in reality:

> Halliday is a sweet, shaggy nerd with a guileless Northern California drawl and a deeply awkward manner, especially around women. Sorrento [the face of IOI] is an autocratic bean counter, a would-be master of the universe who doesn't even like video games. These characters are clichés, but they are also allegorical figures. In the movie, they represent opposing principles, but in our world, they are pretty much the same guy. A lot of the starry-eyed do-it-yourselfers tinkering in their garages and giving life to their boyish dreams

> back in the '70s and '80s turned out to be harboring superman fantasies of global domination all along. They shared their wondrous creations and played the rest of us for suckers, collecting our admiration, our attention and our data as profit and feudal tribute.

The only difference between the two corporations—which, for *Ready Player One* is the *crucial* one—is one of aesthetic preference. It's OK for such figures to exist, the novel suggests, as long as they like the right things.

By winning the contest, Wade preserves the continued functioning of the OASIS *as it is*, in effect saving the (virtual) world from the fate to which the real one has already succumbed. *Ready Player One* is thus able to invoke the world-saving convention of the media Cline loves, to preserve his fantasy of triumph, by displacing it into a different context. Through the OASIS, then, *Ready Player One* constructs a substitute world that, unlike the real one, *can* be saved. In saving the OASIS, *Ready Player One* also evinces a nostalgia for a type of story that is rarely told in the twenty-first century, about a world in which destruction can be averted. Cline's attempt to reproduce this narrative is thus an expression of nostalgic fantasy for an outmoded media convention, a Jamesonian pastiche in which obsolete cultural forms reemerge, hollowed of their original function and redeployed as style.

The question, however, still remains: If not its influences, what delimits the extent of the novel's triumphs and the changes they enact? Here we see contemporary social reality structuring (arguably superseding) Cline's homage. In its reluctance to imagine a better future beyond its virtual world, as well as its retreat into '80s pop culture, the novel expresses sentiments that arose as a result of the conditions of the end of history. In this context, *Ready Player One* doesn't imagine a better future because it can't: because the notion of a better future has lost credibility; because we're already living in a time that was itself another time's "better future" and, in many ways, have little to show for it (whatever one thinks of the progress of the past few decades, it's difficult to say that we've so far lived up to what was imagined for the twenty-first century); because of, ultimately, a sense that the future is already written and nothing else *is* possible. To paraphrase Mark Fisher, it's easier to imagine the complete virtualization of oligarchic capitalism through the construction of a massive, worldwide video game than it is to imagine anything better.

The novel is, in this light, an expression of a feeling of powerlessness so pervasive that even the prospect of becoming the wealthiest person on the planet with a controlling stake in the world's largest corporation is not enough to provide one with the ability to imagine a viable alternative to the status quo: Midway through the novel, Wade's love interest Art3mis asks, "What would you do if you won. . . . How would you spend all that money?" After replying that he'd "move into a mansion. Buy a bunch of cool shit. Not be poor," she presses for more: "Wow. Big dreamer. . . . And after you buy your mansion and your 'cool shit,' what will you do with the hundred and thirty billion you'll have left over?" "Not wanting her to think I was some shallow idiot," Wade explains that he would "have a nuclear-powered interstellar spacecraft constructed in Earth's orbit. . . . I'd stock it with a lifetime supply of food and water, a self-sustaining biosphere, and a supercomputer loaded with every movie, book, song, videogame, and piece of artwork that human civilization has ever created, along with a stand-alone copy of the OASIS. Then I'd invite a few of my closest friends to come aboard, along with a team of doctors and scientists, and we'd all get the hell out of Dodge. Leave the solar system and start looking for an extrasolar Earthlike planet" (97–98). When Art3mis asks if Wade realizes that "nearly half the people on this planet are starving," Wade replies that "the reason so many people are starving is because we've wrecked the planet. The Earth is dying, you know? It's time to leave" (98). Art3mis, often positioned as the novel's moral core, replies that she would use the money to "make sure everyone on this planet has enough to eat. Once we tackle world hunger, then we can figure out how to fix the environment and solve the energy crisis," which elicits an eye roll from Wade: "Right. . . . And after you pull off that miracle, you can genetically engineer a bunch of Smurfs and unicorns to frolic around this new perfect world you've created. . . . You really think it's that simple. . . . That you can just write a check for two hundred and forty billion dollars and fix all the world's problems?" (98). In this, Wade expresses the belief that the only option is, essentially, giving up—the problems are beyond solving. The novel initially poses this as a debate between a supposedly clear-eyed cynicism and lofty idealism, and, at least here, it seems to suggest that neither is totally correct. In the novel's final scene, after they've defeated IOI and won the contest, Wade and Art3mis return to the question:

> "So what happens now?"
>
> I smiled. "We're going to use all of the moolah we just won to feed everyone on the planet. We're going to make the world a better place, right?"
>
> She grinned. "Don't you want to build a huge interstellar spaceship, load it full of videogames, junk food, and comfy couches, and then get the hell out of here?"
>
> "I'm up for that, too," I said. "If it means I get to spend the rest of my life with you." (371)

Cline ultimately avoids declaring one approach correct, dissolving the debate into a romantic appeal. Wade, though, having now learned the meaning of love and friendship, does seem to have developed a desire to think beyond himself, and recognizes the value of striving for something even if the result isn't guaranteed.

If the end of *Ready Player One* seems to leave the door open for the possibility of a better future, Cline's 2020 sequel quickly shuts it and, by the end, locks it and throws away the key. *Ready Player Two,* which takes place three years after the end of the first novel, begins with Wade recounting the group's activities in the time since. Following his victory in Halliday's egg hunt, Wade elected to share his wealth and control of GSS with his three friends who helped him along the way. With their newfound prosperity, each has taken on considerable philanthropic missions aimed at combating pet issues ranging from world hunger to housing discrimination against the LGBTQ community. In true neoliberal fashion (they are, after all, the most powerful people on the planet), they also attempted to solve problems on the level of government itself:

> We'd also started funneling cash to the struggling U.S. government and its citizens, who had been surviving on foreign aid for decades. We paid off the national debt and provided aerial-defense drones and tactical telebots to help reestablish the rule of law in the rural areas where local infrastructure had collapsed along with the power grid. Human law enforcement officers no longer had to risk their own lives to uphold the law. Our police telebots were able to carry out their mission to serve and protect without putting any human lives at risk. Their programming and their operational fail-safes prevented them from harming anyone in the line of duty. (61)

Unfortunately for the so-called High Five, their "noble efforts weren't moving the dial. . . . For the time being we were holding chaos and collapse at bay, but humanity's perilous predicament just kept getting worse." The reason, Wade explains, was "painfully obvious": "We'd already passed the point of no return. The world's population was fast approaching ten billion people, and Mother Earth was making it abundantly clear that she could no longer sustain all of us—especially not after we'd spent the past two centuries poisoning her oceans and atmosphere with wild industrial abandon. We had made our bed, and now we were going to die in it" (61). In response, he has used his considerable wealth to begin construction of the same "nuclear-powered interstellar spacecraft" he fantasized about in the first book, with room for "up to two dozen human passengers" and the goal of finding a new planet fit for human habitation (62). Even as he recognizes the optics of this move, Wade rationalizes it as the only way to ensure a future for humanity, and, thus, "the only responsible thing to do": "With Earth teetering on the brink of destruction, leaving our eggs in one basket was foolish" (65).

The return of Wade's cynicism in the early stages of the second novel is partly driven by the disintegration of his relationship with Art3mis (which was arguably the true source of his newfound conviction anyway); however, despite having won her back by the end of the novel, and having once again beaten back the forces that threaten the future of the OASIS, the spaceship actually remains the group's (and, seemingly Cline's) only tangible solution to the problems the world faces, albeit with a slight twist. Following the discovery of technology that can create sentient AI clones by mapping human brains, which is the catalyst of most of the novel's action, the group decides in the end to send copies of themselves and the OASIS into space to search for a habitable planet while they remain on Earth. The AI copy of Wade's consciousness, who narrates the final chapter, is uncharacteristically hopeful despite recognizing that very little has actually changed: "Things aren't perfect. The people who remain back on Earth are still facing plenty of huge problems. But they also still have the OASIS as their collective means of escape. . . . Even with all of the problems confronting our counterparts back on Earth, it's comforting to know that there are smart, resourceful people back there, doing everything in their power to make life better for their fellow human beings—while digital copies of many of those same people are out here in space, searching to find humanity a new home" (587–588). Here, Cline again slips into the same bystander theory of change that he expressed in the *Slate* interview—*Something, somehow needs to change; hopefully someone will figure it out because I can't*. As in *Ready Player One*, *Ready Player Two* closes with an attempt at an '80s movie morality lesson: "The only thing you can do is keep right on playing. Because the game that is your life still isn't over yet. And there's no telling how far you might be able to get, what you might discover, or who you might meet when you get there" (589). Since Cline has stated that the final book in the trilogy will be a prequel, this is how the saga ends. There are only two options for dealing with the horrors of the modern world: escapism (distraction) and giving up (abandonment).

There is, here and throughout both novels, a paradox: a seemingly unshakable belief in the power of the individual to overcome whatever is laid before them coupled with the sense that we've reached the end of what can be achieved (or, at least, the limit of what can be imagined). As Susan Aronstein and Jason Thompson have argued in their examination of the novel's appropriation of Arthurian legend, *Ready Player One*'s conclusion offers readers "the grail, the ultimate Easter egg, arguing that true meaning . . . lies outside of the world of the game, in the meta-level of genuine human exchange. [Cline] paints our modern world as a wasteland in need of an Arthur to restore it, and no code, trick, or joke—no magic, no memory, and no Merlin—he argues, can do that" (63). And yet, in *Ready Player Two*, no Arthur arrives. Wade may have found the grail—twice—but salvation is not on the horizon.[2] In this, the scale of Wade's success is both massive and minuscule. He has taken on the second most powerful corporation in the world, outsmarted literally everyone else on the planet, and defeated a supposedly all-knowing, all-powerful artificial intelligence, and yet none of it has had any broader impact on the crises faced by humanity that the series, for some reason, cannot let go of. In truth, at the novel's close, *nothing has really happened*: A narrative that begins by invoking a multitude of global catastrophes supposedly ends in triumph despite its champion having made zero impact on any of them. Not only this, but Wade's victories also ensure the survival of one of the major obstacles to real change in the novel: the OASIS itself. The novel makes clear that, more than anything else, Halliday's invention encourages *escapism* (and thus passive acceptance) over *escape* (liberation), placating the masses and leaving them in a state of inertia.

The series is thus an expression of the profound pessimism that has developed as a result of the end of history. Wade synthesizes this view early in the first novel, soberly summarizing the state of the world as he wishes someone else had done for him: "Basically, kid, what this all means is that life is a lot tougher than it used to be, in the Good Old Days, back before you were born. Things used to be awesome, but now they're kinda terrifying. To be honest, the future doesn't look too bright. You were born at a pretty crappy time in history. And it looks like things are only gonna get worse from here on out. Human civilization is in 'decline.' Some even say it's 'collapsing'" (17–18). Because fundamental change is seemingly impossible, and because the system doesn't provide—and, in fact, regularly suppresses—any stories that give meaning to these struggles, this powerful sense of hopelessness emerges. It's no wonder that the novels can only conceive of two approaches: distraction and abandonment. This is what happens when the belief that a system is broken couples with the notion that there is no alternative to it. All there is left to do is either look away or fantasize about escape. A few pages after the description above, Wade explains that Halliday's Easter Egg hunt provided him with precisely this, a way to find meaning in the world through purposeful distraction: "Suddenly, I'd found something worth doing. A dream worth chasing. For the last five years, the Hunt had given me a goal and purpose. A quest to fulfill. A reason to get up in the morning. Something to look forward to. The moment I began searching for the egg, the future no longer seemed so bleak" (19). In the second novel, however, after the excitement of the Hunt has dissipated, Wade drifts back into hopelessness about the future of humanity and begins construction on the aforementioned spaceship. The hunt for the egg is thus revealed to be only a temporary respite from the insurmountable despair facing the planet. Nothing good is permanent, and presentiment of catastrophe always returns.

This inevitable malaise is one of the ways in which the novel's nostalgia interacts meaningfully with its end of history–inflected dystopia. In a time when things only seem to get worse, and the future appears to be written in stone, the past naturally becomes a place of solace and comfort. Importantly, however, this is not actually the function of nostalgia for the novel's characters: Wade and his friends never really express any nostalgic longing. Aside from generally lamenting the present decline and distracting themselves from the present with the artifacts of another time, the characters hold no "I was born in the wrong generation" discussions in either novel, and none of them express a particular desire to "go back" despite the 1980s, for all its (generally unacknowledged) faults, appearing considerably better than the novel's present. The reason for this is simple: Having never experienced the actual 1980s, their entire notion of the period comes from media and consumer products, which, through the OASIS, they can already experience firsthand in perfect simulacra. Wade's best friend, Aech, for instance, has modeled her personal chat room after "a large suburban rec room, circa the late 1980s. Old movie and comic book posters covered the wood-paneled walls. A vintage RCA television stood in the center of the room, hooked up to a Betamax VCR, a LaserDisc player, and several vintage videogame consoles. Bookshelves lined the far wall, filled with role-playing game supplements and back issues of Dragon magazine" (*Ready Player One* 37). What *Ready Player One* stages for its characters is not a nostalgia for events, for a specific time or a place filtered through a particular subjectivity, but an attachment to *things*—which are much more easily reproduced and acquired, and, furthermore, have a particular aesthetic quality. There's a reason the VCR is a Betamax from the 1980s rather than a Toshiba from the early 2000s, though the two objects served the exact same purpose in reality. However, in Aech's virtual chat room, neither serves *any* purpose aside from contributing to the room's aesthetic. As in *Stranger Things* (the subject of chapter 2 of this book), we see here a hierarchy at work, where the aesthetic of an object is its most essential quality: style for the sake of style. It's easy to see why, when the objects of their infatuation are immediately available, these characters don't long for the past that used to contain them. Insofar as one's nostalgia is tied to *things* rather than experiences, the OASIS has, in effect, made longing obsolete. Baudrillard has argued that "nostalgia . . . was beautiful for never being satisfied, as was utopia for never being achieved" (*Illusion of the End* 120). The fantasy *Ready Player One* stages, in which nostalgia *can* be satisfied, is a grotesque revision that simultaneously deprives it of its beauty and its critical potential. *Ready Player Two* takes this a step further, incorporating the creation of technology that enables one to relive memories—their own or someone else's—ultimately transposing intangible events and experiences into products that can be obtained and consumed.

The OASIS itself is also a space that is fundamentally shaped by the end of history. It is a site where the cultural has utterly supplanted the political and the historical. At one point in the first novel, Wade notes that real-world elections were pointless, but that he always voted in OASIS elections. In a reactionary move, Cline, through Wade, also expresses disdain for the fundamentals of democracy, noting that "now that everyone could vote from home, via the OASIS, the only people who could get elected were movie stars, reality TV personalities, or radical evangelists" (201). The OASIS elections exist only in the form of pop cultural artifacts, wholly abstracted from the context in which they were created. Halliday's virtual reality simulation is thus the epitome of what Slavoj Žižek has described as "a place deprived of its history; a *worldless* place" (*Trouble in Paradise* 10) that exists in the postideological world. If, as Fredric Jameson has argued, the postmodern subject is one who has lost their sense of history, the OASIS is the ultimate postmodern space, a posthistorical playground. In Cline's future, all conflict plays out in the artificial world of culture, a literalization of contemporary "culture wars" but further abstracted from political reality in favor of petty disputes over the management of products and aesthetic properties. History, as a result, doesn't really happen anymore. In fact, not only is the OASIS a space where the transplanting of culture for history and politics ensures that nothing meaningful ever happens, stasis is actually its primary function. The OASIS exists to provide stability in a world of decay.

The OASIS works not only to ensure that the world is trapped in a perpetual present, but also to make the utopian(ized) past inhabitable again—an act that takes place both within the world of the novel and for its readers. As a readerly experience, *Ready Player One* promises to immerse its readers in a world of '80s nostalgia through a fantasy of a future where (via simulation) inhabiting the past is physically (or, at least, *visually*) possible. In one part of the novel, Wade visits a planet where Halliday had also sought precisely this result: "In the early days of the OASIS, Halliday had created a small planet named Middletown, named after his hometown in Ohio. The planet was the site of a meticulous re-creation of his hometown as it was in the late 1980s. That saying about how you can never go home again? Halliday had found a way. Middletown was one of his pet projects, and he'd spent years coding and refining it. And it was well known (to gunters, at least) that one of the most detailed and accurate parts of the Middletown simulation was the re-creation of Halliday's boyhood home" (65). For Halliday,[3] Middletown was the literalization of nostalgia: Instead of returning to his home in a memory, he converted that memory into physical space. The purpose of doing so is unclear, since the town was only populated with invented citizens powered by artificial intelligence instead of friends and family (most of whom were, presumably, dead), and, though one wonders what the use of this hollowed-out nostalgic simulacrum might be, it's a question the novel doesn't really interrogate.[4] Nonetheless, with Middletown, the distance that forms the impossibility at the heart of nostalgia seemingly became a little bit less—a tantalizing prospect for readers drawn in by the promise of a romp through the increasingly forgotten media that shaped their adolescence.

Halliday, we're told, devoted a considerable amount of time to the task of creating Middletown, working not only from memory but also from maps, phone books, photographs, and other artifacts to piece together what his memory couldn't render. The goal, Wade explains, was "to make everything as authentic and accurate as possible" (102), which raises an important question: authentic and accurate *to what*? The implication from Halliday's use of these documents is that he was seeking to replicate historical reality by going beyond the limitations of memory; yet, at the same time, nostalgic desire is also shown to have superseded reality as "Halliday had coded the planet so that no matter when you visited or where you were on the surface, it was always a perfect late-autumn afternoon, circa 1986" (101). In this, the supposedly *realistic* recreation is characterized by an impossible subversion of reality designed to *improve* physical reality so that it better reflects the ideal. When Wade arrives in Middletown, he makes note of the AI inhabitants of the town who seem, above all else, designed to evoke *'80s-ness*, producing another evasion of true authenticity in their hyperrealism: "[They were] all dressed in mid-1980s attire. A woman with a giant ozone-depleting hairdo bobbed her head to an oversize Walkman. A kid in a gray Members Only jacket leaned against the wall, working on a Rubik's Cube. A Mohawked punk rocker sat in a plastic chair, watching a *Riptide* rerun on a coin-operated television" (101). Though Wade doesn't notice, the town's AI population, who seem to have been designed based on a list of "80s things," are remarkably unreal, a reflection not of the actual Middletown, Ohio, of 1986 (not everyone in the '80s, particularly in the small industrial towns of the Midwest, looked so stereotypically '80s), but more like a cinematic invention where everything is designed to *signify* for an audience: When he first arrives, Wade notes that it was "like stepping out of a time machine" and, having no frame of reference for the 1980s *except* media, adds a few sentences later that it reminded him of the (fictional) town from *Footloose* (101–102). In this way, Middletown is ultimately an *idealized* version of Halliday's hometown that sought authenticity only insofar as it was necessary to evoke the time and place without contradiction, a means of facilitating immersion.

Cline's novel is predicated on the desire to provide this—the world of *Ready Player One*, and its invention of the OASIS, in other words, exist for the purpose of reanimating the past. This desire is instantiated, at least in part, by the end of history, when the future is no longer desirable in itself and the past has morphed into a site of fantasy. The future is invoked in this novel mainly as a means of creating the conditions for the existence of a technology that enables one to inhabit a time that *is* desirable, one that can, crucially, remake that time in its idealized, ultradesirable form; in short, the future exists in the novel as a mechanism for returning to the past.

If the novel's appeal is that it allows readers to return to the past, then it's worth considering how it does so. Notably, unlike a novel that is *actually* set in the 1980s, either naturally or through some sort of time travel, Cline's series never truly leaves the 2040s. (But, of course, nor does it ever actually arrive at the 2040s; both places are imaginary, one a retrospective simulacrum, the other a prospective projection. The '80s are thus everywhere and nowhere.) Wade's trip to Middletown in the first novel, for instance, is purely simulated, and it is largely a fictional (re)construction even within the novel's fictional world. The sequel comes a bit closer to the actual 1980s as a setting in a few scenes that place Wade in the shoes of other people as he experiences their memories firsthand through the OASIS (similar to the "Flicksyncs" of *WarGames* and *Monty Python and the Holy Grail* from the first novel), but Wade is never *physically* there, and these glimpses of the actual 1980s are brief and deeply personal, which doesn't provide readers much opportunity to fully immerse themselves in the period. The novels' interaction with the past is thus almost exclusively bound up in references to media and consumer products.

In this, Cline's novels evince an extreme form of the same hollowing of allusion that I discuss in greater detail in chapter 2. In *Stranger Things*, another highly referential nostalgic narrative, the main thrust of the relationship between text and referent is presence alone—the text only needs to provide enough to suggest the reference. *Ready Player One* takes this to another level: In *Stranger Things*, these references are often at least partially coded, in the form of trope, narrative structure, sound design, and cinematography (kids riding bikes in the suburbs *evokes* the same in *E.T.*); in the novels, on the other hand, Cline typically just *says the name of the thing* ("Like Marty McFly, I woke up at exactly 10:28 A.M., to the song 'Back in Time' by Huey Lewis and the News" [*Ready Player Two* 39]). It's the authorial equivalent of pointing at an animal in the zoo, saying, "Hey, look, a tiger," and then moving on to the next exhibit. Formally, this also reflects Jameson's claim that postmodernism enacts the abstraction of modernist aesthetics (*Postmodernism* 17). Here, the modernist emphasis on *allusion* becomes the postmodernist emphasis on *reference*, taken to its extreme. Meaning is imparted here through gesture alone, contained in the technique itself rather than in what it produces. The reference, in other words, is not a means to an end, *it is the end*. There is nothing deeper lurking in the technique, and the result is a comparatively impoverished experience. As Laura Hudson explains in her review of *Ready Player Two*, "*There are no pleasures to be had here, only a reminder of things that once produced pleasure.* A random page of dialogue from *The Princess Bride* does not inspire a sense of romantic, swashbuckling adventure. Reciting the names of stars in every John Hughes movie does not convey their adolescent joy and heartbreak. And telling us that a climactic battle 'was like Yoda versus Palpatine, Gandalf versus Saruman, and Neo versus Agent Smith' does not make it feel like any of those far more interesting things" ("*Ready Player Two*"; emphasis added). *Ready Player One*'s deployment of this hollow referentiality in the service of nostalgia is a perfect reflection of the decoupling of nostalgia from experience that I discussed extensively in the introduction. Not only is it alienated from personal experience, but it's also divorced entirely from any sort of meaningful context: a dangling signifier capable only of evoking recognition. Emotion, in this form, arrives solely in the gratification one might feel from getting the reference and, possibly, the jolt of endorphins that comes from being reminded of something you once enjoyed. Pleasure has largely been outsourced to the past.

This system of nostalgia by referential accumulation is not incidental; it is central to the way that *Ready Player One* operates. It's part of the novel's essence, so deeply ingrained that the first trailer for Spielberg's adaptation (co-written by

Cline)—which, in keeping with the spirit of its predecessor, prominently featured a cavalcade of recognizable intellectual properties like Master Chief, Chucky, and the Iron Giant—was mocked by viewers online as *Recognizing Things: The Movie.*[5] The text's encyclopedic approach to homage is without question its most prominent feature. This is borne, at least in part, of the novel's aforementioned lack of context for its references. On nearly every page, the reader is confronted by a series of references that they either understand or don't. As Grady puts it, "The primary aesthetic pleasure [of the novel] is one of recognition: Yes, I know that reference, and yes, I agree that it sucks or rocks."

This has led many reviewers and critics to identify exclusion as the novel's central gesture. Megan Amber Condis, for instance, has argued that "the references serve as a gate-keeping mechanism: readers prove themselves to be a part of the gamer in-group described in and valorized by the novel if they can demonstrate encyclopedic knowledge of Halliday's/Cline's canon" (5). This reading, however, doesn't accurately capture the true character of the novel's system of references. While it might be true that readers who recognize Cline's references will feel a sense of thrill or achievement (and perhaps even belonging), it bears repeating that an overwhelming portion of the references in the series are actually to exceedingly mainstream artifacts, many of which are decidedly *not* classic geek/nerd/gamer texts, and for readers who lived through (or arguably even *near*) the 1980s much of the novel will likely be very familiar, whether they identify as part of Cline's subculture or not. Thus, while classic gaming trivia may not appeal to many readers—even self-identified gamers who were born in the late 1990s and have no experience with Atari games like *Galaga* or *Contra*[6]—it also isn't the primary mode of reference in the novel; instead, gaming is merely a subset of the larger class of references in the novel: the 1980s of Cline's adolescence. More than a novel for gamers or geeks, this is a novel built around a reader (or, arguably, author) of a certain age; *Ready Player One*'s ideal reader is one who, like Cline, came of age in or around the 1980s because simply living through this time grants most Americans automatic familiarity with the overwhelming majority of the novel's canon.

Indeed, despite accusations of gatekeeping, *Ready Player Two* makes abundantly clear that Cline *wants* his readers to be able to enjoy his novels, to take part in his nostalgic fantasy, even without getting all of the references. As Samantha Nelson pointed out in her review, unlike its predecessor, Cline's sequel "reads like a fusion between a Wikipedia page and a video game walk-through: It makes copious references but absolutely ensures readers get the joke by having characters share the source of a quote." Moreover, in addition to the references to games and other more conventionally white, masculine pop cultural artifacts like those we saw in the first novel, *Ready Player Two* also spends considerable time discussing those produced by women and people of color (seemingly as a corrective for the criticism Cline faced in the aftermath of *Ready Player*

One). Though he might prefer that readers automatically get his references, and readers who do are more likely to take pleasure in the work, the expansion of Cline's canon suggests that his goal is actually the opposite of traditional gatekeeping, in that the novels seek to gain validation *through* recognition. The more readers taking pleasure in the '80s nostalgia-fest, the better. The fact that both novels' references are often deployed with a triviality that enables unfamiliar readers to continue the story without substantial loss further emphasizes that Cline's goal is inclusive.

Cline seems to want, and surmises his readers want, above all else, to be *recognized*. It's no coincidence that the two most important characters in the novel are essentially avatars for different elements of their creator. Biographically, Halliday and Cline share a lot: similar birth years, similar hometowns in the same state, similar obsessions with the pop culture of their adolescence. They also share a desire to create a world in which their tastes become dominant. At one point in the novel, Halliday's closest friend and GSS cofounder, Ogden Morrow, explains that "Jim always wanted everyone to share his obsessions, to love the same things he loved. I think this contest is his way of giving the entire world an incentive to do just that" (*Ready Player One* 122). *Ready Player One* is Cline's attempt to do the same. Wade, too, as Nick Schager points out, serves as a kind of stand-in for Cline: "Just as Wade uses his Parzival avatar to create a perfect version of himself, so Cline does the same with Wade—since Wade's boundless, super-radical-amazing '80s erudition is really Cline's, and something the author can't help but brag about in detail. When Wade boasts about his virtual car ('my time-traveling, Ghost Busting, Knight Riding, matter-penetrating DeLorean') one can practically hear Cline squealing with delight over the idea of owning such a fit-for-a-fourth-grader's-imagination mash-up vehicle." In this light, the novels stage a world where its creator is represented by the two most important people on the planet. It's a power fantasy, of sorts, whose source is explicitly cultural, derived from one's mastery of a specific kind of pop culture knowledge. Readers who identify with Wade, Halliday, and Cline—who, in other words, *recognize* themselves within the novel—can also partake in this fantasy. Because this is the foundation of the novel, its popularity is perhaps less a matter of artistic excellence and more a function of its ability to capture readers within this fantasy. It casts Cline as a curator rather than creator, enacting through its gestural referentiality what Mark Fisher has labeled the "transformation of culture into museum pieces" (*Ghosts of My Life* 4), decontextualized artifacts made to be discussed but not experienced. Here, the author has engaged in the same act as his character: Just as Halliday, through his contest, constructs a world obsessed with what he deems valuable, so too has Cline, through his novel, created a narrative built around the valorization of his preferred media. The ultimate effect is to create a platform for recognition, in which praise of the novel necessarily involves praise for Cline's taste and, therefore, as I will shortly show, his *identity*.

Recognition in the novel is not simply a matter of being seen within characters; it is thematically central, and is the element that provides unity to the series. In its focus on recognition, the novel mirrors a larger trend in contemporary culture, which has seen an explosion of recognition claims. As Nancy Fraser explained in 2000, "Claims for the recognition of difference now drive many of the world's social conflicts, from campaigns for national sovereignty and subnational autonomy, to battles around multiculturalism, to the newly energized movements for international human rights, which seek to promote both universal respect for shared humanity and esteem for cultural distinctiveness. They have also become predominant within social movements such as feminism, which had previously foregrounded the redistribution of resources" (107). This tendency, Anna Kornbluh has argued, "deflects struggles over power and resources into struggles over respect and identity." Calls to be "seen and heard" under this rubric have grown in number and intensity in the years since Fraser first described this shift, and recognition has emerged as one of the—if not *the*—central mandates of contemporary social life, "orient[ing] everything from the accumulation of social media likes to university composition pedagogy, from 'I feel seen' mantras to industrial-scale self help, from Hollywood writers' rooms to electoral candidates" (61). Broadly, this shift is concomitant with recent interpretations of identity politics that, as the concept has grown in popularity, have become increasingly detached from its more materialist beginnings. This attenuated form of recognition politics is, in many cases, not even about recognition in the classical sense, but is actually a more superficial call for *affirmation* (Kornbluh 61), which substitutes the immediate pleasures of acquiring individual cultural legitimacy for the deeper resolution of collective material struggle.

The contemporary emphasis on identity and recognition—or, more specifically, their incorporation into mainstream culture outside of the expressly political—has also spawned a number of offshoots that warrant closer attention, especially in the way that they are reflected in Cline's novels. Most notably, as the discourse around identity politics has become mainstream, many Americans now seek to be recognized (or affirmed) based on individual, often idiosyncratic, identities that coalesce around aesthetic taste more than conventional social categories such as race, class, gender, and sexuality.[7] End-of-history neoliberalism, in other words, indexes identity to patterns of consumption (gamer, Marvel fan, hip-hop head, K-Pop stan), and the self, as a result, must then be recognized through the things that constitute it. In order for a Marvel fan to feel validated, for instance, their favorite movies must be appreciated by the broader public. Critique of the product then becomes a critique of the identity of those who like it.[8] Mediated nostalgia, therefore, is just another expression of consumer choice that has come to define the self. Identity, in this formulation, is a product of the products that one enjoyed as a kid. Recognition of that childhood self becomes a matter of the recognition or validation of the consumer's choice, and reexperiencing the media that helped define an adolescence becomes an act of self-recognition and, perhaps more importantly, of cultural validation. To be seen and heard, in this context, is to have memories of favorite childhood TV shows seen and heard. *Ready Player One* exemplifies what happens when the consumer preferences that formed an essential part of adolescent identity become obsolete. Where identity has become tied to patterns of consumption and taste, increasing obsolescence results in the subject's feeling misrecognized. In posthistorical culture, where conventional social structures have become increasingly atomized, cultural irrelevance, when the products that define one's identity are no longer widely recognized (neither understood nor validated), is akin to social death—as Lauren Berlant puts it, "Under capitalism, being in circulation denotes being in life" (42). As a project, *Ready Player One* is thus an attempt to fight against the death of one's identity—to ensure that it remains not only culturally relevant but, most of all, dominant; it is an attempt to reassert the primacy of (a certain kind of) Gen-X pop cultural heritage.[9] As a work of fiction, *Ready Player One* stages a utopian fantasy where this kind of social death never occurs because the world has become enraptured by the increasingly outmoded tastes and pop cultural objects of its creators' adolescence. The novel imagines a future where Gen-X pop culture, and the identities that are tied up in it, are not only still relevant but actually reassert themselves as the dominant force.

This situation arises at the end of history because, in the absence of systemic political alternatives, and with the attendant foreclosing of possibility, neoliberalism suggests instead a marketized solution to social stratification: The way to gain recognition is to vie for status in the realm of culture. Thus, whether or not recognition is the structuring mechanism of History as Fukuyama contended, he was, nonetheless, correct to identify recognition as a fundamental force in life at the end of history. Specifically, Fukuyama claims that the innate desire for recognition, modified by the conditions of the end of history, will produce a return to Hegel's originary battles for pure prestige: "Liberal economic principles," he explains, "provide no support for traditional communities; quite the contrary, they tend to atomize and separate people", and thus the decline of community life in the universalized liberal state at the end of history, coupled with the lack of urgent sociopolitical action, may lead to "bloody and pointless prestige battles" (*End of History* 325, 328). While he imagines these battles taking the form of literal combat between individuals or groups, the posthistorical outsourcing of conflict to the realm of culture, which Fukuyama didn't quite foresee, has instead led to discursive battles over petty cultural disputes with only prestige at stake. All of this arises out of what Fukuyama terms *megalothymia*, a term he coined in *The End of History* for "the desire to be recognized as superior to other people" (182), a state which, he contends, is fostered by the conditions of the end of history. Though not explicitly antagonistic toward a particular opponent (other than the aforementioned "poseurs" who only pretend to like his favored IP), *Ready Player One* essentially serves this function for Cline and his audience: In its insistence on the greatness of its canon, the novel itself becomes a claim for prestige. Its status as a best seller then serves to bestow the novel's canon—and, more importantly, the identities it represents—with the recognition they seek. Recognition of the canon's superiority imparts recognition of the subject's superiority.

Ready Player Two then plays out as a corrective to *Ready Player One*, in which the freshly recognized subject confers recognition to groups whose contributions might have been excluded previously, but whom he deems worthy of validation too. Cline's sequel, in other words, is really a book about identity. As such, it reads like a response to criticism leveled at the first novel, which, despite its best-seller status, also met with considerable resistance, especially for the construction of its aforementioned canon. Condis effectively summarizes the opposition the novel faced: "The pop culture 'syllabus' embedded within *Ready Player One* [is] almost exclusively white and male because it reflects and reproduces the historical and material conditions that led to the creation of its featured texts. . . . By lending its authority only to certain texts (texts by and about those who inhabit historically privileged positions within gamer culture) and by excluding, ignoring, or ghettoizing texts by and about those who inhabit other positions, *Ready Player One* reproduces the social system that produced it, a social system in which true, archetypal geeks are modeled on their progenitors: white males" (10). Ultimately, for many, the novel is premised less on providing the fun action-adventure novel Cline intended, and instead imagines "a world of elitist gatekeeping . . . a world in which a person's value is determined by their knowledge of esoteric cultural trivia, where those of lesser value must be defeated and wiped away, and where gaming is all that matters. And, crucially, it is a world specifically for straight white men" (Grady). "The main thing *Ready Player One* is doing," Grady concludes, "is telling those '80s-boy-culture-obsessed gamers that they matter, that in fact they are the most important people in the universe."

Ready Player One pivots on Cline's tastes, which are those of a stereotypical straight white male geek of a certain age; the novel is, undoubtedly, a power fantasy built *especially* for those who embody that identity. In defense of its alleged homogeneity, however, proponents of the novel might point out that the novel's characters are relatively diverse. The High Five is composed of a white man, a white woman, a Black lesbian, and two Japanese men, and, while none are as important as Wade—unambiguously the novel's hero, whose perspective alone focalizes the story—their contributions are essential. These characters, moreover, can be viewed as making the novel's intention to welcome everyone into its fantasy (ignoring the fact that the novel's fantasy is not one in which everyone would want to participate since it is structured in a manner that necessarily excludes—not everyone *likes* this stuff—despite the author's apparent intention).

Ready Player One's treatment of Aech's race and sexuality showcases both the author's "good" intentions and the failures that result from the ideology that shaped his project. Throughout most of the novel, Aech, Wade's best friend and fellow gunter, is referred to using masculine pronouns in response to her avatar's appearance ("a tall, broad-shouldered Caucasian male with dark hair and brown eyes" [38]). Because the two have never met in real life, not until the final third of the novel does Wade (and the reader) learn that Aech is actually, in her words, "a fat black chick" (519). Aech explains her decision to present as a white man in the OASIS:

> Her real name, she said, was Helen Harris, and she was only a few months older than I was. She'd grown up in Atlanta, raised by a single mother. Her father had died in Afghanistan when she was still a baby. Her mother, Marie, worked from home in an online data processing center. In Marie's opinion, the OASIS was the best thing that had ever happened to both women and people of color. From the very start, Marie had used a white male avatar to conduct all of her online business, because of the marked difference it made in how she was treated and the opportunities she was given.
>
> When Aech first logged into the OASIS, she followed her mother's advice and created a Caucasian male avatar. 'H' had been her mother's nickname for her since she was a baby, so she'd decided to use it as the name of her online persona. (320)

Here, Cline acknowledges the privileges accorded to his own identity that are denied to others. However, as Condis explains, while "one might think that Aech's story could open up space within the narrative of the novel to critique such a non-inclusive definition of gamer culture. . . . Cline [instead] forecloses this possibility by focusing more on how Aech's masquerade affects his narrator, Wade, than on how it affected her as she lived it" (14). Indeed, the novel follows Wade's reactions very closely as he moves from shock and betrayal ("How could he—*she*—deceive me all these years?" [318]) to forgiveness ("We'd connected on a purely mental level. I understood her, trusted her, and loved her as a dear friend. None of that had changed, or could be changed by anything as *inconsequential* as her gender, or skin color, or orientation" [emphasis added; 321]), but outside of telling her life story, *Ready Player One* pays little attention to the seriousness of the issues Aech's reveal invokes, and these concerns don't arise again until Cline revisits them in the sequel. Further, Wade's framing of Aech's masquerade as "inconsequential"—which "confuses the notion that Aech's race, gender, and sexuality don't matter to [Wade] with the notion that they do not matter generally" (Condis 15)—perfectly encapsulates the novel's essential ideology: What matters are your tastes rather than your place in any conventional social categories; (pop) culture, again, is everything. With Aech, Cline's point is the *erosion* of difference rather than the equal recognition of it. By dismissing differences of race, gender, and sexuality as immaterial, the novel attempts to pave the way for anyone who enjoys its canon to partake in its fantasy.

The issue, of course, is that the novel is still inherently hierarchical, built around the notions that some cultural artifacts are superior to others and, subsequently, that the identities tied to the appreciation of these *worthy* artifacts are also superior. At the same time, no matter what he says, Cline can't make race immaterial, and he can't truly create an inclusive canon composed of media that overwhelmingly favors one group. In other words, there is a fundamental contradiction between the novel's desire for inclusion and the entries in its canon. *Ready Player Two* is an attempt to resolve this conflict: If the first novel is an effort to gain recognition for its author and for the readers who share his tastes, its sequel seeks to distribute the same cultural capital to those who might have felt left out based on identity differences.

In *Ready Player Two*, Cline's efforts to remedy this incongruity take two primary forms: recognition through empathy and recognition through media. The former arrives mainly through revelations Wade experiences as a result of the OASIS Neural Interface (ONI), a new technology introduced at the beginning of the novel that "allows an OASIS user to see, hear, smell, taste, and feel their avatar's virtual environment, via signals transmitted directly into their cerebral cortex. The headset's sensor array also monitors and interprets its wearer's brain activity, allowing them to control their OASIS avatar just as they do their physical body—simply by thinking about it" (8–9). More importantly for Wade's (and the novel's) emotional development, "The ONI allows you to relive moments of other people's lives. To see the world through their eyes, hear it through their ears, smell it through their nose, taste it with their tongue, and feel it through their skin" (9). As Aech explains, this has led to "a drastic increase in empathy and environmental conservation among daily ONI users, along with an overwhelming drop in racist, sexist, and homophobic ideologies. And that's all around the world, across all age groups and social strata. For the first time in human history, we have technology that gives us the ability to live in someone else's skin for a little while. And we've seen a huge drop in hate crimes around the globe too. And crime rates in general" (108). All it takes to solve these centuries-old social conflicts, the novel suggests, is the ability to walk a mile in someone else's virtual shoes; the ills of the world are not produced politically, socially, or systemically, but are instead conceived of as *purely* individual phenomena resulting from a deficit of empathy that can be corrected through access to the right experiences. Accordingly, Wade explains, this has had a major impact on his own emotional development:

> Thanks to years of surfing the ONI-net [an online database of curated ONI files that allow the user to experience events from a variety of identities and social positions], I now knew what it felt like to be all kinds of different people,

> having all different kinds of sex. I'd experienced sex with women while being another woman, and sex with men as both a woman and a man. I'd done playback of several different flavors of straight and gay and nonbinary sex, just out of pure curiosity, and I'd come away with the same pure realization that most ONI users came away with: Passion was passion and love was love, regardless of who the participants involved were, or what sort of body they were assigned at birth. (145)

This part of the novel reads like a direct response to Wade's homophobia in the first book, which comes out as anxiety over Art3mis's real identity. The two have never met IRL, but Wade has a "massive cyber-crush" on her nonetheless (35). Though he claims to be certain that she's female, and imagines her looking exactly like her avatar, he also acknowledges multiple times that this might not be true: "I reminded myself that the person operating the avatar in front of me might not be a woman at all. This 'girl,' whom I'd been cyber-crushing on for the past three years, might very well be an obese, hairy-knuckled guy named Chuck" (88). This Chuck figure shows up as the embodiment of Wade's sexual anxiety each time he considers the issue. At one point, after telling her that he doesn't "want to find out that I've got a crush on some 300 lb. dude named Chuck who lives in his mother's basement in suburban Detroit," he also falls into transphobia, asking, "Are you a woman? And by that I mean are you a human female who has never had a sex-change operation?" (173). The ONI's revelations about gender identity and sexuality are, in this light, an especially pointed apology for moments like these.

The novel doesn't shy away from the implications of the ONI on sexuality and gender identity, either, leading, as Wade explains, to a new category: øgender. "People who identified as øgender," he says, "were individuals who chose to experience sex exclusively through their ONI headsets, and who also didn't limit themselves to experiencing it as a specific gender or sexual orientation" (145). This was not a rare designation:

> Coming out as øgender became incredibly common in the wake of the ONI's release. For the first time in human history, anyone eighteen years of age or older could safely and easily experience sexual intercourse with any gender and as any gender. This tended to alter their perception of gender identity and fluidity in profound ways. It had certainly altered mine. And I was certain that it had done the same thing for every other ONI user with even a mildly adventurous spirit. Thanks to the OASIS Neural Interface, your gender and your sexuality were no longer constrained by—or confined to—the physical body you happened to be born into. (145)

We see deployed here the same kind of liberatory utopian premise that Cline lays out for minorities in the first novel. The OASIS allows you to be whoever you want to be; all you have to do is climb into the right skin: Race, gender, sexuality, all of these things are *purely* performative, based in doing rather than being—aesthetics rather than content. Difference, again, is immaterial, and utopia is construed as a place where everyone is, essentially, free to be the same.

This is, of course, *not* the reading Cline seems to intend. The novel is unambiguous in claiming the benefits of these developments, and the affordances of the ONI for individual identity. To show this, *Ready Player Two* introduces a new character, L0hengrin, who was "famous for changing her avatar's gender, unexpectedly and without warning—sometimes in mid-sentence. When she transformed into a male, she seemed to prefer the likeness of a young James Spader, especially his look from the 1985 film *Tuff Turf.* Regardless of her avatar's current gender, L0hengrin's public profile specified that her preferred gender pronouns were she and her" (131). After using his OASIS admin powers to snoop through her school records, Wade discovers that L0hengrin had been assigned as male at birth. Thanks to the ONI, however, Wade was unperturbed by this news: "Discovering this minor detail didn't send me spiraling into a sexual-identity crisis, the way it probably would have back when I was younger" (145).

The revelations that Wade attains from the ONI are not confined to fleeting moments like these. They are, instead, built into the novel's central quest. At the end of each stage, Wade is thrust into the ONI-captured memories of Kira Morrow, the deceased wife of Halliday's former partner and the object of his unrequited love. These moments chart the emotional history of Halliday's relationship with Kira, which, when he experienced them from her point of view, Halliday truly understood for the first time. Wade's journey is meant to provide the same revelations about the inner lives of women that Halliday had gleaned, namely, that they have their own thoughts and feelings, and aren't simply objects of male attention. There's a fundamental crudeness, both philosophical and formal, to the process of empathy the novel lays out—as Samantha Nelson puts it, Wade can't help but point out Kira's breasts each time he's placed within her body. The novel, Hudson notes, "revolves around the idea that after reliving the recorded memories of women, supposedly clueless men experience a moment of enlightenment and now realize that women are people. It never occurs to [Wade] that he also could have come to the same conclusion about [Halliday's misogyny] by using the greatest empathy machine of all, his brain, and running the . . . program that is listening to other people and believing them about their experiences" ("*Ready Player Two*"). Only by (virtually) becoming someone else can these men understand the experiences of others. Further, the novel's need to point out that women are people is decidedly retro, out of place in the 2020 literary and cultural milieu and more befitting the '80s movies of Cline's adolescence. The author's obsession with the nostalgic pop culture he grew up with has seemingly produced a kind of arrested development, in which his understanding of these issues has not advanced beyond the time they were first revealed to him.

As part of its discussion of the validity of minority identities, *Ready Player Two* also introduces a reexamination of its canon and the history that underpins it. The novel repeats its predecessor's questing structure, with the "search for the seven shards" replacing the "hunt for the golden eggs." This time, however, rather than sending Wade on a journey through his own favored media as before, Halliday's second quest is built around the media that Kira loved (which, not coincidentally, is also quintessentially '80s). As a result, the stages of the search are more focused on the media that would be relevant to a stereotypical (white and straight) '80s girl. The novel spends considerable time celebrating these texts, while also using them as an opportunity to critically explore how they reflect the experiences of women, people of color, and members of the LGBTQ community.

Cline's gestures toward inclusion, however, are always filtered through the same flattened neoliberal consumption-recognition matrix: The works of minority artists, and the minority identities (Cline believes) they represent, are recognized in the terms already established by the first novel, that is, their contribution to the pop culture of Cline's adolescence. Instead of validating elements of uniquely Black and queer culture, for instance, the novel merely highlights (tenuously) the contributions members of these groups have made to the preestablished '80s pop nostalgia canon; rather than attempting to recover artistic contributions that were stifled, in other words, *Ready Player Two* only includes references to elements already included, which the previous novel overlooked, such as Prince and, even more problematically, John Hughes movies. "Look," the novel seems to say, "there's something for everyone here." These diversification efforts are also often coupled with dialogue recognizing the representational injustices of the '80s canon, which are named and then quickly discarded—a permissive act, much like *Stranger Things*' acknowledgment of unconscious racial bias that I analyze in chapter 2. A central aim of *Ready Player Two* is maintaining the integrity of Cline's original canon through incorporation by absorbing more artifacts (and identities) into the existing setup instead of reconceiving the project.

This effort plays out most extensively when the novel's action moves to two planets, Shermer and Afterworld, where the knowledge and experiences of Art3mis and Aech are fully recognized for the first time. The former planet, Wade explains,

> was home to a lovingly detailed, decades-in-the-making Oasis re-creation of Shermer, Illinois, the fictional Chicago suburb where the filmmaker John Hughes set many of the movies he wrote and/or directed over the course of his celebrated career. . . .
>
> The simulated suburb had a scaled-down replica of Lake Michigan along its northern and eastern borders, and a shrunken version of downtown

> Chicago bordering it to the west and the south, so all the '80s Windy City landmarks featured in *Ferris Bueller's Day Off* could be incorporated in the simulation, too, including the Sears Tower, the stock exchange, Wrigley Field, and the Art Institute of Chicago. And out beyond the lake and the Chicago city limits, there was a ridiculously abbreviated version of the United States, so that the simulation could incorporate cities and locations from Hughes's scripted *Vacation* and *Home Alone* films. (292–293)

On Shermer, "interactive re-creations of all of these movies were constantly playing all around you. And the events depicted in those films played out over and over again simultaneously, day after day and week after week, on an endless loop" (296), allowing players to watch their favorite films from new angles or even disrupt the narratives.

Upon the group's arrival, Wade's description of the idyllic town is undercut by critique from Aech and Art3mis:

> The sun was rising above the lake to the east. A beautiful spring morning in an upscale Midwestern suburb at the height of Reagan's America. Period-appropriate cars and trucks—1989 or earlier—filled the tree-lined streets.
>
> "Look at this lily-white hellscape," Aech said, shaking her head as she stared out her own window. "Is there a single person of color in this entire town?"
>
> "Sure," Art3mis replied. "But most of them hang out at a place called the Kandy Bar over in Chicago. This place does have a serious diversity problem—like the whole of '80s cinema . . ."
>
> Aech nodded. "Well, maybe the next shard will be hidden in the kingdom of Zamunda." (302)

This kind of critique is also coded into the planet's structure: After opening a map of the town, Wade notes that "Shermer had a set of railroad tracks running diagonally through its middle, dividing the town into two more-or-less equal halves, which were labeled RICH and POOR" (296).

Strangely, however, this critique is embedded in a planet designed as an homage that, we are told, was constructed by "legions of fans" over the course of several decades (292). In this, there is an odd tension between the obvious affection Cline and his characters have for Hughes's films, and the way that the novel frames them. If we take *Ready Player Two* seriously, we're left wondering why those who love Hughes's films enough to dedicate years of their life reconstructing the town in the OASIS would so pointedly undercut it. (This question can also be asked of Cline himself.) One way to resolve this quandary is to consider the possibility that this kind of crude critical ventriloquism is actually part of the homage. In this scenario, the presentation of the politics of Hughes's films is to be read as kitsch, a knowing acknowledgment of a shortfall rendered in such a way that it not only fails to undermine the work, but actually enhances it. What was, in its time, a sincere (if cynical) attempt to depict life in America becomes instead a site of humor, a way to laugh at how silly we used to be (which, in turn, subtly promotes the notion that we no longer *are* that way). This procedure also effectively obscures the fact that the reactionary politics of Hughes's films coincided with the ideological project of a burgeoning right-wing movement that has only grown more powerful in the years since. Therefore, by reframing Hughes's politics as a joke, the novel's critique is effectively defanged at the moment it is uttered, with the fundamental crudeness of "RICH" and "POOR" sides of the tracks serving as a mechanism that enables ironic detachment for readers at the expense of a deeper reckoning with the period. This framing, however, though not exactly inaccurate, is also somewhat of an oversimplification, insofar as Hughes's films are often about imagined conflicts between the middle and upper-middle classes rather than a simple dichotomy between rich and poor. The novel's criticism likewise mystifies a key premise of the filmmaker's ideological investments. Shermer's geography thus invokes the kind of relationship between fan and reference that is central to *Ready Player Two*'s revised approach to its nostalgic canon, staging the struggle to find pleasure in a problematized past. If you can laugh off the *bad* parts, the novel suggests. you can still enjoy the *good* ones.

These critiques are voiced in the first ten pages of the Shermer section of the novel and then largely abandoned, although midway through the section, the novel adopts a critical pose one final time, as Art3mis debates whether Duckie from *Pretty in Pink* deserves sympathy based on the way that he treats women in the film (317). Otherwise, the novel proceeds unabated as the group (led by Art3mis, who, as a girl, is naturally *the* expert on Hughes's films) spends the next four chapters on Shermer, dressed as the "Dork Squad" from *Sixteen Candles*, trying to solve the latest clue by rearranging events on the planet to reflect the original casting of Robert Downey Jr. (inhabiting the planet as his character from *Weird Science*) as Duckie in *Pretty in Pink* while restoring the film's ending to an earlier version that Hughes supposedly favored but was disliked by test audiences. In other words, the novel retains an overt attachment to Hughes's work, and desires to languish in the nostalgia Shermer induces despite acknowledging the reasons it shouldn't. Importantly, however, though *Ready Player Two* takes steps to point out the flaws in Hughes's oeuvre, and to some extent indicts itself for loving these films anyway, the novel fails to identify, much less reckon with, how they shaped its understanding of the world. In other words, while much of the series is dedicated to surface-level reference, the ideological underpinnings that are shaped by its canon are largely omitted from the moments of critique. The novel's engagement with Hughes's world(view), in other words, runs deeper than it lets on, particularly in its narrow construction of the social world, which borrows heavily from films like *Home Alone* and *National Lampoon's Christmas Vacation*. While in one section the novel appears to mock the vulgar "RICH" vs. "POOR" framing these films sometimes employ, the series also earnestly reproduces this kind of simplification elsewhere in its insistent belief in the redemptive power of pop culture and teenage rebellion; in its reductively positing race, gender, and sexuality as merely superficial, performative differences, divorced from one's true *inner* self;[10] and in its casting Wade's victory over IOI as a win for the little guy, obscuring the fact that GSS, the most powerful corporation on the planet, was already under the control of the supposed little guy whose influence on the cultural field, now near total, had made zero difference to the rapidly deteriorating state of the world (and, in fact, coincided with it). While *Ready Player Two* works to problematize some of its predecessor's tendencies, it primarily voices superficial critiques of the texts it references, while the ideological and philosophical dimensions of these works are reproduced with little alteration.

Ultimately, the novel tries to have its cake and eat it too: It recognizes the complaints levied against its predecessor and then attempts to reconfigure the objects of its attachment so it can partake in the same nostalgic fantasy anyway (while subsequently obscuring its attachment to the more heinous elements of its canon). Rearrangement and realignment in the service of maintaining the integrity of the existing project, in other words, substitutes for fundamental change. In this regard, the novel enacts the same "We see you and we hear you" response model increasingly deployed by corporations and public officials embroiled in scandal. Witnessing (itself a form of recognition) takes the place of material action—a hallmark of the posthistorical moment.

Cline modifies this strategy on Afterworld, a planet built around the music of Prince. "The Afterworld's surface," Wade explains, "is covered with a stylized re-creation of downtown Minneapolis in the late 1980s, along with locations from Prince's other movies and music videos. You can walk into a simulation of every club gig and concert he ever performed during his career" (371). This is a welcome change of scenery for Aech, who "probably know[s] more about Prince and his artistic output than any other human being in history" (370). As with Shermer, Afterworld is Cline's attempt to dive into nostalgic artifacts that he presumes would be more relevant to groups (Black people, women, the LGBTQ community) that might've felt excluded in the first novel, as well as an opportunity for the author to consider again the way that heteronormativity shaped his original work. Aech voices this critique by chiding Wade for previously dismissing *Purple Rain* because of latent sexual confusion:

> "And do you remember how many times you actually sat through the entire film with me? Nada. Never. *Not once.* And we both know why, don't we? It was because Prince always made you feel a little sexually confused and uncomfortable, didn't he?"

> The old Wade would have denied this. But like I said, the ONI had broadened my horizons. Enough, at least, for me to recognize the truth about my adolescent self.
>
> "Ok, maybe that's a *little* true," I said, smiling. "Whenever I was watching old episodes of Friday Night Videos and 'When Doves Cry' came on, I always averted my eyes when he was getting up out of that bathtub. Every single time." (370)

However, though initially presented as an olive branch to readers of color and a challenge to heteronormativity, Prince's inclusion in the novel also becomes an opportunity for Cline to reflect critically on homophobia. Before finding the Raspberry Beret and defeating the final boss on Afterworld, Aech explains:

> "Later in life, after he became a Jehovah's Witness, Prince came out as antigay," she said. "He believed that God didn't approve of homosexuality, so he couldn't either. Can you really believe that, Z?" She shook her head. "For decades he was an icon and a role model to generations of sexually confused kids and adults. He spoke for us, through his lyrics: '*I'm not a woman, I'm not a man. I am something that you'll never understand.*'"
>
> She started to get choked up and had to pause for a few seconds to collect herself.
>
> "Then, one day," she went on, "Prince suddenly changes his mind, and says, 'No, no. I was wrong all along. You really should hate yourself for being gay because God says it's a sin for you to be the person He made you to be . . .'" (428)

Cline's treatment of Prince in this section relies on a problematic conflation of gender and sexuality that again belies the author's misunderstanding of the issues the novel raises: The lyrics of "I Would Die 4 U," referenced in the passage above, pertain to gender identity, while the rest of the discussion relates to sexuality (Wade's sexual confusion, Aech's lesbianism). Though the two issues may be linked, they are also discrete, and sections like these not only blur the lines between them, but do so from a place of profound misunderstanding, steeped in a decidedly retrograde conception of identity. Further, in light of the critique voiced by Aech, it's somewhat curious that Prince was even selected to begin with, as these biographical realities seem to undercut the value of his inclusion in a way that wouldn't necessarily be true for other figures, particularly ones who actually identify as queer, and don't come with the same antigay baggage. If the purpose of including Prince was to reference an artist whose identity and fandom weren't sufficiently invoked in the first novel, to offer Others a chance to celebrate their parts of the '80s, the homophobia discussion in effect undermines the effort. Then again, there are few figures who tick boxes as Prince does, and fewer still who are recognizably part of the '80s canon. Recognizing an artist who fundamentally isn't part of the existing cultural formation of '80s pop culture would disrupt rather than maintain its integrity, and such an act would be at odds with the fundamental purpose of *Ready Player Two*'s expansion. As on Shermer, Afterworld is Cline's misshapen attempt to celebrate and criticize all at once—this time, an effort made even more incoherent by its bizarre insistence on using a single object to serve multiple, contradictory functions.

This effort illuminates another way to read the novel, which further clarifies the role that its nostalgia plays at the end of history. *Ready Player Two* has been criticized for lacking the charms of its predecessor, and it's easy to see why when you consider the task the book undertakes: Its particular combination of homage and critique reads like a misshapen attempt at simultaneous reiteration, apology, and penance. It seeks, in other words, to apologize for the thing it wants to continue doing—sometimes right in the middle of it. Cline still loves the movies and games of his adolescence, but he also seems to believe those who argued that he shouldn't. The novel is therefore riddled with guilt, plagued by intrusive critical thoughts, such as, "We don't have time for literary criticism right now, Aech, valid though it may be! OK?" (466). It tries but fails to reconcile this contradiction. Perhaps, then, Cline's sequel is less an act of gatekeeping, or chauvinism, than an act of melancholic desperation, an effort to try to make what used to work *work again*. The novel is nostalgic, in this sense, not just for the '80s, but also for the conditions of the first novel's 2011 release, a prelapsarian paradise where nostalgic longing is unimpeded by criticism.

Midway through *Ready Player Two*, one of its villains (ventriloquizing Cline's critics) asks, "Don't you kids ever get tired of picking through the wreckage of a past generation's nostalgia? . . . I mean, look around. The entire OASIS is like one giant graveyard, haunted by the undead pop-culture icons of a bygone era. A crazy old man's shrine to a bunch of pointless crap" (435). On the face of it, the novel's answer is pretty firmly *no*, but *Ready Player Two* is also haunted by the idea that maybe the answer should be *yes*: Nostalgia in Cline's series *is* a kind of graveyard, a catalogue of dead things, and *Ready Player Two* contributes to the death of the artifacts it reveres by focusing so closely on their limitations. Even *Ready Player One*, in trying to reassert the relevance of its canon, tacitly acknowledges its demise. In a way, Cline won the battle but lost the war: *Ready Player One* staved off death for just a little while, but, as it always does in the real world, death returned. In the end, the series is all about death: The reinvigoration of dead styles on a dying world with a dead-end future is inaugurated by Halliday's death, and, in its invention of AI copies of human consciousness, the series ends with what Wade describes as the end of death: "We might be part of the last generation ever to know the sting of human mortality. From this moment forth, death would have no more dominion" (578). No longer, the book explains, will people experience loss. Ironically, by defeating loss, *Ready Player Two* also effectively ends nostalgia. The novel, in other words, ends by hoping for a future where it would never need to exist. "I want to give the world the means to ensure that no one will ever have to lose someone they love again," Wade explains. "I think this will make life a lot less painful for most people" (546). Styles die out more quickly than the average person, so, for a life defined by them, nostalgia is all the more vital as a means of escaping the inevitable. Nostalgia, the desire to recover that which has been lost by temporarily reviving the dead, is, in this light, ultimately about pain management, a way to manage death in a time when there's nothing else to turn to.

CHAPTER 2

Stranger Things, Nostalgia, and Aesthetics

In the summer of 2019, the Netflix series *Stranger Things* partnered with Eggo for a marketing campaign in the buildup to the release of its highly anticipated third season. The show, which follows a group of teens and adults in small-town 1980s Indiana as they struggle to keep at bay a succession of supernatural forces unleashed following the opening of a portal to an alternate dimension, had become a surprise hit following its 2016 premiere, and quickly became the streaming service's most recognizable original production. Eggo waffles—a favorite of Eleven, one of the show's teen protagonists—had seen a surge in sales following the show's premiere and gained iconic status within its fandom, so a partnership capitalizing on the hype represented a logical next step. The two franchises had previously collaborated on a trailer for the series' second season, which premiered during Super Bowl LI, in which a vintage "L'eggo my Eggo" commercial was progressively interrupted and eventually overtaken by scenes from the show's upcoming season. The much more elaborate 2019 campaign featured a variety of tie-ins including an Eggo-branded *Stranger Things* spoiler blocker for fans' internet browsers, recipes tied to each of the upcoming nine episodes, and instructions for making costumes using Eggo boxes. Eggo also bought billboards in towns across the country named Hawkins, the fictional town in which the series is set. These billboards featured the Eggo logo with blood dripping from the E—a nod to Eleven's frequent nosebleeds.

This marketing effort culminated in two larger releases. In June, Eggo claimed to have unearthed a series of unreleased advertisements from 1985 featuring hidden teasers related to the show, which they subsequently posted across social media platforms. Following this, the company also created limited edition boxes replicating the look of the ones sold in the 1980s—identical save for the "Limited Edition 1985 Graphics" label at the top. Initially, these retro Eggos were only available online through Amazon, but they saw a larger release in select stores across the United States following the series' July Fourth debut.

The latter two examples, the ads and the box, provide an acute illustration of the hyperaestheticized nostalgia for which *Stranger Things* is the archetype. The ads, for instance, hinge upon a nostalgia for consumer products and advertising that is entirely mediated and thus based upon the recreation of an aesthetic object; the nostalgic allure of the ads, in other words, derives from their replication of the stylistics of '80s ads. Grainy visuals and tape distortions blanket one video showing a "typical" middle-class suburban breakfast table featuring milk, orange juice, and, of course, Eggos before cutting to a screen that reads "One Eggo Can Change Everything." These visual imperfections exist even though the ad was produced digitally and published exclusively online, thus bypassing the analog processes that created them in the ads being copied. The ads, in this way, have a simulacral core: a detailed recreation of an object that never existed but is meant to appear as though it did in order to replicate the same response one would have had toward the original, had it ever existed. The ad is, in other words, a thing that serves, at best, as a vague *reminder* of the thing it is parodying, and therefore the nostalgia it seeks to produce is further removed from its actual object.

The boxes also emphasize aesthetics as primary content: While the packaging is retro-styled, the waffles inside—supposedly the product—remain unchanged. The only difference between the Limited Edition 1985 Graphics Eggos and regular 2019 Eggos is the package itself, and thus, as it relates to the function or quality of the product, nothing substantial is different. The aesthetic, therefore, *is* the substance. Consumers don't buy Limited Edition 1985 Graphics Eggos for the Eggos, but for the Limited Edition 1985 Graphics. As with the ads, the sole draw of the product derives from its visual recreation of something from the past. The irony, however, is that this recreation is inherently imperfect because the Limited Edition 1985 Graphics label announces the boxes as a recreation, which breaks the illusion of visual fidelity, signifying that it is, in fact, *not* the thing it is meant to look like. The Limited Edition 1985 Graphics Eggos are, therefore, a reproduction whose status as reproduction is built into its appeal—it's not the real thing, but it sure looks like it.

This is *Stranger Things* in a nutshell. The series' nostalgic appeal derives from its seemingly faithful recreation and reassembly of a variety of tropes and aesthetic norms common to '80s media, representing a hyperrecombinatorial approach to the past, in which the past is configured merely as the particular confluence of genres, tropes, and stylistics. Its nostalgia is thus primarily oriented toward cultural ephemera rather than grounded in past experiences. Though there is potential overlap between lived experiences and those represented in cultural ephemera for viewers of a certain age, it is significant that the lens the show provides for those viewers to reminisce about their lived experiences is explicitly tropological and mediated—it is accessed, if at all, through reference, genre, narrative structure, sound, and visual style. As in the Eggo ads, *Stranger Things* aims to recreate a thing that never truly existed, 1980s childhood, but only as it was depicted in films of the era, and only through a kind of mimetic pastiche—childhood in a hundred references. To the extent that the show depicts seemingly generalizable nostalgic experiences (e.g., children riding bikes in the suburbs), it regularly converts those realities into mediated references (*E.T.*, *The Goonies*), distancing the nostalgia those moments induce from its mnemonic core, which is always already framed by media. Like the Limited Edition 1985 Graphics Eggos, *Stranger Things* is all about recreation: a copy whose entire function is to call attention to itself as copy. Yet, in doing so, it also announces itself as decidedly *not* the thing it is aiming to recreate. For *Stranger Things*, therefore, looking like it (sounding like it, feeling like it) is everything; as with the box, the aesthetic *is* the substance.

Stranger Things and the 1985 Limited Edition Graphic Eggo boxes, therefore, are essentially the same product: hyperaestheticized containers whose draw and value lie more in the exterior than the interior,[1] whose form supersedes their substance, and whose interior qualities are artificially[2] elevated by the nature of the exterior. In addition to the stylistic similarities, *Stranger Things*' design shares an aesthetic paradigm with the Eggo boxes. *Stranger Things* is not simply an Eggo box; rather, it is functionally akin to a 1985 Limited Edition Graphic Eggo box whose contents are (for the sake of analogy) unknown: They could be plain, blueberry, chocolate chip, or perhaps some special *Stranger Things* tie-in flavor—or, better yet, the box could be empty. An evocative exterior coupled with an indeterminant interior allows—even encourages—the consumer to project into the box whatever its graphics elicit for that individual, and the box is crucially never opened to reveal its actual contents. What one imagines inside the box is overdetermined by what one sees on the outside, and the limits of this act of imagination—or *interpretation*—are only partially demarcated, allowing for a wide range of possibilities. *Stranger Things* thus produces a system of meaning-making through suggestion and accumulation; it is a pastiche whose signification allows for a seemingly endless range of interpretations.

In this way, *Stranger Things* is the archetype for the aesthetic logic that underpins reflective-age nostalgia. By substituting hollow allusions to media and other temporally coded signifiers for a deeper engagement with the historical period it purports to capture, the series exemplifies both the posthistorical flattening of politics and history and the concomitant elevation of cultural objects as the defining markers of the past that are, in many ways, the primary features of the reflective age. If *Ready Player One* shows how the conditions of the end of history have produced this particular turn to the past, *Stranger Things* illuminates how these conditions have resulted in a cultural paradigm whose stylistic reliance on surface-level reproduction leaves it mired in the past.

In the relatively short time since the release of its first season—despite what I have argued above (or, as I will shortly show, *because* of it)—the series has become the subject of surprisingly diverse readings by fans as well as critics both popular and academic. A gloss of the interpretive frames into which viewers have placed the show offers a glimpse into this myriad and often contradictory landscape: The series has been seen as a distinctly and celebratory nostalgic vision of the 1980s and its media (Chaney; Genzlinger; McCarthy); a critique of the 1980s, Reaganism, and middle-class suburbia (Burges; R. Butler; Nussbaum; Smith); an allegory or metaphor for the traumatic experience of coming-of-age and entering into a world of adult conformity (R. Butler; Khan); a form of digital gothic or an expression of longing for the analog in a digital world (Landrum; Rust); an exploration of queerness past and present as well as a critique of straight nostalgia (Berns et al.; Briefel; Burges and Middleton; Roach); an example of a distinctly white nostalgia (Bering-Porter; Giovannone); and a critique of white nostalgia (Reich).

A list such as this would seem to illustrate that *Stranger Things* is a rich, complex, and perhaps even profound series. While there is textual evidence supporting any of these interpretations, taken together the readings reveal that the core function of the series is to reconstruct a version of the 1980s in which every major narrative incident or component, by replication or divergence, cites some "source," weaving together potential meanings so vast as to embrace numerous, self-contradictory interpretations, for which the show offers no path to a final judgment or method for achieving argumentative clarity. *Stranger Things*, in other words, relies on ambiguity produced through connotation, and, beyond overly familiar maxims such as "friendship is important" and "growing up is hard," it provides no clear denotations. To the extent that we consider meaning to be a text's content, the series' reliance on stereotype, trope, and genre, then, provides both its form *and* its primary content. Put simply, it *suggests* a lot but *says* very little, and each new suggestive connotation diminishes its capacity for *saying* anything.

The abundance of critical readings, overwhelmingly devoted to elucidating the meaning encoded by the aesthetics, often mistake aesthetic posturing for thematic substance. Aviva Briefel's *Post45* essay "Familiar Things: Snow Ball '84 and Straight Nostalgia" exemplifies this mistake in its reading of season 2's closing sequence, which takes place at a school dance. On the surface, the scenes that occur at "Snow Ball '84"—including, most notably, a dance between two of the series' adolescent protagonists, Mike and Eleven, which signals the culmination of a heterosexual coupling the show had been building toward since early in the first season (and one of the central narrative components of season 3, which was released concurrently with *Post45*'s special issue and is thus not incorporated into Briefel's analysis)—depict a conventionally nostalgic vision of adolescent romance that can be found in many films produced before, during, or after the '80s. Briefel argues, however, that the scenes pointedly "invoke the iconic and distinctly non-nostalgic prom scene from Brian De Palma's *Carrie*,[3] which subtly counteracts the forced identification of Snow Ball '84." *Carrie* and *Stranger Things*, she argues,

> Both show characters grooming in front of mirrors in preparation for the big event, deploy overhead establishing shots of the glittery gym and its painfully invested teenagers, and rotate the camera around the dancing couples. At the center of both sequences is a "pity" dance that serves as an initiation into heterosexual rituals: Tommy's girlfriend, Sue, forces him to ask Carrie to the prom to compensate for her own prior bullying of the outcast girl; in Stranger Things, Nancy invites Dustin to dance after he has been rejected by several girls his age. In both cases, the pitying character teaches the pitied one to dance through instructions to "just listen to the music."

Briefel seems to have fallen into *Stranger Things*' referential trap. As the above evidence inadvertently indicates, there is no obvious visual link to *Carrie* in the scene unless one counts establishing shots and basic camera movement employed in practically every school dance scene in recent film history. The focus on *Carrie*, while ignoring more obvious links to '80s films such as *Footloose* and *Pretty in Pink*, seems to derive especially from the "pity" dance, which, although not unique to *Carrie*, is admittedly a more selective reference point. However, such a reading relies heavily on a flimsy correlation (that the dances are out of "pity") that ignores key differences. In the scene, Mike's older sister Nancy—one of the show's unambiguously "good" characters—notices Dustin crying alone on the bleachers after his crush chose to couple up with his friend Lucas, and his subsequent offer to dance was crudely rejected by another girl. After convincing Dustin to join her on the dance floor, Nancy offers advice: "Girls this age are dumb," she explains as Dustin, now smiling, holds her waist. "Give them a few years, and they'll wise up. You're gonna drive them nuts." Unlike Tommy, who, as Briefel notes, was "forced" to dance with Carrie, Nancy dances with Dustin out of sincere sympathy, and Dustin appears genuinely reassured. In contrast to *Carrie*, whose scenes of relentless bullying prior to the dance give audiences every reason to be skeptical about Sue and Tommy's intentions, there is nothing sinister or foreboding in Nancy's encouragement, and the show itself provides no reason to doubt Dustin's newfound resolve. In fact, Dustin's trajectory over the third season unambiguously validates Nancy's mid-dance counsel and, in doing so, further distances their dance from Mike and Carrie's and thus from the critique of heteronormativity Briefel reads into it. *Stranger Things* season 3, which takes place a year after Snow Ball '84 and follows the gang as they once again try to stem the tide of the Upside Down—this time while also grappling with the Soviet Union, which has set up its own research facility deep below the town's new shopping mall—concludes with the revelation that Dustin's mythical "girlfriend from camp" is, in fact, real, and climaxes with the two performing a ham radio duet of the theme from *The Neverending Story.* Heteronormativity may be omnipresent in both texts, but in *Stranger Things*, its attainment is a source of triumph.

Nonetheless, Briefel concludes, "With these *allusions*, the audience is invited to recognize the oppressiveness of dominant nostalgia narratives and turn to the cinematic memory of a horror film in which heterosexuality is an undeniable source of terror" (emphasis added). In other words, Briefel's reading requires an intertextual relationship in which the entirety of the scene's "meaning" is revealed by the reference: Although it shows one thing, an intertextual reference proves that it is saying the opposite. *Stranger Things*, in other words, merely has to *look* like something else in order to borrow its message. The fact that the series elsewhere shows little interest in such a critique of heteronormative nostalgia (and, indeed, often celebrates it) is seemingly unimportant because of its *reference*—or, to more precisely lower the allusive bar, because of its *referential environment.* Where everything is a reference, all potential meanings are subordinated to its connection.

Briefel's article, therefore, typifies an apparent desire throughout *Stranger Things* scholarship to make the show transcend the confines of nostalgic pablum and to *say something*, even if that means upending its own nostalgic premise. The series, in this light, is functionally a husk that allows viewers to find within its panoply of '80s cultural ephemera whatever they want to see. To be sure, *Stranger Things* is not unique in generating contradictory and/or mutually exclusive critical readings. What *is* unique, however, is that the source of this trend in *Stranger Things* criticism can be tied to specific trends that have implications for posthistorical culture as well as critical discourse on nostalgia more broadly.

At a fundamental level, the series converts nostalgia and the 1980s into aesthetics, participating in the same system of reference that, as Joel Burges and Jason Middleton have argued, distinguishes *the 1980s* as a historical period from *the '80s* as a phenomenological object. *Stranger Things* is, in other words, not interested in investigating the 1980s as it was actually lived, nor in reflecting the period beyond its invocation of cultural ephemera. In this process of aestheticization, in the move from the 1980s to the '80s, cultural artifacts and historical realities become de- or re-contextualized markers—kids ride bikes as in *E.T.*, otherwise apolitical families have Reagan-Bush'84 signs in their yards—hollowed of purpose and thus endlessly signifying. This vagueness produces a vision of the '80s that is more indeterminant and thus more alienated from historical reality than traditional nostalgic texts.

The series' indeterminacy, however, is one of its central draws. Because its intertextual accumulation provides limitless interpretive ground, the series' nostalgic charm and denotative vagueness facilitate prolific sites of viewer identification. *Stranger Things* is, in this way, a kind of choose-your-own interpretive adventure. This is what encouraged, for instance, Burges and Middleton to dedicate over half of their intro to the *Post45* special issue to critical reflections on their own experiences as adolescents in the '80s, framed by a passing reference in the series' pilot to a particular issue of *X-Men* with which both writers were familiar; it is what, in the same issue, enabled Elizabeth Reich to read the Upside Down as "a metaphor for the extra-temporal, perpetually endangered, and suffocating existence of black life in the US" while at the same time allowing David Bering-Porter to identify the show's tokenizing treatment of race and its neoliberal brand of white nostalgia.

While divergent readings are not unique to *Stranger Things*, there is something greater to reckon with here. As Amy Rust and others have noted, series creators Matt and Ross Duffer and executive producer Shawn Levy have continually emphasized their desire for total authenticity and fidelity, manifest in efforts to meticulously reproduce the '80s through set design and props. While one might argue that the inclusion of extradimensional demons in the series signals its divergence from objective reality, these elements are, in fact, discrete from its historical setting—there is, in other words, no sense that the series is diverging from its historical setting despite this, and so these overt gestures of subjective imagination don't infect its temporal verisimilitude. Obvious acts of divergence from the real ultimately reinforce the *realness* of the elements that remain unaffected. Further, the overwhelming emphasis on '80s media—where strange things are actually quite common—also works to normalize the existence of the paranormal within the real. This emphasis on authenticity obscures the brushstrokes of historical recreation in order to impart the notion that we are really seeing the '80s and not simply an interpretation of it.

This also marks a contrast with the reflective mode employed by films and television from an earlier nostalgic paradigm, such as *The Wonder Years* and *A Christmas Story*, which I discussed in the introduction. In these examples, memory serves as the authorizing mechanism for turning to the past, highlighting the subjective nature of the historical reconstructions contained within. While texts like these gained popularity because, for many viewers, they distilled some essential quality of the past they reconstructed, it is nonetheless significant that, in contrast to *Stranger Things*, they made clear efforts to delimit interpretation through this framing. This difference highlights what is borne out elsewhere in the series: a focus not on depicting supposedly generalizable individual experiences but on capturing the essence of the phenomenon directly. The '80s, in other words, is contained not within the lives of the people who lived it but in the tropes and stylistics that governed them—or, more precisely, that governed their *depiction*.

Despite *Stranger Things*' deep investment in accuracy, however, its vision of fidelity (i.e., the location of the '80s phenomenon that it posits) is overwhelmingly superficial, made up of sound and vision, haircuts and products. It's worth noting here that the Duffer Brothers, for all their investment in '80s nostalgia, were actually born in 1984, a full year after season 1 is set. So, while Mike, Eleven, and the gang were learning about love and going on shopping trips to the Starcourt Mall in season 3's 1985, Matt and Ross Duffer were teething. Their experiences as fifteen-year-olds in 1998 were surely quite different from those they've nostalgically created for their characters thirteen years earlier, and so their sense of the *authentic* '80s is therefore almost entirely drawn from film and television rather than memory and experience.[4] It's no surprise, then, that the series sees the '80s as a matter of styles and things, access to which can be granted simply through reference and resemblance. The '80s for the Duffer Brothers—excepting whatever memories of kindergarten they may have retained—was never really anything other than a mediated object, pure aesthetic and affect. *Stranger Things*' interest in other forms of reproduction, its attempts at capturing some kind of '80s zeitgeist or detailed historical reality, are similarly always borne of and/or filtered through media and thus are attempts at directly recreating not a historical reality itself but the historical reality supposedly captured within the media of the period. The result is a series that seeks to reproduce in "objective" terms but does so through a necessarily subjective process. This is true not only in the creators' act of deciding *what* captures the '80s, but, as the diverse critical readings above indicate, also in the series' process of making meaning through vague intertextual reference that leaves interpretation fully up to the viewer. Though the series positions itself otherwise, *Stranger Things*' recreation of the '80s is thus a doubly subjective act.

Through its focus on the '80s as phenomenon, its emphasis on reconstruction through hypermediated reference, and its evasion of denotative clarity, the series cedes interpretive ground to its audience. By deemphasizing the inherent subjectivity in its own act of representation and turning to media as the "objective" foundation for its reconstruction, the series ironically configures the past as a subjective phenomenon instead of a historical period. For *Stranger Things*, in other words, the '80s is whatever you want it to be: Reagan, neon and synths, yuppies vs. geeks, *The Breakfast Club*, bicycles, Duran Duran, stifling heteronormativity, triumphant heteronormativity, unparalleled freedom and/or danger, and on and on. There is no *there* there, just a listicle of events, traits, and tropes.

Stranger Things therefore presents an interesting study of the conflict between nostalgia and history that emerges in the posthistorical world. Conventionally, nostalgia follows an Edenic structure, with the past configured as a kind of prelapsarian paradise in contrast to a fallen present. As Philip Roth pointed out in *American Pastoral*, one can map the same pre- and postlapsarian model onto narratives of American history in the latter half of the twentieth century, with the fall of the belief in an American paradise coming at the hands of 1960s political unrest that fundamentally altered how the nation is able to see itself.

Reagan's nostalgia for the '50s similarly positioned the '60s and beyond as a time after the fall, and revisionist films like *Back to the Future* reflect the same perception through their desire to repair the damage by returning to the moment just *before*. There is a sense that America as a notion never fully recovered, and that things have only gotten worse in the years that followed—a status continually reinforced by 24/7 news coverage and a media landscape that thrives on the spectacle and sensation of the horrors of modernity. As in Eden, the fall comes with knowledge, and a recognition of oneself as fallen. In the twenty-first century, when the American public is constantly reminded, by films, television series, and the news, of the sins of its past, conventional nostalgia poses a problem: How can viewers, especially the more socially progressive millennials and zoomers who make up the plurality of *Stranger Things*' audience, maintain an awareness of the AIDS and crack epidemics while simultaneously looking back longingly on the period in which they were most prominent? How can they yearn for a time of laxer parental supervision without being reminded of the horrifying reason that the practice has disappeared? The answer, for *Stranger Things*, is that they can't—at least not at the same time. The series' aestheticization is its greatest resource for preserving its nostalgia, providing an answer to the question "How does one long for a time that is itself already fallen?"

This is most acutely exemplified by one of the series' simplest and most frequent images: kids riding bikes. Although markedly nodding to Spielbergian adventure films, even without their mediated reference, shots of the *Stranger Things* kids pedaling through town have broad nostalgic resonance; for many viewers, moments like these recall specific lived experiences. At the same time, as with all nostalgic objects, these memories are haunted by the notion that they contain a now-impossible experience. Unlike arcades and acid wash jeans, however, changes in attitudes toward childhood autonomy are not simply a matter of the passage of time, of fading styles and fads, but rather derive from the emergence of historical realities: namely, the rise in reports of child abductions and murders in the '70s and '80s and their intensified coverage on television news.[5] There is, in this way, an additional, terrible layer to the series' evocations. Rather than trying to ignore this unsavory resonance, *Stranger Things* acknowledges it. Season 1 of the series revolves around the disappearance of Will Byers, one of the show's protagonists, who goes missing in the pilot while riding his bicycle home after a night of playing *Dungeons & Dragons* at Mike's house. The show redirects the historical fact of abduction that haunts the incident onto the aesthetic supernatural, with the disappearance coming not at the hands of a child predator, but from a demon ripped from the pages of a *D&D* handbook—a revision of the substitution found in Stephen King's *It*, but divorced from the novel's more deliberately metaphorical resonances.[6] The series thus offers a knowing nod to one of the decade's horrors while also mapping it onto genre, and the threat of child predation to the show's nostalgia is thus removed by means of aesthetic displacement. Child abduction at the hands of the Demogorgon is therefore a stand-in for the real that, in the end, suppresses it.

Season 3 takes the series' aestheticized abstraction of historical conflict to another level with its *Red Dawn*-esque Soviet invasion plot, which introduces the idea that the USSR is also conducting secret experiments involving the Upside Down deep beneath Hawkins. The season opens on a shadowy lab filled with workers in hazmat suits using some kind of ray gun to create one of the portals that link to the Upside Down while uniformed military officials watch from a glass-enclosed control room. After the experiment goes awry, vaporizing several scientists and destroying most of the tech, a brooding Soviet general inspects the wall where a portal failed to open fully. "We are close," the head scientist nervously protests. "You can see our progress. We just need more ti-." His pleas are cut off as the general's buzz-cutted henchman reaches out to choke him, lifting him off his feet as the Soviet marching song "The Red Army Is the Strongest" begins to play. "You have one year," the general tells a second scientist as the first lifelessly falls to the floor.

Stranger Things season 3 is thus inaugurated with the replication of a particular kind of '80s Cold War narrative, a cartoonish vision of unflinching Soviet bad guys determined to do evil whatever the cost. This thread continues throughout the season, but is most visible in Grigori, the aforementioned henchman who is later sent to kill Sheriff Hopper following his discovery of the Soviet operation. The ensuing action casts Grigori as one part Terminator, one part Ivan Drago, synthesizing the robotic, amoral determination of each, and the series, once again, relies on a preestablished trope for its resonance—one that is, in this case, particularly divorced from its historical context. In the series, the Cold War generally only loomed in the background through passing references until the third season—brief gestures toward verisimilitude but little more. The conflict thus represented a largely untapped well of '80s phenomena for the series to exploit in its perpetual quest for material to revisit.

Stranger Things' expanded treatment of the hostilities is particularly interesting because, more than any of the series' other sociohistorical inspirations, the Cold War resonated in the 1980s in a very different way than it did in the 2010s, and the series' re-vision of the conflict is a product of that distance. For many Americans—and, seemingly, for the show as well—because the threat of nuclear annihilation at the hands of the Evil Empire never came to pass, its dissolution marks the Cold War as a closed narrative event. We know, in other words, how it ends, and the Red Menace no longer looms large.[7] Indeed, not only has the threat long been dissipated, but in the age of terror attacks and forever wars, a war that never came to pass might seem quaint by contrast, producing for many viewers—especially those who didn't live through it—a kind of anachronistic dramatic irony within the series. The reality, of course, is that even though direct combat between Soviet and U.S. ground forces never came to pass, events such as the Korean and Vietnam wars, the Cuban Missile Crisis, U.S. involvement in Latin America, Africa, Central Asia, and the Middle East—not to mention the array of domestic policies and practices that emerged as direct or indirect consequences of the conflict—all certainly had, and continue to have, a profound impact nationally and globally. In *Stranger Things*, however, the Cold War threat is confined to the Soviet Union's desire to acquire advanced weaponry in its quest for the total annihilation of the United States. As such, *Stranger Things*' representation of Cold War anxieties neither addresses nor invokes these broader legacies—and is, in fact, invested in the notion that the conflict was contained purely within the geographic borders of the United States and the USSR—pivoting instead on a shallow caricature drawn from action movies. Grigori is a perfect representation of this, a trope derived from two characters initially constructed as vessels for specific cultural fears subsequently redeployed in an era where those fears no longer have any cogency. In the end, he's nothing more than an ahistorical sideshow oddity, a kitschy testament to how silly it all was.

This is also reflected in the third season's more extensive turn toward the conventions of '80s action movies. Though the series had always featured action sequences, in the first two seasons they veered more toward those found in horror and science fiction, almost always pitting humans against monsters rather than against one another. Hopper's plotline in season three, which casts him as a hard-nosed detective working to uncover the secret behind the Soviet presence in Hawkins, breaks this pattern with the inclusion of numerous action tropes. One such scene features an especially over-the-top interrogation, in which Hopper nearly dismembers the mayor with a cigar cutter ("Are you insane?" the mayor asks. "I don't know," Hopper replies. "Let's find out"). In another sequence, Grigori and Hopper pursue one another with silenced pistols in a hall of mirrors, a scene whose neon lighting, coupled with Hopper's pastel Hawaiian shirt, nods more to *Miami Vice* and *Magnum P.I.* than anything Spielberg ever produced. The season's penultimate scene is a fistfight to the death between Hopper and Grigori whose blocking and cinematography recall late-'80s action staples like *Die Hard* and *Lethal Weapon*. These scenes, and the generic shift they signify that accompanies the series' turn to the Cold War, are yet another instance of *Stranger Things*' reluctance to confront history without invoking trope, genre, or style.

As with its treatment of missing children in season 1, season 3's turn to trope in its confrontation with historical reality is ultimately a surface-deep misdirection, one that neutralizes a threat to the show's nostalgia—who wants to go back to worrying about nuclear war?—by means of aesthetic displacement. More importantly, however, *Stranger Things*' nostalgized Cold War illustrates precisely why this effort to nullify challenges to one's rosy view of the past is so problematic: The turn toward a temporally specific trope in the representation of a historical period produces a kind of feedback loop wherein the redeployment of the trope reinforces the notion that it was, at least in some way, accurate, which then lends a sense of authenticity to the trope and the reconstruction it's contained within. This kind of reductive shorthanding, directed toward something that is conventionally viewed as settled history, serves to produce and/or perpetuate ahistorical perceptions of the past.

Nostalgia often relies on these misconceptions. It requires the past to be better than the present, so if the past really *wasn't* better than the present, or if the notion has lost cogency, the nostalgiac needs to remake it. Nostalgia is, of course, always about remaking the past to varying degrees, but the degrees and methods haven't always been the same, and what we have seen with nostalgia for the 1980s and beyond in media like *Stranger Things* is markedly different than what has traditionally come before, especially in the realm of film and television. Historically, nostalgic revision was a process of subtraction (intentionally or through selective forgetting), creating a coherent vision of the past by subordinating, or outright removing, its conflicts. Classically nostalgic films such as *American Graffiti* and *Dazed and Confused* as well as shows like *Freaks and Geeks* do this by enacting a narrowing of scope, focusing, for instance, on one group of high schoolers in a specific place at a specific time, which enables them to avoid directly invoking the broader conflicts of the period (insofar as the group in question can be seen as insulated from them), even as those experiences coalesce to posit a generalizable zeitgeist for the era. Recent "nostalgic" series such as *Mad Men*, *Glow*, and *The Americans*, as well as the remake of *It*, confront this process directly, drawing viewers in by invoking the preestablished affective and stylistic allure of the era before deconstructing the premises that underride them and drawing to the surface the conflicts they subordinate. *Stranger Things*, however, engages in a newer phenomenon, one that began to emerge in the early 2000s with shows like VH1's *I Love the '80s/'70s/'90s* (2002–2005) and the *Vice City* (2002) and *San Andreas* (2004) entries in the *Grand Theft Auto* franchise, as well as a series of retro and revivalist developments in music, seen in garage rock acts like the Strokes, the White Stripes, and the Hives; and, at the end of the decade, in the arrival of '80s-influenced genres like outrun, synthwave, and vaporwave. As Simon Reynolds has noted, "The 2000s were dominated by the 're-' prefix: *re*vivals, *re*issues, *re*makes, *re*-enactments. . . . The 2000s was also the decade of rampant *re*cycling: bygone genres *re*vived and *re*novated, vintage sonic material *re*processed and *re*combined" (xi). Artifacts like these reveled particularly in a phenomenological nostalgia that, although it also engaged in subtraction, was animated more by an infatuation with style and spectacle than by a rosy view of the past—or, better yet, its emphasis on style enabled its rosy re-vision.[8] In these examples, nostalgia is manifested less in a sense of longing and more in mimesis, in pointed efforts to directly reproduce temporally coded aesthetics drawn largely from media.

Broadly, this emphasis on retro aesthetics can also be seen in a number of areas within contemporary popular culture, from pseudotraditionalist niche movements online like cottagecore and tradwife, to the resurgence of lo-fi and analog styles in music and "vintage" filters on Instagram and TikTok. Most notably, there has emerged online, particularly among zoomers on YouTube and TikTok, a particular interest in what is known as "aesthetic" (often stylized as "A E S T H E T I C" and sometimes deployed as a general quality, as can be seen in numerous "How To Be Aesthetic" guides). Aesthetic, in this context, extends beyond the mere relabeling of sartorial "style," representing the conversion of all facets of life into a generic formation ("vintage," "hypebeast," "baddie," "artmom," "kidcore"), marking everything from clothing and hairstyles to accent, bodily comportment, and even social media fonts as signifiers of selfhood that can and should be actively cultivated from a list of curated options (sometimes called "starter packs"). It is, in other words, the intentional conversion of oneself into trope—fitting, in some ways, for a life posted and viewed as much as lived. The logic of Gen-Z aesthetic, crucially, extends backward, with numerous videos that assemble the styles and things of the past into a coherent "type" for which there is no true original. One TikTok (since deleted) began with the caption "*rare aesthetic* Actually growing up in the 2000s" followed by a montage of pop cultural artifacts from the period, including Avril Lavigne, Nintendo GameCube, *The Cheetah Girls*, the wall of a Blockbuster Video store, an AIM chat room, and glittery lip gloss. In videos like these, the past and the subjects that occupied them are both rendered tropologically, defined by a particular confluence of aesthetic markers.

Ready Player One similarly conceives of the 1980s as a confluence of mediated objects disconnected from lived experience, a time period (re-)constituted through pop culture reference. The quest at the story's core, and the herculean labors that follow, hinge upon Wade's absorption of unexperienced 1980s popular culture. The novel thus represents the same kind of nostalgia that we see in *Stranger Things*: alienated from personal experience and abstracted from lived reality, subsequently flattened into an infatuation with aesthetics and style. Notably, Steven Spielberg's 2018 adaptation revises the novel's focus on the '80s to include a wider collection of nerd culture references from the 1970s to the 2000s, substituting *The Iron Giant*, Master Chief, and the T-Rex from *Jurassic Park* for more oblique references to *Joust*, *Max Headroom*, and Rush. What persists across both film and novel, however, is the notion of a past remembered and reassembled through reference and recognition; moreover, Spielberg's substitutions reveal just how hollow this nostalgia is, irreverently re-skinning objects for a broader target audience with little narrative consequence—Spielberg notes in a *Los Angeles Times* article that the production team was unable to secure the rights to *Blade Runner* for a sequence that takes place within the world of the Ridley Scott film, so, rather than cutting the scene, *The Shining*'s Overlook Hotel was substituted instead (Rottenberg). In this nostalgic formulation, differences between objects are of little consequence, so long as both are recognizable and signify pastness.

Stranger Things is the apotheosis of these trends, merging a formal attachment to style and genre more commonly found in nonnarrative television, music, consumer products, and social media with a sense of longing enabled by processes of substitution and subordination most commonly found in narrative cinema. In this way, *Stranger Things* is distinct from most of its predecessors as well as its contemporaries in television and film; though borne of the same reverence for style, synthwave, a genre that provides much of the series' non-'80s soundtrack, including its theme, does not posit a vision of the 1980s in its attachment to the aesthetics of the era—there is, in other words, little sense that this kind of retro-inflected musical movement has any bearing on one's understanding of the period from which its stylistics are derived. There's a limit to its mimesis. Though paradigmatically similar, the same cannot be said of *Stranger Things*. The mélange that results from its particular merging of aesthetics, history, and nostalgia produces a past that is more malleable and alienated, and whose acts of emphasis and historical omission are, at the same time, less noticeable and more powerful: If the past is no longer primarily about lived and historical realities, but about a style, and if that process involves the conversion of those lived and historical realities into tropes and genre elements, then it can easily retain its affective allure. If what you love about the '80s is turquoise, arcades, and *Ferris Bueller*, then why pay any mind to the War on Drugs?[9]

This system of abstracting the conflicts of the '80s is not limited to the tropification of historical events. While the series broadly functions as an empty container, the cinematic influences out of which it is constructed often impose meaning onto the characters, narratives, and iconography that *Stranger Things* essentially lifts wholesale. This model of replication without revision reproduces the implications of the original, in effect reifying the notions they encode—not only as components of the reality of the '80s, but as generalizable truths. Critics often point to nostalgic media's pattern of "imagining contemporary values . . . in the context of the past" (Bering-Porter). While *Stranger Things* certainly participates in this process, its mode of pastiche is more strikingly engaged in the opposite maneuver: laundering ideological constructs of the past into the present. Most notably, from its pilot, which opens on a dark and ominous building labeled "Hawkins National Laboratory / Department of Energy," *Stranger Things* has engaged in a pattern of uncritically borrowing political framing from the films that influenced it. For instance, *Stranger Things* essentially lifts wholesale the central conflict of *E.T.*, pitting children against nefarious government agents determined to wrest control over the supernatural entity at the narrative's core. Eleven, the series' E.T. substitute, spends much of the first season on the run, having escaped from the government facility where she had been held since infancy, subjected to various experiments using her telekinetic abilities. Like Spielberg's Elliot, Mike offers Eleven shelter and attempts to teach her about American life—"This is my living room, it's mostly for watching TV"—while government agents attempt to locate and recapture her by any means necessary. Unlike *E.T.*, however, *Stranger Things*' depiction of the federal government doesn't neatly fold into a larger opposition between the cynical adult world and childhood innocence[10]—in fact, it doesn't appear to have metaphorical value at all. In this, despite its liberal gestures toward inclusion and feminism, the series offers a strikingly conservative vision of the federal government as an overbearing, immoral, and oppressively paternalistic institution. "[*Stranger Things* is] especially refreshing for libertarians," Matthew McCaffrey explained, writing in 2016 for the right-wing conspiracy blog *InfoWars*. "[They] can finally enjoy a show where the main villain is government itself: at last, the antagonist isn't the market or even a corrupt politician, just government. Maybe its best plot twist is that there's nary an evil corporation to be seen." Insofar as one can derive a coherent set of claims or values from the series' depiction of this conflict, *Stranger Things* is essentially indistinguishable from the conservative politics that dominated the decade, encapsulated by Reagan's mantra "The government *is* the problem."

In some instances, the series' conservatism surpasses the kind embedded in its Spielbergian inspirations—showcasing, inadvertently, the unprogressive nature of these nominally liberal influences. This is most notable in its Reaganesque vision of competing paternalisms. The show provides a contrast between federal and local government filtered through Eleven's two father figures, Dr. Brenner and Sheriff Hopper. Brenner, the face of the shadowy government agency running mind-control experiments deep in the bowels of the Hawkins National Laboratory, who had abducted Eleven shortly after her birth in an effort to harness her telekinetic powers for use as a superweapon, is referred to as "Papa" by Eleven throughout the series. Flashbacks show their relationship to be emotionally neglectful, psychologically abusive, and physically exploitative. One scene early in the first season shows Eleven seated before a caged, hissing cat as Brenner watches from a control room. As Eleven has previously crushed a soda can with her mind in another flashback, the scene implies that Brenner expects her to now use her powers on a living creature. After Eleven refuses, she's dragged kicking and screaming by two orderlies to a small, dark room and thrown inside. As the door closes, Eleven rises to her feet, and uses her powers to knock one of the men against the wall and snap the neck of the other before collapsing to the floor in despair. After Brenner approaches, we see a close-up of Eleven's face as his hands slowly move into the frame and caress her head. He then carries her body, limp with exhaustion, back to her room. This scenario is repeated in the season 1 finale, where Brenner finds Eleven, once again collapsed from exhaustion, having used her powers to fend off the Demogorgon. "Eleven, Eleven, can you hear me?" he says as he cradles her head in his hands while the camera looms over his shoulder, framing a close-up on Eleven's face. She replies, weakly, "Papa?" and he responds with a subtly sinister imitation of care: "Yes, yes, it's your papa." Eleven becomes unsettled once she notices her friends being forcefully restrained, with Mike yelling, "Let her go you bastards!" As she begins to writhe, Brenner caresses her face and seeks to assure her, "Shh shh, you're sick. You're sick, but I'm going to make you better. I'm going to take you back home where I can make you well again, where we can make all of this better so no one gets hurt." Eleven, having now learned the true meaning of love and friendship, rejects his overtures: "Bad . . . bad," she says, turning to Mike and then calling his name. The scene is interrupted by the reappearance of the Demogorgon, which attacks Brenner and the agents, giving the kids cover to escape; it concludes with the monster tackling Brenner, presumably killing him. Though he doesn't play an active role in the series' second and third seasons, Brenner does reappear in flashbacks and hallucinations, highlighting the traumatic impact that he continues to have on Eleven's psyche. In all of this, *Stranger Things* repeatedly emphasizes the notion that Brenner, and the federal government for which he is the series' most prominent representative, are cold, manipulative, and overbearing—ill-suited fathers for a child or a nation, affirming Reagan's critique of what later came to be known as the "nanny-state."

In contrast, the series offers a Reagan-inspired elevation of local government through Sheriff Hopper, a caring and good-hearted man hardened by the trauma of his daughter's death. Following Eleven's disappearance in the season 1 finale, Hopper assumes a paternal surrogacy role for her in seasons 2 and 3, first leaving boxes of Eggos in the woods where she's presumed to be in hiding, and later offering her shelter in his cabin. In order to protect Eleven from the government agents who remain intent on recapturing her, Hopper initially forbids her from leaving the cabin, which becomes a source of tension throughout the second season. On Halloween, for instance, Eleven, in a homemade ghost costume, asks to go trick-or-treating:

HOPPER: You want to go *trick-or-treating*? You know the rules.
ELEVEN: Yes, but—
HOPPER: Yeah, so you know the answer.
ELEVEN: But they wouldn't see me . . .
HOPPER: I don't care. I don't care. Alright? You go out there, ghost or not, it's a risk. We don't take risks, alright? They're stupid. And?
ELEVEN: We're not stupid.
HOPPER: Exactly.

In this, the series creates a parallel between the confinement Eleven experienced at the hands of the government and the one instituted by Hopper. While both are overbearing, the show makes clear that Brenner's captivity is abusive while

Hopper is responding to very real concerns about Eleven's safety. Though this situation is frustrating for Eleven, *Stranger Things* clearly views Hopper's concerns as much more permissible, thereby elevating Hopper's model of paternalism and (if inadvertently) the local government he represents. Though he is at times impulsive and overprotective, the series ultimately depicts Hopper as a model of oversight and protection based on genuine desire for Eleven's well-being. If he's overbearing, it's not to exploit Eleven, as is the case with Brenner, but because he cares too much.

The series' replication of '80s politics under the guise of trope also extends to its sense of place, as Hawkins reproduces the heartland-centric, Morning-in-America vision of the country that Reagan and numerous '80s films worked so hard to foster, imbuing small towns with a special status not afforded to other locales. Here, the cultural narrative suggests, is where *real* Americans live, where the nation's true spirit resides, and where "monsters are twice as horrifying when they attack those good solid people and shatter what we falsely perceive as the innocence of small-town America" (Smokler). It's a familiar trope, one that can be found in different forms throughout films of the period, from *Back to the Future*'s Hill Valley and John Hughes's Shermer, Illinois, to David Lynch's Lumberton and Twin Peaks.

This mediated configuration of the American small town has been central to the Duffer Brothers' project from the beginning, and, though they regularly draw parallels between it and their hometown in interviews, the Duffers' vision of Hawkins and small-town America in the 1980s is, on the whole, less a mnemonic exercise and more a cinematic (re-)creation. From its initial sale to Netflix under the title *Montauk*—an homage to the coastal New York of *Jaws* and the New England settings of King's novels—the series' sense of place has always been tied, directly or indirectly, not to the places where its creators grew up (as one might expect with a conventionally nostalgic tale of childhood), but to those in the films they loved. Though the coastal setting was eventually abandoned due to the complications of shooting on Long Island in the winter, the idyllic small-town setting remained as principal filming was moved to Atlanta, Georgia—a location that, as Matt noted in an interview with *The Hollywood Reporter*, much more closely resembled their own childhood in Durham, North Carolina (Fienberg). Despite acknowledging this similarity, however, the Duffers ultimately chose to set their fictional town in Indiana. The decision to bypass North Carolina, where the Duffers grew up, and Georgia, where the series is filmed and that apparently resembles their hometown, in favor of a third location that, in reality, has very little in common with either is a microcosm of the shift away from memory and toward mediation that I discussed in the introduction: *Stranger Things*' nostalgia is oriented more toward the imagined small towns its creators saw on television and in films than the one they actually lived in.

And yet, there's more to the series' construction of Hawkins than just the nostalgic hierarchy it implies. As with much of *Stranger Things*, what distinguishes Hawkins from the fictional towns that inspired it is that, unlike its predecessors (which are set at the time of their creation), *Stranger Things* takes place thirty years before the time in which it was made. Thus, instead of attempting to reflect its own contemporary reality, Hawkins is a recreation of a setting from a different time, and therefore the product of a different cultural and historical context. While this is true for nearly all works involved in historical recreation, the Duffers' fictional town is particularly interesting because it is an attempt not simply to recreate a historical environment, but rather to recreate a historical environment that was itself already an act of creative imagination—Hawkins, in other words, isn't set in the 1980s as much as in the '80s of the movies it borrows from. As Lacey N. Smith has pointed out, though images like the white picket fence, orderly supermarket shelves, and downtown movie marquee "coalesce to form an imaginary ideal suburbia, it is a mediated imaginary, inspired more by a proliferation of portrayed suburban environments across a variety of media than by the material, inhabited suburbs of everyday life" (217). The small towns upon which Hawkins is based, in other words, did not exist except in fiction. In a sense, this means that *Stranger Things*' "historical" setting is doubly fictional: based on examples drawn not only from media, but from media examples that were themselves not drawn from reality. With its quaint Main Street ripped from *The Andy Griffith Show* and its quiet, well-manicured lawns, Hawkins actually represents a dying vision of Americana that was already the subject of nostalgic yearning in the 1980s. The small-town and suburban images that permeate the '80s media that the series draws upon were, even then, less a historical fact (insofar as they represented some kind of norm of national experience) and more a function of an ongoing ideological project that sought to revive cultural and historical conditions, based in large part on television and cinema. This ideological project was, in other words, more interested in the representational value of these small towns than in the locations themselves, and their revival was more conceptual than materially executed (Smith 217).[11] As Alan Nadel has argued, this nostalgia for a cinematic or televisual reality is, in fact, one of the defining features of Reagan's presidency, and movies of the period are replete with narratives and images seeking to naturalize filmic paradigms as historic ones. Thus, in borrowing from these films, what *Stranger Things* presents as an *accurate* depiction of small-town life in the 1980s is instead merely a simulacrum of '80s cinema, mistaking mediated fantasy for historical reality. *Stranger Things*, then, like numerous '80s films before it, represents the attempted establishment of a fiction as history, an effort to make something that *wasn't* seem as though it *was*. Critically, in the case of *Stranger Things*, this means that its nostalgic suburbia is doubly removed, further alienated from its (increasingly obscured) origins and therefore less recognizable for what it is.

The elevation of small towns, Middle America, and suburbia was, more than anything else, an effort to mark boundaries, to delineate what was and was not American. In its wholesale replication of these spaces, *Stranger Things* doesn't just work to naturalize the '80s suburban fantasy as a historical reality, it also grants validity to the ideas the fantasy was constructed to represent. In light of this, one must ask, What other notions are naturalized in Hawkins's reproduction of the trope of the '80s small town? What does Hawkins reinscribe in its efforts to construct the "ordinary"'80s suburban childhood? It's worth emphasizing here that the series' setting does not hinge upon a single point of reference, but is instead a pastiche constructed through an assembly of aesthetic ideas, "a representation of suburban-ness, meshed with small-town-ness, and Midwest-ness, and other simulacra that coalesce under the guise of a coherent visual past informed by the 1950s but colored by the aesthetics of 1980s pop culture" (Smith 220). Though each of these components is, at least in some ways, discrete, they nonetheless converge around a few shared traits: As Smith has pointed out, these concepts primarily serve to "reinforce ideologies that sustain late capitalism and the suburban consumerism built to foster it," such as the nuclear family, patriarchal gender roles, and liberty through mass consumption (217).

Most of all, the influences that produced Hawkins pivot upon an exclusionary brand of white nostalgia, a notion that is evident not simply in the overwhelming lack of diversity in both Hawkins and the towns that influenced it, but also in the positions that the few characters of color occupy within these spaces. Hawkins is defined as much by its demographics as by its aesthetic markers (lawns, bicycles, mom-and-pop shops)—its demographics, in this sense, function as yet another aesthetic marker, linking the series to its mediated and ideological forbearers. As a location, Indiana is especially useful to the series because it approximates the Americana triumvirate (Midwest, small town, suburban) that *Stranger Things* relies upon while also offering a historically very white population. Like Hughes's Shermer, Illinois, and King's Castle Rock, Maine, before it, Hawkins is therefore a setting where an overwhelmingly white population can be convincingly placed without its lack of diversity seeming like a contrivance (which would unsettle the series' liberal aspirations). *Stranger Things*' vision of its idyllic small town is, in this way, inseparable from its racial politics—and both are functions of its aesthetically driven and tropologically dependent nostalgia. Whiteness, in other words, is part of what makes Hawkins *Hawkins*.

This is reflected both in the town and in the series' central cast. Its core group of children and adults notably contains only one nonwhite member, which simultaneously represents a seemingly purposeful gesture toward diversity *and* a nod toward the token minority cliché from classic '80s films such as *The Goonies* and *Ghostbusters*. Like many of the tropes that *Stranger Things* relies upon, the inclusion of Lucas in the show's group of adolescent protagonists serves no broader narrative or thematic purpose, and, aside from his race, Lucas is arguably the least distinct character in the group. That Lucas is fairly one-dimensional is not unusual for the series, as most of the teen characters, at least initially, conform to a particular type: Mike is the headstrong leader, Will is the sensitive one, Dustin is the late bloomer, Nancy is the good girl, Steve is the bad boy, Jonathan is the outsider, Max is the tomboy; in Lucas's case, however, his "type" is not tied to personality traits, but to his race. It is perhaps not a coincidence, then, that Lucas is also the least developed character over the course of the show. As the series progresses, the other teens each come to transcend their initial type in one way or another: Steve goes from being the coolest guy in class to working at an ice cream shop in the mall and hanging out with kids several grades below him; Jonathan comes out of his shell and begins dating Nancy, who has shed her "good girl" attitude and fixation on popularity, and the two begin transitioning into the adult world as interns with the local newspaper; Dustin finally gets a girlfriend; Will tries to overcome his trauma and assert himself. In the show's three seasons, there is no significant change in Lucas's attitude, his standing within the group, his social circumstances, or anything else that might constitute development for a teenage character. His only growth arrives in the form of a relationship with season 2 newcomer Max (who, in the space of one season, goes from an unsociable tomboy who loves skateboarding and arcades to a girly-girl who teaches Eleven about the wonders of the mall while "Material Girl" plays in the background). Because his type is, essentially, "Black," and because the films that *Stranger Things* is so reliant upon don't offer any other types of Blackness or minority status to which he could pivot, Lucas is seemingly unable to progress beyond his initial role.

As Bering-Porter has noted, "Lucas replaces Data, the Asian character from *The Goonies*, with a black character, but one who serves a similar purpose, unintentionally highlighting a certain display of whiteness and white culture that is often hidden in plain sight." His presence within the group also completes the parallel with the Losers Club from *It*—which the Duffer Brothers lobbied to remake before turning their attention to *Stranger Things* (Fienberg)—composed of five white boys, a Black boy, and a white girl. In this way, Lucas's presence is dictated by, and derives meaning from, its reference. This is particularly evident in the first season, where Lucas's Blackness is only an allusion that provides a superficial notion of diversity to an otherwise all-white production—or, more cynically, deflects the series from charges of exclusion.

In the second season, the writers attempted to respond to allegations of tokenism with a scene that more critically highlights Lucas's role in the group. Mike and Lucas get into an argument when they meet up before school on Halloween in homemade *Ghostbusters* costumes. Mike takes offense at the fact that he and Lucas have inadvertently chosen to role-play as the same (white) character. Mike, their conversation reveals, had assumed that Lucas would be Winston, the sole

Black Ghostbuster. The ensuing exchange reveals Mike's implicit racial bias, and calls into question the logic of tokenism that Lucas, as a character, himself exemplifies:

LUCAS: No one wants to be Winston, Man.
MIKE: What's wrong with Winston?
LUCAS: What's wrong with Winston? He joined the team super late, he's not funny, and he's not even a scientist!
MIKE: Yeah, but he's still cool.
LUCAS: If he's cool, then you be Winston.
MIKE: I can't.
LUCAS: Why not?
MIKE: Because . . .
LUCAS: Because you're not black?
MIKE: I didn't say that.
LUCAS: You thought it.

The conversation is replaced by embarrassment when they notice that the other students are arriving without costumes. Although Lucas and Mike later reconcile, the topic of racial prejudice never reappears. This episode, as Bering-Porter points out, reflects the show's ultimate failure to reckon with the issues it raises: "The inclusion of Lucas, first as a token, then more fully, serves as a weak gesture towards diversity. The show's acknowledgment of its mistake is a familiar gesture, rooted in sympathy that does little to change the conditions through which people of color are othered. . . . His more fulsome inclusion becomes a way of marketing *Stranger Things* as 'diverse' and revealing its own awareness of this gesture towards diversity, allowing the audience to take a certain pleasure in the show's white nostalgia." As this passage suggests, the series' engagement with this critique is limited to acknowledgment alone—Lucas's role in the show did not change, nor did the series abandon the racial ideology that governs it.

Despite its acknowledgment of the inherent flaws in its earlier approach, *Stranger Things*' third season illustrates that the series cannot conceive of race beyond trope. Its elevation of Erica, Lucas's younger sister, from a minor character in the first two seasons to a major player in its third, creates a binary where Blackness is either empty token or stereotype. In seasons one and two, Erica's role is confined to brief comedic appearances as a feisty sibling, mocking the dorkiness of Lucas and his friends. "God you are such a nerd," she says to Lucas in his *Ghostbusters* costume. "No wonder you only hang out with boys." By the midpoint of the third season, however, Erica has become enmeshed in the adventure, accompanying Dustin, Steve, and Robin in their accidental descent into the secret Soviet bunker below the mall. Although heightened character development could accompany this increase in screen time, Erica remains largely the same: a boisterous, no-nonsense, sassy Black girl, a pint-sized Madea primed for comic relief. In one episode, the trio attempts to convince her to investigate a mysterious air duct that none of them can fit into:

> ERICA: Yeah, I don't know . . .
> DUSTIN: You don't know if you can fit?
> ERICA: Oh, I can fit. I just don't know if I want to.
> ROBIN: Are you claustrophobic?
> ERICA: I don't have phobias.
> STEVE: Ok, well, what's the problem?
> ERICA: The problem is I still haven't heard what's in this *for Erica.*

The scene then cuts to a shot of Steve sliding a comically large ice cream sundae across a table. "More fudge please," Erica replies as she slides the sundae back to him. "Go on," she urges with an exaggerated hand gesture. Later, after Erica reluctantly agrees to help out, they find themselves trapped in an elevator. After Robin discovers a bottle containing a strange green substance, Erica attempts to smash it: "It could be useful," she explains. "We could survive down here a long time without food, but if the human body doesn't get water, it will die. . . . If it comes down to me drinking that shit or dying of thirst, I drink," she concludes with a cheeky grin.

The only revelations about Erica in the third season are that she's good at math and likes *My Little Pony* (unexpected, based on Dustin's reaction, because she's Black and has an attitude). Erica is coded as Black in a way that Lucas—whose affect is indistinguishable from that of his "ordinary" white friends—and their parents aren't. This is apparent both in her characterization and in the series' mise-en-scène. Unlike Lucas, whose nonfamilial interactions are always with white people, Erica first appears in season 3 accompanied by four unnamed and previously unseen Black girls who have no lines. When she reappears in the following two episodes, she's again surrounded by three Black girls who, despite several minutes of screen time, still don't speak. Who these girls are and why this population of ten-year-old Black girls equals the rest of the show's Black population combined is apparently unimportant; all that matters is how these girls frame Erica, the Blackness they confer, and the "diversity" they add to the show's cast. Race, in this light, is a matter of utility.

This form of diversity, Bering-Porter correctly notes, identifies a central impetus in the series: to maintain the power of its nostalgia by protecting it from critique. For *Stranger Things*, the value of Blackness lies in its ability to authorize contradictions, as the inclusion of Black characters and brief forays into critical discourse enables the series to maintain its white nostalgia without outwardly appearing to do so. Just as capitalism suppresses challenges to its dominance by incorporating dilutions of them into itself, so too does *Stranger Things* absorb and then defang its contradictions in order to maintain its nostalgia. Race functions like child predation and the threat of nuclear annihilation: a threat to its nostalgia that must be acknowledged and then cast aside. The parallels with '80s films then serve as a cover for the series' replication of a regressive racial politics.

Because the series conflates the 1980s with its depiction in the media of the period, a hierarchy emerges, with cinematic precedent at the top. In this way, the white Americana of Spielberg, King, and Hughes is more central to the '80s than any historical or mnemonic reality, and fidelity to these sources is more important than whatever political sympathies the series may have. The exclusionary whiteness of the American small town, and the racial politics encoded within it, therefore comprise yet another '80s trope that *Stranger Things* uncritically reinforces in its pursuit of accuracy. This is the particular danger of *Stranger Things*' brand of mediated nostalgia: The series is so focused on style that it ultimately loses sight of the implications produced by the aesthetic elements it borrows. While the series' liberal gestures suggest that it may not intend to say the unsavory things that its references imply, these notions nonetheless come to fill the empty space created by its reluctance to offer anything substantial of its own. *Stranger Things*' nostalgic deference to the paradigms established by its influences buries any potential for the series to offer critique in its own contradictions. Ultimately, the series finds itself trapped within the confines of the past it reimagined.

As Noah Berlatsky has pointed out, *Stranger Things* is stuck in a loop: "It defeats the monsters and creates a better future. Then it looks around . . . and has to wearily jump to the past to try to get back to a better future all over again." Victories are always conditional and short lived: They save Will in the season 1 finale, and a month later he coughs up a slug-like creature triggering a menacing vision of the Upside Down; Mike and Eleven share a dance at Snow Ball '84 after defeating the Mind Flayer, and then the camera slowly backs out of the gym, inverts itself, and reveals the Mind Flayer still alive in the Upside Down. *Stranger Things* thereby imports the logic of closure more commonly found in cinematic sequels, relying on an escalation of conflict and a broadening of scope with each successive entry. Every season has a new monster, each less specific than the next—demonic Eggo boxes, built to contain whatever horror one wants to map onto them. The result is a narrative that, as it progresses, piling on newer and greater horrors with each episode, suggests that all things will only get worse, that decay may be slowed down but never stopped, and that the horrors will always return in one form or another. Though its characters persist, the series doesn't appear to believe that a better future is actually possible; its nostalgic attachment to a particular bygone childhood and its insistence upon the death that growing up brings seemingly won't allow it. But even if it wanted to repair the damages of the past and present, *Stranger Things*, and the hypermediated nostalgia for which it is the archetype, is structurally incapable of pursuing such a project, even symbolically, because its insistence on style means that there's nothing to point to as *the* thing to conquer, only form. *Stranger Things* fears anything that lies beneath the surface, whether it's the subterranean Upside Down or the horrors of the modern world that it hides beneath metaphor and trope. Because the series cannot conceive of the past as anything other than an aesthetic, there's nothing material for it to confront, only un- or rearticulated doom. This is the true death of its reflective-age nostalgia: a cycle intent on endlessly reproducing dead styles as the world burns in the distance.

CHAPTER 3

Twin Peaks: The Return, Nostalgia, and Fantasies of Repetition

"Our Very First Show, Again," the first episode of the Netflix series *Fuller House* (2016–2020)—a revival of the popular ABC sitcom *Full House* that aired from 1987 to 1995—begins by replaying the opening credits of the original series, featuring shots of late-1980s San Francisco as the Tanner family crosses the Golden Gate Bridge in a vintage convertible and frolics in the park while the original theme plays out its familiar opening lament: "Whatever happened to predictability? / The newsman, the paperboy, evening TV." The new-old intro is truncated, however, when, in place of the actual credits, the show cuts to an establishing shot of the famous house, beneath the words "29 years later." Inside the house, viewers are reintroduced to the core cast from the original series, who, we learn, have gathered to help DJ, the eldest child in the original Tanner family, following the death of her husband. ("Our Very First Show," the *Full House* pilot, takes place three months after the death of DJ's mother as her father's best friend, Joey, and her maternal uncle, Jesse, move in to support the family.) As the original cast (re)appears, one by one, we learn that Danny, Uncle Jesse, Aunt Becky, and Uncle Joey are all departing later that day, to resume their (old) new lives in other cities, leaving DJ alone for the first time since her husband's death. (The first scene of the series' original pilot features Danny and the kids bidding farewell to his mother in a similar context). The family, gathered around the dinner table, share brief bits of news updating viewers on what has happened since the show went off the air: Danny and Aunt Becky now have a morning show in Los Angeles (they cohosted *Wake Up, San Francisco* in the original run); Jesse is a composer for *General Hospital* (a knowing nod to the fact that John Stamos got his big break on the series); Joey (a struggling stand-up in *Full House*) works as a comedian in Las Vegas; DJ is a veterinarian; Stephanie is a DJ in London; Michelle, the cast announces and then breaks the fourth wall with a sarcastic glare into the camera, has a successful fashion career in New York (the Olsen twins declined to participate in the new series)—all, we are assured, are living the lives fans would have imagined; they have not, it seems, sold their dreams. After the scene concludes, the new-new-old opening credits begin, accompanied by a version of the iconic theme, with slightly altered verse lyrics, now sung by pop star Carly Rae Jepsen:

"Everywhere You Look (*Full House* Theme)," written by Jesse Frederick, Bennett Salvay, and Jeff Franklin	**"Everywhere You Look (*Fuller House* Theme)," written by Jesse Frederick, Bennett Salvay, Jeff Franklin, and Butch Walker**
Whatever happened to predictability?	Whatever happened to predictability?
The milkman, the paperboy, the evening TV?	The milkman, the paperboy, the evening TV?
~~Clouds as mean as you've ever seen~~	Everybody eventually
~~Ain't a bird who knows your tune~~	Says that they're as lost as you
~~Then a little voice inside you whispers~~	So everybody shout it together
"~~Kid~~, don't sell your dreams so soon!"	"Hey, don't sell your dreams so soon!"

As the music plays, fans are treated to a medley of new, old, and new-old images, beginning with a computer-generated picture frame on a computer-generated wood-paneled wall showing the cast from the original first season, followed by a photo of the cast from the original final season against the same false background. These images give way to a sprawling reshot look at the Golden Gate Bridge, presented in high definition from an angle that mirrors the helicopter shot early in the original credits. The intro then segues, as each member of the cast is introduced, into sequences merging past and present: The core returning cast members (Candace Cameron Bure [DJ], Jodie Sweetin [Stephanie], Andrea Barber [Kimmy]) are superimposed on montages of their characters from the original introduction; new characters (children of the core returning characters) are superimposed over their baby pictures; "special guest stars" (Stamos [Jesse], Bob Saget [Danny], Dave Coulier [Joey] et al.), appear in split-screen shots showing clips from the original introduction alongside footage of them repeating the same actions (Stamos plays guitar on a bench, Saget catches a football, etc.).

After the credits, we find DJ and Stephanie in their old bedroom, talking about the passage of time. "Isn't this crazy? I wound up living back in my old bedroom. I moved in here when I was five," DJ says. "Yeah," Stephanie replies, "then I moved in. Now here we are again. Circle of life." The two reminisce about an incident from the original pilot, in which, after being asked to share a bedroom, they got into an argument that ended with Stephanie clinging to the top of the curtains, a pose she attempts to reenact. That evening, at a going-away party (which takes place in the family living room), when Stephanie, DJing for the group, announces it's "time to take it back to the late '80s when this party got started—New Kids on the Block!" the women all congregate to perform the choreography from the video for "You Got It (The Right Stuff)." Later, Uncle Jesse sings the song "Forever" to Aunt Becky, with everyone looking on—just as he did at their wedding in the original series. Eventually, the whole group joins in. We meet Comet Jr. Jr., the granddaughter of the family's original dog, who gives birth to a litter of puppies near the end of the episode. We also see DJ's best friend and family pest Kimmy get a hug from Danny: "I've been waiting twenty years to hug the king of huggers," she says. In the final scene of the episode, Danny, Uncle Jesse, Aunt Becky, and Uncle Joey offer to extend their stay in order to help the increasingly overwhelmed DJ. Danny, who was previously planning to sell the house, announces that he has changed his mind, saying DJ and her kids can stay as long as they like. Their new plans are quickly scuttled, however, when Stephanie and Kimmy (like Jesse and Joey before them) offer to move in instead. DJ agrees. Moments later, when the baby starts crying, Joey says, "I know how to handle this" and begins to sing the theme song from *The Flintstones.* (In the original pilot, when Michelle starts crying, Joey also says, "I know how to handle this," and sings the same song.) As in the original pilot, the family gathers around the crib, and the camera cuts to an overhead shot of the baby as they all circle the crib while singing along. Also, as in the original, DJ and Stephanie perform the "a dabba-doo time" line in duet, and Stephanie yells, "Wilma!!!!" This all appears in split-screen format, with the new footage replicating the old, shot for shot and gesture for gesture. The audio is also doubled, such that the slightly quieter original sing-along forms a haunting echo of the new track. After they finish singing, hug, say farewells, and Danny, Uncle Jesse, Aunt Becky, and Uncle Joey depart, the new-old Tanner family—DJ, Stephanie, Kimmy, and their children—gather around the crib to sing the Flintstones theme once more. The camera fades to black and the credits roll.

The *Fuller House* pilot thus concludes, having reestablished, through repetition, the order of the original series: Everything has been revived, recycled, reassembled, reunited, and reinstated.

The paradox of culture at the end of history is that nothing ever really ends anymore. Though characterized by (a certain kind of) stasis, the posthistorical world is also marked by the constant ebb and flow of preexisting artifacts and styles, such that when one fades out of fashion it is always replaced by another reiteration. What came to an end at the end of history, in other words, was (a certain kind of) progress, a belief in a progressive political teleology, rather than change itself. Change, at least on the level of culture, has instead accelerated at an unprecedented rate. Old things are constantly returning anew, such that in place of modernity's implicit forward velocity, cultural change has manifested its energy in the circular fashion of a treadmill. The end of history is, in this way, a (pseudo)cyclical temporality, and we find ourselves caught in its pattern of infinite recursion. This chapter will, as a result, be especially attentive to the prefix re-, particularly when it indicates cyclicality, recycling, a process of repetition, or a return to prior states, or accompanies instances of doing again.

In his 2011 retrospective *Retromania*, Simon Reynolds called the 2000s the "re-decade." Though, at the time, Reynolds was right to recognize the increasingly backward-glancing nature of postmillennium Anglo-American pop culture, the following decade proved even more deserving of the moniker. Already, by the middle of the 2010s, the various retro movements in music and fashion that, Reynolds correctly pointed out, dominated the 2000s had given way to more straightforward acts of recycling, rebooting, and revivalism. In other words, the popularity of artists like Adele, the Strokes, and the White Stripes whose vaguely vintage homages (the primary focus of much of Reynolds's analysis) provided the foundation for otherwise novel songwriting was on the wane (with fewer and fewer retro acts popping up each year), replaced by even more targeted efforts to reproduce what-used-to-be with even greater fidelity; the artifacts of bygone eras served less as inspiration than as products, full stop. The prevailing production process, in other words, was no longer to make new from old, but instead to make the old new.

In one sense, this is nothing new, as remakes in film and television, alongside covers and commemorative rereleases in music, had been major parts of the American mediascape for most of the twentieth century. What is novel about this period, however, is the sheer volume of mediated reproductions that emerged in the second decade of the twenty-first century after a period of relative scarcity. Additionally, the present situation is distinct from previous historical examples, particularly in film and television, due to the widespread availability of the originals thanks to streaming. In the classical Hollywood era, for instance, remakes were being produced at a time when most people had no access to the originals, and, even later on as television gained access to film libraries, availability was determined by station programming rather than the consumer. In music, rereleases were often little more than marketing gimmicks aimed at ensuring that older releases made their way back onto the shelves of brick-and-mortar stores. The rise of home cinema, video rental, and, even more significantly, streaming platforms like Netflix and Spotify, saw control shift to the hands of consumers, who now found themselves able to access originals in a way they never had before. These technological developments meant that reproductions were now more redundant than ever, as their earlier justification (lack of access) was no longer operative. The role that remakes and other reproductions play in the media landscape of the twenty-first century, therefore, has been fundamentally altered.

This shift, from creating new-from-old to creating new-old or reproducing old anew, became particularly noticeable in film and, especially, television.

Accelerated by the persistent quest for content amid the streaming wars, retro-inspired but nonetheless novel IPs like *Mad Men* and *Stranger Things* were eventually outnumbered by a slew of revivals, reboots, and remakes. An article from 2018, for instance, offered a list of 121 movie remakes and reboots currently in development, from *Clueless* and *Blade* to *Das Boot* (Brew and Harley). A similar list published in March 2021 identified twenty-five TV reboots either premiering or beginning production that year alone, featuring several influential titles like *Sex and the City* and *Beavis and Butt-Head* (Spencer). In another example of doubled nostalgia for nostalgia, *Field of Dreams* was revived in 2021 when the New York Yankees and Chicago White Sox played a regular-season game on the titular field in Dyersville, Iowa (the park itself is an homage to Comiskey Park, where the White Sox played from 1910 until 1990), dressed in throwback uniforms just like those in the film. As in the film, the two teams were led onto the field by Kevin Costner, who then gave a speech repeating some of his famous lines ("Is this heaven?") while a portion of the film's score played in the background. The ABC *Live in Front of a Studio Audience* specials, which premiered in 2019, present another layer of abstracted televisual repetition. In this series, single episodes of hit shows from the '70s and '80s, such as *All in the Family* and *The Facts of Life*, are performed word for word and shot for shot on perfectly recreated sets before a live audience by a new cast made up of familiar stars of today, none of whom had any connection to the original shows (Woody Harrelson plays Archie Bunker, Jamie Foxx plays George Jefferson, etc.). It's unclear, in an era where the shows of the past are so easily accessible via streaming services, what the draw of this series is supposed to be, particularly when much of the action falls into (inadvertent?) irony—the performance of Kevin Hart, cast as a child pretending to be a superhero in the first scene of the *Diff'rent Strokes* episode, resonates very differently than when Gary Coleman, an actual child, initially performed the part, which would seem to undercut the sincerity of the original show and its nostalgic draw. Nonetheless, the show was a relative hit for ABC, raking in top viewership numbers and winning multiple Primetime Emmys. Extreme examples such as these aside, '80s and '90s TV, following the conventional twenty-five-year nostalgia cycle, was the largest source of material during this period. Since 2016, when *Fuller House*—arguably the first of its kind[1]—premiered, *Roseanne, Punky Brewster, Night Court, That '70s Show, Saved by the Bell, The Fresh Prince of Bel-Air, Mad About You, Will and Grace, Sex and the City, The X-Files*, and *Twin Peaks* have each reappeared in one form or fashion. Thus, by the end of the 2010s, though more conventional homages still proliferated throughout film, television, and music, in terms of sheer volume the balance had overwhelmingly shifted toward reproduction—a trend that has continued into the first few years of the 2020s and shows no signs of slowing down.

This onslaught is not just a response to the fact that nostalgia is trendy; there is, as always, an economic imperative behind such a move. Premised on the extraction of profit from all it can touch, capitalism's expansionist logic sees existing IPs lying dormant (i.e., not producing anything new and thus not making as much money as it could) as an untapped resource. This notion is underscored by the fact that these intellectual properties typically have established communities of fans, which is especially important for television, a medium that relies on creating and sustaining connections between audiences and characters and is therefore more likely to produce the kind of deep nostalgic attachments that bring viewers back. It is no coincidence, in this light, that (as the list above indicates) the overwhelming majority of televisual reboots and revivals are shows that originally centered on the family or on teens whose age cohort is now well into adulthood. These situations provide another layer of nostalgic resonance for returning viewers, who find occasion not just to reconvene with their beloved characters, but also discover new avenues of identification (viewers who watched *Full House* as children may now find parallels with DJ's adventures in parenting; they may also come to better appreciate characters, like teachers and other authority figures, whose lives in the original run seemed distant from their own). Nostalgia TV, in other words, promises returning viewers the opportunity to again see their lives reflected on the small screen. The strength of these attachments makes revived and rebooted IP a treasure trove for studios. In part for these reasons, nostalgia TV is also relatively less risky to produce, since new projects don't carry the same guarantee of an audience (and, therefore, have a greater potential for total failure). The profit projections for making something new, in other words, are often tighter than they are for remaking something old. Not coincidentally, the end of history exists in the context of a broader economic model that also seeks to minimize cost and risk, setting aside, where possible, the question of quality and long-term outcomes. As Zygmunt Bauman has pointed out, "It is the mind-boggling speed of circulation, of recycling, ageing, dumping and replacement which brings profit today—not the durability and lasting reliability of the product" (*Liquid Modernity* 14). The end of history is an era of rampant recycling and refashioning, one that is, increasingly, uninterested in (or unwilling—even unable—to sanction) the kind of novelty that defined much of the twentieth century. This is the perpetual condition of the reflective age: an endless procession of the same things happening again.

It is interesting, in this light, that reboots and revivals are almost always set in the present. Rather than picking up where the originals left off, revivals like *Fuller House*, *Punky Brewster*, *The X-Files*, and *Gilmore Girls: A Year in the Life* begin in the present day, often devoting much of the first episode to filling in the gaps between the years of production. Reboots like *Bel-Air* and *Saved by the Bell* likewise eschew the original's now-nostalgic settings in favor of the present, attempting to refashion the original's formula for contemporary tastes along the way (*The Fresh Prince*'s fish-out-of-water comedy of manners becomes a drama about race and class difference; *Saved by the Bell*'s cast of wealthy straight kids adds poor and queer characters). The returns of both revivals and reboots are, therefore, less explicitly nostalgic for the time period of which they are avatars. Instead, they satisfy nostalgia for a product that contains a particular set of forms, styles, and systems of relation that together reflect a particular time. The overall gesture of the reboot/revival, therefore, is to merge these forms, styles, and systems of the past into the present. This effort is perfectly captured in *Fuller House*'s *Flintstones* split-screen scene, which expresses the essence of the impulse driving the revival/reboot. By reenacting the past, with the original cast alongside itself, the scene emphasizes at once both change and its lack—a cinematic *plus ça change*. The differences between the past and its present reiteration, the scene suggests, are merely superficial. The effect of the second repetition, with the new-old cast, is to elide differences full stop, with each character reinterpreted as an earlier form: The daughter becomes her father, the aunt becomes her uncle, the goofy female friend becomes the father's goofy male friend, with old framed as new, new reframed as old. The effect is to erase difference (is the daughter-turned-mother really the father?) and highlight sameness, to produce continuity where it doesn't necessarily exist.

The relationships between nostalgia, repetition, and the end of history are more complex than they might first appear: On one hand, the conditions of the end of history provide the catalyst for expressions of nostalgic longing, dictating what is longed for; on the other hand, nostalgia also (re)produces the political, social, and cultural values of the very same posthistorical world it is a reaction to. "Everywhere You Look (Fuller House Theme)" is a good example of this. The song is doubly nostalgic (nostalgic for a time that was itself nostalgic), an expression of longing for how things used to be as well as an expression of nostalgia for an earlier expression of nostalgia. The song's opening two lines, lifted directly from "Everywhere You Look (Full House Theme)," mourn the disappearance of a way of life that had already, the original song tells us, been lost ("Whatever happened to . . . ?"). Just as the original song implied that the original show offered a televisual antidote to the loss of traditional American family values, the revitalized song suggests that the revived show will recapture the original show's reactionary paradise of milkmen, paperboys, and evening TV. The new song also suggests that the problems that plagued society in the '80s and '90s remain unresolved today (it's unclear if they were resolved while the show was airing and then simply returned, or if they ever went away to begin with), leaving it caught in a double bind: The song seeks to acknowledge its heritage by comparing the problems of the past and the present, but to do so it must, like the original, also invoke the idea that the series provides some kind of redress for the losses named by the song. This is an example of the way that nostalgia internalizes the end of history's contradictions: It expresses a need to recycle the past in order to remedy the present even though the same forms and objects were around when the problems began (and were specifically premised on counteracting them). Put another way, it suggests that things will improve if we simply redo the same things over and over, even if the past three decades have been, more or less, an exercise in just that to no avail.

The theme is also an expression of another problem: Repeating the original's opening lament flattens the distinction between the two periods, while also, ironically, undercutting the complaint about the loss of predictability—how long must the milkman, paperboy, and evening TV be missing before their absence becomes predictable? When does the new normal stop being new? The end of history, once again, presents a complication here, with its paradox of endless change in the midst of grinding stagnation. On one hand, the end of history is nothing if not predictable, and the neoliberal order that was reshaping America when the original song was penned (the true source of much of the sociocultural upheaval in the period) had been firmly in place for decades by the time *Fuller House* arrived. In this light, very little has changed, and the predictability complaint rings false. On the other hand, many of the same sociocultural upheavals that occasioned nostalgic responses in the '80s and '90s have only accelerated in the time since the show ended. In this light, the complaint has at least a logical foundation. Here, again, is a state of confusion brought about by the end of history's mystifying conflation of the cultural and political, which the *Fuller House* theme perfectly reproduces.

It is in the context of this uniquely posthistorical moment of seemingly endless nostalgic repetition, reboots, and revivals that season 3 of *Twin Peaks* was released. Following a twenty-five-year hiatus, the show, often referred to as *Twin Peaks: The Return*, returned on Showtime as an eighteen-episode miniseries on May 21, 2017, continuing the storyline of *Twin Peaks* twenty-five years after it began—just as Laura Palmer had enigmatically promised in the original series, whispering, "I'll see you again in twenty-five years." Repetition, a thematic interest for the series since its inception, plays an even more crucial role in *The Return*, forming the backbone of its commentary on the nature of nostalgia and televisual reboots/revivals. In doing so, the series not only sheds light on the nature of nostalgia at the end of history, but also offers a salient critique of the fantastic attachments produced in this cultural context.

The original series, which premiered on ABC on April 8, 1990, followed FBI special agent Dale Cooper's investigation into the murder of a young girl in the seemingly idyllic titular small town in the Pacific Northwest. Along the way, audiences were introduced to a slew of idiosyncratic characters, surreal imagery, and generic pastiche, learning that the mystery of Laura Palmer's death went in directions darker and more unexpected than they could have imagined. Following a labyrinthian series of twists, including the revelation that Laura's murder at the hands of her incestuous father was actually part of a deeper struggle between supernatural forces of evil that inhabited the town, the series concluded one season later, with Cooper, having (at the urging of ABC executives) solved the show's central mystery several episodes earlier, being trapped in the interdimensional Black Lodge, while a doppelgänger, possessed by the evil spirit BOB, had returned to Twin Peaks in his place. The show ended with the doppelgänger smashing his head into a mirror, whose reflection shows the grinning face of BOB rather than Cooper's, and laughing maniacally as blood drips down his forehead. The enigmatic cliffhanger conclusion of the show's original run was followed almost immediately by a cinematic prequel, *Fire Walk with Me*, which largely avoided resolving the remaining mysteries established in the series, opting instead to explore Laura's final days and the events leading up to her death. Though its critical assessment has warmed in the years since, the film was almost universally panned upon release, and, though it remained an influential cult classic, public interest in the series, once a must-see event and bona fide cultural phenomenon, quickly faded.

The premiere of *The Return* opens with footage from the original series, in which Laura says, "I'll see you again in twenty-five years" before fading to black. In lieu of conventional exposition, *The Return* reminds viewers of its catalyzing events through a montage featuring a mist-covered forest canopy, an abandoned mill, the empty halls of a late-1980s high school, a girl running in slow motion with her hands covering her face, and a slow zoom on Laura's infamous homecoming photo in the school's trophy cabinet that ends with a close-up. The words "Twin Peaks" appear across Laura's face, and the opening credits begin, featuring new (but familiar) images of a waterfall, red curtains, and a black-and-white zig-zag floor, all accompanied by Angelo Badalamenti's original score. Agent Cooper, we learn in the next scene, is still trapped in the Black Lodge and, as we see a few scenes later, his doppelgänger has been living in his place for the last twenty-five years.

Though familiar, the new season, shot from a single eighteen-hour script and subsequently edited into episodes (officially titled "Part One," "Part Two," etc.), takes time to return fully to its original state (but, arguably, never really does). Like *The Odyssey*, whose similarity to the series has been noted by several critics[2] and that cocreator Mark Frost has cited as an inspiration, *The Return* is not so much about the return's completion as about the process of returning. Agent Cooper, Frost and Lynch's Odysseus, spends most of the series trying to return not only to Twin Peaks but also to his old self and, in another sense, to return *The Return* to the conditions and conventions that characterized the original series. This process lasts most of the season and occupies the majority of his narrative arc. In typical Lynch fashion, the process is also not straightforward: Although Cooper appears in the second scene of the first episode, he is still trapped in the Black Lodge, which he doesn't exit until the third episode; once out, Cooper erroneously replaces Dougie, a lookalike living in Las Vegas who was "manufactured" by the original doppelgänger to allow him to remain outside the Black Lodge longer than his initial twenty-five-year mandate. As a result of this confounded process, Cooper returns in a bewildered state, unaware of who he is, unable to speak in complete sentences, and only capable of repeating phrases (particularly those that stir his recognition of his original life). In this stage, Cooper's activity is defined by repetition—he slowly becomes himself again by repeating the tropes and traits that defined him in the original run. This fulfills a central desire for fans of the series, some of whom had been longing for the return of their beloved character for two decades. Cooper spends the following thirteen episodes absently meandering through Dougie's life, variously encountering abstracted elements of his original persona such as coffee, pie, or law enforcement. Not until the sixteenth hour of *The Return* does Cooper fully return to the character in the original series. After waking up from a coma and remembering who he is (simultaneously adopting his old, familiar mannerisms), Cooper books a flight to Twin Peaks to resume his quest to save Laura, whose murder twenty-five years ago, he has become convinced, can still be prevented. He arrives at the Twin Peaks Sheriff Station just in time to reunite with the old crew, help defeat his doppelgänger, and destroy BOB. Having reestablished the order of the original series, Cooper's Homeric return to Twin Peaks/*Twin Peaks* has succeeded. Like *Fuller House*, everything has been revived, recycled, reassembled, reunited, and reinstated.

His triumphant return to Twin Peaks (and *Twin Peaks*) is relatively short lived, however, as within minutes of the show's reconstitution Cooper again leaves Twin Peaks/*Twin Peaks*. As though driven by the need to undo the damage done in the original series (or, we might say, the past), Cooper travels through a portal in the basement of the Great Northern Hotel that eventually takes him back to February 23, 1989, the night Laura Palmer was murdered, and the day before the series began. There, Cooper is digitally edited into now-black-and-white scenes from *Fire Walk with Me* as he watches Laura in the woods with James hours before her fateful encounter with Leo and Jacques. After they fight, James leaves, and she returns to the woods, where Cooper reaches out to her. The scene cuts to a shot from the original series showing Laura's hair in close-up as her body, wrapped in plastic, has washed ashore. As before, the camera surveys the body, before cutting to a wide shot. This time, instead of being discovered by Pete Martell as he heads out to fish, the body fades away, leaving no trace. Now in color, Laura, in the woods, asks Cooper, "Where are we going?" and Cooper replies, "Home." *The Return* then reairs the opening scene of the original pilot, showing Josie looking at herself in the mirror, and Pete greeting Catherine before leaving to fish. As Pete walks outside, we can see that Laura's body is no longer there, and, unlike in the original, Pete carries on with his day. When we return to the woods, Cooper is leading Laura through the darkness. At one point, however, he looks back and sees that, like Eurydice, she has disappeared. *Twin Peaks*, which *The Return* had only just returned to, has vanished; the entire narrative has been rewritten.

In the finale, Cooper and Diane (Cooper's formerly unseen secretary to whom he dictates taped messages in the original series, now played by frequent Lynch collaborator Laura Dern) drive into the desert, enter a portal of some kind, and find themselves on a dark desert highway. They get a room at a motel and have sex, and in the morning Diane has disappeared. Cooper finds a letter addressed to "Richard" from "Linda" that says, "When you read this I'll be gone. Please don't try to find me, I don't recognize you anymore. Whatever it was we had together is over." Bemused, Cooper (Richard) heads to Odessa, Texas, and enters Judy's Diner, which, unlike Twin Peaks' idyllic Double-R Diner, is dingy and patronized by three aggressive men who are harassing their waitress. After (uncharacteristically) beating the men, Cooper (Richard) gets the address of another waitress who works at the coffee shop but isn't there that day. When he knocks on her door, a woman played by Sheryl Lee (the actress who plays Laura Palmer) opens it and identifies herself as Carrie Page. When asked if she is Laura Palmer, she says, in a Texas accent, "No, I'm not her." After Cooper fails to stimulate her memory, she asks what's going on, and Cooper replies, "As strange as it sounds, I think you're a girl named Laura Palmer. I want to take you to your mother's home—your home, at one time. It's very important." He shows her his FBI badge, and she agrees to leave with him, citing a need to "get out of Dodge" anyway. They return, once more, to Twin Peaks, drive past the Double-R (which she says she doesn't recognize), and arrive at the Palmer house. When they knock on the door, they're greeted not by Laura's mother, but by a woman who identifies herself as Alice Tremond, played by the home's real-life owner (who had never appeared in the series before), who says that she doesn't know of anyone by the name of Sarah Palmer, and that she bought the home from someone named Chalfont. (Mrs. Tremond and Mrs. Chalfont are names given to an elderly woman to whom Laura used to deliver meals, who appeared in both the original series and the film.) Confused, Cooper and Carrie turn from the house and walk back onto the street. Cooper, walking as if in a daze, asks, "What year is this?" Carrie looks at the house, and we hear the sound of Sarah Palmer yelling "Laura" on the morning she disappeared, taken directly from the original series. Carrie, who seems to have heard it too, starts shaking and then violently screams. There is a loud electrical pop, then the lights in the house cut out, and the show cuts to black. After thirty seconds, an image of Laura whispering in Cooper's ear fades in and the credits roll.

This is the end of Agent Cooper's long-awaited return to Twin Peaks, the end of *Twin Peaks: The Return*, and, in more ways than one, the end of *Twin Peaks*. In his desire to revitalize the past by preventing the demise of one of its artifacts, Cooper has seemingly undone everything: The end of *Twin Peaks: The Return* thus marks the end of *Twin Peaks* the show as well as the obliteration of the universe the show depicted, both literally (the show is over) and diegetically (everything that happened from the original series until the finale has, apparently, been undone). Cooper's attempt to revive Laura has inadvertently created a rupture, distorting the past, and everything that followed, beyond recognition: Nothing is as it was, everything is now something else, all stability and coherence have been lost. Revival, in this way, is configured as an act of destruction rather than creation; the process of doing over again that is endemic to televisual reboots and revivals is as much, the show seems to suggest, about erasing what came before as about making something new. And yet, as Carrie's scream illustrates, traces of the past still haunt these redacted versions anyway—the past can never truly be undone, only repressed. (Carrie, one might argue, is a frame that masks Laura's original trauma, a cinematic staging of Freud's return of the repressed.) Ultimately, *The Return* tells us not only that you cannot return home, but also that you cannot bring home back by revising the conditions that led to its disappearance.

This discussion also illustrates how nostalgia serves as a sustaining fantasy of the end of history. Nostalgia is symptomatic and generative of the end of history because it both reproduces and is an example of the kind of fraying fantasies of American life that permeate the period: security, stability, progress, and coherence, most of all. Nostalgia is a fantasy of reproduction and impossible return, one whose impossibility is contradicted by the return of styles and shows, which seems, in turn, to suggest the possibility of a deeper return, one that lies beyond style and form. Structurally (and contradictorily), nostalgia provides the potential for a dual fantasy: Nostalgia, especially in the form of reboots/remakes, invokes progress even as it actually more broadly signifies return/recursion, and, in doing so, it enables one to produce a version of the past that identifies (increasingly superficial/aesthetic) differences while typically not providing the space for one to consider why they are different (because, as *Stranger Things* shows, in the process of aestheticization, or of marking difference through mediated objects, those things are mystified). In short, it allows one to believe that select things are improving—or at least changing. At the same time, as *Ready Player One* illustrates, nostalgia also provides a fantasy world through which one can escape an increasingly pessimistic reality; nostalgia TV, in particular, promises to provide stability and the comfort of the familiar in the face of the seemingly unending cultural change and sociopolitical decay. In the end, nostalgia at the end of history promotes the fantasy of a progressive social world while at the same time providing a fantastic escape from the reality of decay and decline.

This produces a fraught double bind, in which people are caught between two contradictory fantasies that cannot be resolved, and find themselves helplessly attached to ideas, attitudes, and ways of being that no longer work, but that they are nonetheless compelled to repeat (often without even realizing it). The end of history inspires nostalgic thinking in part because it produces a desire to escape the present despite simultaneously refusing refuge in the future, while the same turn to nostalgic fantasy—particularly the kinds of hyperaestheticized, nonreflective ones that have overwhelmed the cultural landscape of the past two decades—also impedes any efforts actually to improve the conditions that drew one to it in the first place. As I pointed out in the introduction, the end of history is, above all, marked by stagnation and decay, the dissolution of progress; the solution to such problems, though politically complicated, is certainly not to turn to fantasies of the past[3] (least of all, the past's own fantasies), particularly when they are founded in notions that have already failed to prevent the present state from emerging. To put it another way: If the fall came before 1987, as the *Full House* theme suggests, what sense does it make to return to 1987, as the revival urges?

But making logical sense is not the point; the function of fantasy is not to fix reality as it actually is, but to provide an outlet for unsatisfied desires by reconfiguring or recalibrating one's image of their life so that it satisfies what they find lacking in reality; "[Fantasy] supplements the functioning of ideology and keeps subjects relatively content with an imaginary satisfaction," as Todd McGowan has explained (*Impossible David Lynch* 15). More specifically, as Lauren Berlant points out, "Fantasy is the means by which people hoard idealizing theories and tableaux about how they and the world 'add up to something'" (3). Nostalgia, a response to a pessimistic reality that ultimately obscures the real cycles of decay and stagnation that produced it, feeds on the feeling that the world increasingly does not add up to anything coherent and stable, and is not itself desirable (and, thus, desire must be fulfilled elsewhere). Fictive narratives are powerful conduits for this process because, as Jameson (drawing on Louis Althusser) points out in *The Political Unconscious*, they resolve at the fantasy level conflicts that do not allow resolution in the realities of everyday life. The function of nostalgia and nostalgic media, in other words, is not to create logical consistency but to provide space for the psychological fulfillment of certain desires, even as this fantastic fulfillment has no bearing on the material world (and possibly impedes it).

This predicament recalls Berlant's notion of cruel optimism, which describes a relation where "something you desire is actually an obstacle to your flourishing. It might involve food, or a kind of love; it might be a fantasy of the good life, or a political project. It might rest on something simpler, too, like a new habit that promises to induce in you an improved way of being. These kinds of optimistic relation are not inherently cruel. They become cruel only when the object that draws your attachment actively impedes the aim that brought you to it initially" (1). Nostalgia at the end of history, in this light, is perhaps the ultimate example of the phenomenon Berlant has identified: A form of cruelly optimistic fantasy that "recalibrates what we encounter so that we can imagine that something or someone can fulfill our desire . . . project[ing] qualities onto [the past] so that we can love . . . and manipulate it for having those qualities—which it might or might not have" (122), a process that ultimately "blocks the satisfactions [it] offers" (51) but nonetheless binds the individual to the promises it has come to represent, whose contours are a direct result of the social conditions that led to its emergence. Nostalgia at the end of history is, in short, a cruelly optimistic attachment to things that no longer work that is accompanied by a compulsion to repeat them anyway.

This turn to cruel optimism is not simply for the sake of establishing a categorical parallel; rather, it provides another way of considering the nature of nostalgic repetition at the end of history. The cruelness of reflective-age nostalgia lies in its invitation to return and repeat, to try to make what (seemingly) used to work work again, or to recapture what has been irrevocably lost, in order to, in one way or another, repair that which has become broken (a process that is always doomed to fail). Conceptually, nostalgia is premised on the notion of *nostos*, the (continual, insatiable) return home that one longs for precisely because it is impossible. This is nostalgia's cruel, unresolvable paradox: It is occasioned by the same conditions that prevent its fulfillment. Yet, as I noted in the introduction, this is a process that is complicated when irrecoverable pasts are represented by recoverable, mediated objects. The '80s will never actually return, and you can never be a kid again, but, thanks to Netflix, you can watch *Full House* again, and even consume new versions of it. This only serves to strengthen the nostalgic bind by giving viewers a way to indulge in a version of the fantasy that simultaneously makes its larger aim seem more realizable—you no longer need to imagine returning home, *Fuller House* gives you a portal to achieve it (in thirteen twenty-two-minute increments per year).

Cooper's failed homecoming demonstrates the confounded premise of the reboot/revival's repetitive, cruelly optimistic nostalgia. He's determined to return out of an optimistic belief that he can fix what has gone wrong; and yet, as the show demonstrates, this belief is precisely what brings the ultimate downfall of *Twin Peaks*, seemingly (re)writing the show out of existence. Before heading to the Great Northern Hotel in Part 17, Cooper says to his friends in the sheriff's office, "The past dictates the future," a notion that lays out the logic of what follows: If the present (the future of the past) is in disarray, then it must be the result of events that occurred in the past; the logical conclusion of this claim is that, in order to resolve the conflicts of the present, one must return to the source of its undoing (the past). Cooper is bound to this logic early in the season, when, in the process of leaving the Black Lodge, he's led by a strange figure into what appears to be outer space. The figure urges him to jump. Clearly disconcerted by the prospect of leaping into the unknown, Cooper turns back and continues his attempted return. In this moment, we see Cooper's deep attachment to what is familiar, and his compulsion to move backward instead of forward. As a result, the scene reflects the binding logic of posthistorical nostalgia's cruel optimism: The future represents uncertainty; the fantasy world of the past, on the other hand, represents the opposite. Cooper's tragic flaw is not his belief that he can change the past and defeat the causes of the losses he laments—he ultimately does—but rather his unshakable attachment to retrograde problem solving. This is his ruin and the ruin of *Twin Peaks* as a whole. Most concerning of all, this ruin brings no change to the larger state of affairs. The world that Cooper (Richard) and Carrie occupy in the finale—presumably, the one in which Laura's murder has been erased from existence, which, Cooper's logic suggests, should improve the present—is pointedly shown to be no better than the scenes of Twin Peaks and Las Vegas that we get prior to the finale (which are both shown throughout to be in states of decay): The diner where Carrie works is patronized by a group of abusive cowboys whose sexual harassment of their waitress recalls Laura's treatment by many of the men in the original timeline, and Cooper finds Carrie in dire straits, cooped up in a house with a corpse with a bullet in his head sitting in the living room. Nothing is really better, as far as we can tell; the misery has only been rearranged and/or repressed. For every Laura we remove from history, the show seems to suggest, there will always be a Carrie. "The final defeat of the forces responsible for loss . . . does not eliminate loss," McGowan explains. "Rather than saving Laura and delivering them from loss altogether, the path to salvation that Cooper plots leads only to its repetition. In this way, *The Return*, by playing out the logic of fantasy to its end point, shows how fantasy exposes the inescapability of traumatic loss" ("Waiting for Agent Cooper" 125). Cooper's bemused "What year is this?"—the final line of the series—invokes the fatal flaw in his logic: If the past dictates the future, but the future is not what his revised past was supposed to produce, then is this somehow not the future? It's the wrong question, of course, but Cooper, still bound to his original attachments, fails to see it.

The return of Laura's repressed trauma in this final scene, encoded in her mother's call and Carrie's scream, also calls into question the gender and racial dynamics of nostalgic returns. As Franck Boulegue points out, "Instead of building a new home for Laura, Cooper is obsessed with taking her back to the one that was the source of all her troubles" (16). While Twin Peaks was a place of safety and comfort for Cooper—a town where, as he put it in the original series, "A yellow light still means 'slow down,' not 'speed up'"—Carrie's haunting cry reminds us that it was nothing of the sort for Laura. Indeed, it is hard to imagine that Laura, not only a murder victim, but also subjected to repeated sexual assaults by lascivious men throughout the town, including her own father, would have any interest in returning. For her, in other words, Twin Peaks was not the quirky, charming town it was often represented as in the show and pop culture, and her home, where her father repeatedly raped her, is a far cry from a nostalgic object—a notion that is central to *Fire Walk with Me*, which shows the world of Twin Peaks "from the perspective of the fantasy object herself" (McGowan, "Waiting for Agent Cooper" 127). And yet, as Cooper recognizes, Twin Peaks is not Twin Peaks (or *Twin Peaks*) without Laura. As McGowan has pointed out, "Throughout the series, Laura Palmer functions as the lost object within the collective fantasy. She has this role only insofar as she is lost. . . . When she is alive [in *Fire Walk with Me*], she is just a normal troubled teenager. Her loss, however, enables her to function as the object within the fantasy that structures the world of *Twin Peaks*" ("Waiting for Agent Cooper" 125). Her presence (and, by extension, her suffering) is an essential element of both the town and the series, and so his homecoming is necessitated by hers—she is the homecoming queen, after all.[4]

Before leaving Twin Peaks in Part 17, Cooper says, "We live inside a dream," and his face becomes superimposed on the scenes that follow (a sequence lasting nearly five minutes). This moment can be read as a kind of metafictional break in the series, with Cooper's visage, observing the proceedings, announcing his recognition of the fantastic nature of the events that both precede and follow. In this reading, Cooper is not reaching back to save Laura Palmer, the girl who lived in Twin Peaks, but Laura Palmer, the character who lived in *Twin Peaks*. In the second episode, for example, Laura tells Cooper, "I am dead, yet I live," a status that reflects her reality as a mediated object: The character is diegetically dead, but also repeatedly revived by scenes like these each time viewers watch the show. Cooper is not rescuing her from actual death, in other words, but from the narrative death depicted in *Fire Walk with Me*. *The Return*, as such, dramatizes the revisionist act inherent in nostalgia TV. We can read the final section of the finale, with Cooper (recast as Richard) trying to return Laura (reframed as Carrie) to *Twin Peaks*, as an effort to reboot the show under a new premise.

This effort evokes an important distinction between the processes of the revival and the reboot: Revival brings back from the dead and attempts to restart where it left off; reboot restarts anew. In this light, Cooper's first attempt to save Laura is akin to a revival, literally bringing her back from the dead by preventing her murder in the first place. The second attempt, in the finale, resembles a reboot, as Cooper and Laura are no longer the same characters, but rather new ones recreated from the ashes of the originals, containing echoes of their previous forms but repackaged in a fundamentally altered state that reflects its new moment of creation. In this "new" version, Cooper, rebooted as Richard, maintains his original mission but is uncharacteristically brutal—a brutal man for a brutal age, one might say—and becomes confused when his mandate, conceived in 1989, becomes unresolvable; Laura, rebooted as Carrie, is middle aged, works as a waitress in another part of the country, and only recalls her past as Laura in the final seconds of the series. Neither of these attempted restarts succeeds: Cooper's revival of Laura loses sight of the original as it tries to drag an artifact of the past into the present, removing it from its proper context and undoing all that made it what it was. Cooper's reboot falls apart when the pair reach the Palmer house and find that it is inhabited not by Laura's mother, but by the home's real-life owner. Having broken free of the "dream" of the televisual reality he previously inhabited, and having remade the televisual past, Cooper, as Richard, now confronts the real world, which is uncanny, recognizable only through echoes with the original "dream" (same house, different owner). He's left stunned by how incompatible the fantasy, both the original and the revision, is with reality. The turn to the televisual past, and the effort to retroactively refit it, have ultimately unmoored them from reality, and his final question ("What year is this?") takes on another meaning, evoking the confounded temporality produced when a fantastic attachment to the media of the past is confronted by the real. Cooper's attempted reboot only partially obscures, but in no way resolves, the reality that it was created to overcome, and it subsequently fails to be reconciled with the real world. Cooper, an artifact from the 1990s, created for a purpose that has already reached its conclusion, is lost in the present (the "real" present, not the fictional "dream" one), out of place and out of time. Dale Cooper, and the mediated fantasy he represents, are unorientable in the present.

Reparative returns like these, which dominate nostalgia TV, are premised on a belief in the power of repetition with a difference, but these efforts, optimistic though they may be, inadvertently trap participants in a cycle of repetition in which nothing is ever fully resolved. These fantasies, *The Return* illustrates, "cannot ultimately save us from loss but [create] the structure through which we can unconsciously repeat loss" (McGowan, "Waiting for Agent Cooper" 122). Projects seeking this kind of procedure are fundamentally driven by a reconstructive rather than reflective (to use Boym's paradigm) impulse, seeking to rebuild what was instead of considering more deeply what ends such repetition serves—in part because such reflection would emphasize the fundamental incompatibility of the fantasy and the reality it purports to represent. This raises an important question: Of what use is it to revise a fantastic, mediated past if it is so radically incompatible with reality? What, in other words, is the purpose of trying to repair the past? Nostalgia TV, particularly revivals and reboots, provides a fantasy version of both reality and history; however, as the finale demonstrates, reality, history, and televisual fantasy, though they may resemble one another in superficial ways, are ultimately irreconcilable.

This irreconcilability marks a stark contrast with most televisual revivals and reboots. The split-screen scenes that form the end of the *Fuller House* pilot, for instance, suggest the opposite: The fantasies of the past are not only reconcilable with the present, but are also an essential element of it because the present is merely a repackaging of the past. An attachment to the past that leads one to endlessly repeat it, the show suggests, is not only a good thing, but also borders on an immutable law. *Fuller House* invests in fantasies of stability, coherence, safety, and continuity provided by doing the same things over and over. *The Return*, on the other hand, reflects the despair that arises from nostalgia-induced stasis, showcasing how ill equipped a strategy of comforting repetition is for the crises at hand. That the series again ends on a borderline-incomprehensible, resolution-defying cliffhanger (after returning from one twenty-five years earlier) also presents a stark contrast with the process of closure and reopening brought about by conventional revivals and reboots. As such, *The Return*'s evasion of closure reminds us of its role in sustaining the kinds of nostalgic fantasies that these shows rely on, which are also essential to the end of history writ large (in the way that the posthistorical world relies on a false perception of ending and resolution).

To fully understand this, and what it illuminates about the end-of-history repetition compulsion, it's worth considering in more detail the context that shapes Cooper's odyssey. Whether you read the finale as an exercise in metafiction, a journey into an alternative timeline created by meddling with the past, a turn to an alternative dimension within the multiverse, or a signal of the end of a cycle in the Vedic cosmic order, it's clear that Cooper's quest to return to Twin Peaks—and to return Twin Peaks to what it once was—ultimately fails. I have already discussed several ways in which we can read the failure itself, but more can be said about the context in which Cooper's journey is situated. As Boulegue and Martha Nochimson have each pointed out, Cooper's quest, in both its structure and its allusions to Greek myth, recalls the classical epic, in which a hero, emerging into a world of disarray, endeavors to return it to its original order. Cooper's failure in the end is one obvious way in which *The Return* deviates from the conventional epic formula, but what is most novel, and therefore most interesting, is not so much that he fails as the conditions of his failure. Nochimson argues that "the classical epic reveals how all the pieces of the universe and culture, seemingly in conflict, are actually part of a harmonious whole in which the epic hero is able to fulfill epic tasks. The opposite is true in Lynch's modern American epic. Misrule through discontinuity and fragments that are incapable of fitting together is the rule on all levels of reality" (249). The world of *Twin Peaks: The Return*, in other words, is shown to be necessarily dissimilar to its classical counterpart, fundamentally, irreconcilably disordered rather than temporarily disunified. This is not incidental, but an essential part of the story the series is trying to tell, and *The Return* continually returns to scenes of sickness and decay: Foreclosed houses dot the landscape of the Las Vegas suburbs where Cooper first reemerges; a drug-addled mother squatting in one of the homes ignores her son, almost leading to his death; the sociopathic son of one of the show's original characters runs over a child at an intersection and flees the scene; a kid finds a gun in his family's van and shoots the windows out of the Double-R; a woman caught in traffic shrieks that she is running late while a young girl in the passenger seat vomits bile. As Emily VanDerWerff pointed out in her review of the finale, "You never get the sense of a warm, goofy place that so dominated the original series' depiction of the town (and made its sinister undercurrents all the harder to shake). Something broke here, long ago, and the connections between these people have been severed" ("Potentially Frustrating").

Unlike *Fuller House*, which emphasizes how wonderful everyone's lives are now, most of *Twin Peaks*' returning favorites are either treading water or worse off than when we last saw them: Shelly is a divorced single mother, still chasing the bad boy even as she's confronted by her daughter repeating the same mistakes; though Shelly insists he's "still cool," James works the night shift as a security guard at a warehouse; Sheriff Truman is taking a leave of absence to recover from illness; Sarah Palmer sits in her living room alone, drinking and chain-smoking while watching looped images of a boxer being knocked out and a pack of lionesses devouring a gazelle on TV; Ed is still trapped in a loveless marriage with Nadine; Norma, poring over financial statements instead of making her famous pies, has franchised the Double-R, and is increasingly concerned by the drop in quality resulting from cost-cutting; and Audrey is apparently locked in a mental institution after suffering a breakdown following her rape by Cooper's doppelgänger. The Log Lady, frail, on oxygen, dies midway through the season. (Catherine E. Coulson, the actor who played the Log Lady, died only four days after filming.) The cast list is, in fact, littered with deaths.[5] The past twenty-five years have not been kind to the population of Twin Peaks; virtually everything is worse off than it was when we left it. The town, once marked by its idyllic charm and oddball sensibilities, is a shell of its former self.

These developments stand in stark contrast to *Fuller House*, which begins with an offscreen tragedy that the rest of the pilot attempts to remedy, an effort that is, even in the show's first half hour, stunningly successful. This effort also mirrors the role that the series promises to play in its viewers' lives, offering salvation from the traumatic events and absences that have plagued their lives since the show ended. Though perhaps unsurprising given the conventions of the sitcom genre, it's nonetheless notable that such crises are not given the space to fester in *Fuller House*, because they are antithetical to the show's nostalgic mandate. On the other hand, by leaving events unresolved, *The Return* again is distinct from typical narratives of revival, rejecting, along the way, the fantasy of therapeutic televisual nostalgia. Its setting aligns the show with a distinctly postmodern ethos, reflecting the fragmentation, discontinuity, and chaos that has become a hallmark of postwar American fiction's response to the emergent world order.

The series deviates from (or expands upon) more traditional postmodern framing, however, in its responses to the specific conditions of the end of history; the series is, in other words, better understood not as a postmodern epic, but a posthistorical one. What makes this epic posthistorical is not that it fails (a trait shared by many modern and postmodern "epics"), or that it depicts the world as fragmented and dis (or un)ordered, but that its failure arises from an attempted return both to a past and to a mediated state in an effort to repair the present's malaise. Unlike the epic hero, Cooper fails to return order to the world, and, unlike the postmodern hero, he fails specifically because of his optimistic attachment to reviving and revising the past. He actually saves Twin Peaks, in a sense, by helping defeat BOB, but it is a victory that, because of this framing, he doesn't recognize as such.

Misrecognition, a hallmark of the reflective age as previous chapters have illustrated, is a central problem throughout *The Return*, especially when, as is the case with Cooper's failed quest, misrecognition derives from an attachment to a process of repetition or belief in a false version of reality. Like the original series (whose title announces its thematic interest in doubling), instances of repetition, particularly ones that are either false or unnatural, permeate the series. As I previously noted, the scenes of Laura's mother Sarah watching television in her living room reveal that her gaze is fixed on unnatural looping scenes of violence. These scenes, reflecting her traumatized psyche (her daughter was murdered by her husband, following years of incestual rape), highlight the unsuitability of television as a means of recovery because its looping of the same acts over and over obstructs progression. Midway through the season, audiences are also treated to a repeat of James's performance of "Just You" from season 2 of *Twin Peaks*. In the original, James performs the song in the living room of the Palmer home, accompanied by Maddy, Laura's identical cousin (an impossible copy), and Donna. The effects on the recording make the performance uncanny: Not only is James obviously lip-syncing the vocals, but through postprocessing his voice has been pitched into an unnatural falsetto, with each syllable repeated by an echo. The trio's performance (it's unclear if Maddy and Donna are the voices in the recording, but they're obviously lip-syncing on screen) is also backed by drums and bass that are clearly not present in the room where the performance is supposedly taking place. When James performs the song on the Roadhouse stage in *The Return*, all of the uncanny elements are repeated: He is still obviously lip-syncing and, because he is much older, the artificially pitch-shifted falsetto seems even stranger. It is, moreover, the same recording from the original series, and he is accompanied by two unnamed backup singers who are not Maddy (murdered by Leland in season 2) or Donna (Lara Flynn Boyle did not return for the new season), but whose voices are the same, as are the unseen bass and drums. The scene, in other words, doubles the sense of unreality: It repeats a scene from the original, which was built on an act of obvious imitation. The repeat performance is even more estranged from reality than the initial one, which was not original, since it was a recording. The scene, in other words, is a copy of a copy of a copy with no stable point of origin (when was this originally "performed"? By whom?). In this scene, *The Return* once again evokes the disconnect between reality and televisual fantasy, exemplified in the obvious disparity among what we see, what we hear, and what we know. Television, in other words, makes impossibility seem possible—a notion that mirrors the same end-of-history fantasy of nostalgic repetition exemplified in scenes like the *Fuller House* split-screen, which attempts to naturalize a premise (endless repetition and stasis) that is only possible through media.

The Return's doubled characters constitute its most significant examples of repetition. In addition to Richard, Linda, Carrie, Cooper's evil doppelgänger, and

Laura's doppelgänger in the red room (also in the original series), *The Return* introduces the concept of "tulpas," or copies created through mystical means who, unlike doppelgängers, are seemingly unaware of their inorganic status. These are examples of what FBI director Cole labeled "Blue Rose Cases," so named, Agent Preston offers, because "a blue rose does not occur in nature, it's not a natural thing; [the tulpa] was not natural, conjured." Dougie Jones, who Cooper's doppelgänger created in order to delay his return to the Black Lodge, is one such example. We also learn toward the end of *The Return* that Diane, who in the original series was the unseen recipient of Cooper's tape recordings) was actually a tulpa, also created by Cooper's doppelgänger. When the two are removed from the world, they are transported to the red room where MIKE informs them, "Someone manufactured you," again emphasizing the constructed nature of these copies, whose existence is defined by the very thing that their false appearance is meant to obscure.

Repetition like this, the show stresses, is not natural, and it can be manufactured to support a fantasy that leads one to misrecognize reality. Dougie's wife, Janey-E, seemingly falls into this trap. Despite a series of sudden, inexplicable differences, Janey-E willingly partakes in the fantasy of new-Dougie because it offers her financial stability (Cooper-Dougie wins enough money gambling to cover the debts they owed), kindness, and attractiveness. Though every available sign points to the reality that he is not the same Dougie she knew before (he lost considerable weight seemingly overnight, has jet-black hair, and can barely even speak in full sentences), she falls back in love with him anyway. These deceptive doubles suggest how nostalgia entices people to fall in love with simulations, copies, and fantasies. More specifically, they mirror the idealization process essential to the reboot/revival, which produces fantastic "replicas" of the past that are designed to fulfill desires unmet by the present or the past. Janey-E's and Sonny Jim's lives have been so improved by Cooper-Dougie's presence that Cooper initiates the manufacture of a new Dougie tulpa, made in his image, to replace him once he awakes from the coma and leaves for Twin Peaks. When we see Janey-E for the last time, she's embracing this new copy-of-a-copy Dougie, who has returned to Las Vegas to take the place of the Cooper-Dougie they came to love, and who no longer resembles the original Dougie in any way beyond his face. What is staged as a joyous family reunion is, in truth, the lamentable embrace of a copy of a copy of a copy.

Audrey Horne's scenes in *The Return* provide a much darker reflection on misrecognition and, particularly, on mediated fantasy's capacity for obscuring a traumatic reality. In the original series, Audrey was a vivacious, headstrong, precocious teenager who, like many following Laura's murder, sought to dig into the town's hidden secrets. The original series finale leaves Audrey, by that point a fan favorite, possibly dead after a bomb explodes at the bank where she had handcuffed herself to a vault in protest of a forest development project. When she reappears in the twelfth episode of *The Return*, she clearly is not the Audrey we remember, nor is she living the kind of life we might have expected. Spread across five episodes, Audrey's scenes revolve around an argument with Charlie, who is supposedly her husband (though the two have an odd rapport), about Audrey's desire to go to the Roadhouse to look for Billy, her lover, whom she claims has gone missing. (No character named Billy appears in the original series, the film, or *The Return*, though Audrey's lover in season two was played by the actor Billy Zane.) After quarreling with Charlie in his office, they eventually head to the Roadhouse, where she has a breakdown during a musical sequence (featuring "Audrey's Dance," her theme from the original series) and is instantaneously transported to a white room where she looks at her face in a mirror and, in a panic, asks, "What?" With support from *Twin Peaks: The Final Dossier*, a companion to the new season published by Frost, Audrey's final scene has often been interpreted as indicating that she is in a mental institution, engaged in an elaborate fantasy. Audrey's scenes thus constitute an act of misrecognition engineered to replace a painful reality with a fantasy. Crucially, the show does not allow the viewer to differentiate Audrey's fantasy from her reality. If we accept the premise that Audrey is in a mental institution, we are left with two scenarios: Either we saw what happened to Audrey or we saw her fantasy. The velocity of the final cut from the Roadhouse to the white room suggests that Audrey did not actually visit the Roadhouse. The scene suggests, instead, that Audrey is brought back to "reality," as in hypnosis, with a snap of the fingers. This notion is reinforced by Audrey's crisis of recognition, which extends not only to herself, but also to Charlie and to her sense of place.

Like Cooper (as Dougie) before her, Audrey reconstitutes herself as the character from the original series through repetition. Following her mental breakdown, Audrey's mediated fantasy has led her to misrecognize her life on nearly every level, and the lines between diegetic and nondiegetic worlds, between fantasy and reality, have become disordered—a process not dissimilar to the one induced by the influence of nostalgia TV. Popular notions of "the past," it is worth pointing out, are constructed through repetition and recitation, through media (and of media), of events/traits/tropes. Emily VanDerWerff argues, in her recap of episodes 3 and 4, that *The Return* "is about the formation of identity. Are we ourselves? Or are we a collection of outside influences that we trick ourselves into thinking is a coherent person?" In light of the connections the show forges among identity, the past, and mediation, we might expand this question: Was the past we saw on TV actually the past? Or was it a collection of tropes and events, ossified in media, that we tricked ourselves (or were tricked) into thinking was a coherent whole? *The Return*, for its part, seems to suggest that this is at least partially the case, and Audrey's apparent institutionalization parallels how reboots and revivals, and even original series like *Stranger Things*, seek to rehabilitate the past through this substitutional process.

The Return's treatment of nostalgia and fantasy marks an important departure from Lynch's earlier work. Though Lynch's expressions of nostalgia never go unproblematized,[6] *Blue Velvet* and the original run of *Twin Peaks*, in particular, nonetheless demonstrate the filmmaker's belief in the virtue of idealized fantasy. The robin that symbolizes optimism and the triumph of good over evil at the end of *Blue Velvet* may be obviously fake, in other words, but there remains, the filmmaker contended, value to be found in the aspirations it symbolizes. Here, and elsewhere, the film acknowledges that its turn to '50s sentimentality is fantasy, a cinematic invention and thus not reflective of the real, while at the same time pointing to the positive elements contained within that sentimentality. Lynch's film, in other words, does not mistake its nostalgia for reality, nor does it attempt to mystify this substitution; rather, *Blue Velvet* highlights the beauty of the aspirations contained in the artifice (even if the nation wasn't actually as hopeful or kind as it presented itself, or if the hope and kindness were built on false or otherwise corrupt foundations, hope and kindness, the film attests, are good things for a society to aspire to). Lynch's early work, in other words, views mediated nostalgia with optimism, as a positive force so long as it is properly recognized as fantasy and, crucially, not falsely separated from—or used to mask—the horrors of reality.

This is seemingly no longer the case in *The Return*. As I pointed out in discussing the end-of-history decay that afflicts the town in 2016, Twin Peaks in the original series and Twin Peaks in *The Return* are quite distinct, and the optimism contained in the fantastic nostalgia of *Twin Peaks* has turned cruel in *The Return*. While the original series seeks to highlight the aspirational within its mediated, artificial fantasy, *The Return* repeatedly suggests that such a maneuver is no longer useful at the end of history, where the rot and decay brought about by neoliberalism has become so pervasive that fantasies of the Good Life ring false, and where stable grounding in reality has been wholly overtaken by the same kind of mediated, idealized fantasy that Lynch's work previously championed—such that aestheticized fantasies of the past are often no longer recognized for what they are and are instead mistaken for representations of historical reality. So often at the end of history, as we have seen in chapters 1 and 2, in substituting nostalgic fantasy for historical reality, the horrors of the past are separated from the idealized reconstruction, and are subsequently either obscured or symbolically repaired. Thus, the dialectic of the idealized and the horrific that Lynch's philosophy previously relied upon becomes inoperative, as the ideal fantasy has not only overtaken the horrific, but also masquerades as reality, and the sense of artifice underscoring the fantasy has been lost. Cooper's failed attachment to the reparative power of repetition and revision, in this light, indicts the original series and Lynch's own optimistic attachment to nostalgia.

"In the end," as Timothy William Gallow points out, "[Cooper] finds himself chasing a 25-year-old tragedy as the world becomes increasingly unrecognizable"

(216). His downfall, in other words, is that his attachment to the past and desire to repeat it have led him to misrecognize reality—or, perhaps, to recognize that reality was never recognizable to begin with—and he ultimately becomes unmoored from the world around him. To borrow a metaphor from Boulegue, the series is an exercise in squaring the circle, an impossible attempt to re-form (reform) a past that has already taken shape. If, as the series suggests, these cycles of nostalgic repetition, instigated by the conditions of the end of history, invite us to mistake fantasy for reality, and to subsequently misconstrue the relationships between past and present, then nostalgia TV poses a considerable problem for the posthistorical subject. As chapter 1 points out, recognition is a constitutive element in the kinds of nostalgia that have emerged in the past decade or so. This chapter extends this argument by showing that these acts of recognition are, more often than not, actually acts of misrecognition, borne of a process by which nostalgic fantasies modify the past so that its repetition can fulfill our desires. Problems arise when this process is no longer understood as fantasy (or as a process at all), and misrecognition is mistaken for recognition. These repetitive acts of fantastic misrecognition can only end in the death of recognition itself, and the result is a posthistorical subject who, like Agent Cooper, is thrust into a world where they are fundamentally unorientable, alienated from both the past they crave and the present they are fleeing, asking, "What year is this?"

CHAPTER 4

Hillbilly Elegy, Nostalgia, and Right-Wing Melodrama

Nostalgia—historically, a lament for loss—is a natural partner for narratives of disappearance. This is evident even at the end of history, when nostalgia often morphs into attachments to style and conventional objects of nostalgic longing, such as a lost way of life, become detached from the historical context that gave rise to them. In this process, lost realities (as much as they were even *real* to begin with) are often flattened into types and tropes, more symbolic than actual. What emerges, as chapter 2 illustrates, is a kind of hollow notion of the past into which a host of characteristics can be placed.

Accelerated by socioeconomic decline wrought by decades of neoliberalism, nostalgic fixation based specifically in narratives of disappearance plays an especially significant role in right-wing politics of the 2010s and beyond. Though this book takes its title from one side of Svetlana Boym's taxonomy, reflective nostalgia is therefore not the only tendency that warrants closer inspection during this period. Throughout much of the twentieth century in Europe and the United States, the right has engaged in what Boym refers to as "restorative" nostalgia, which "proposes to rebuild the lost home" (41). This tendency, Grafton Tanner explains, is "marked by a fear that the present is in danger and that something nefarious is afoot, an evil conspiracy that threatens to shatter the unsecured homeland, sully its purity, and call its safety into question" (32). Right-wing movements respond to these threats by investing in rhetoric that imagines a prior state that, they urge, must be returned to. In an American context, this can be seen in various right-wing tendencies that have emerged since the Second World War, from evangelical movements that rally against a culture of degeneracy and the John Birch Society's conspiratorial anticollectivism, to the Great Society revanchism of the Reagan administration and the xenophobic populism of the Tea Party. In the present context, the most obvious extension of this tendency is Donald Trump's infamous "Make America Great Again" (MAGA) slogan, which, similar to *Stranger Things*, relies on an ambiguity that enables audiences to combine whichever causes from the previous list that they favor: America can no longer be great for any number of reasons, any "past" can be used to support a vision of America's fall, and the restoration of American greatness can be enacted through any number of policies. Crucially, each of these tendencies presents a vision of the present as fallen and in desperate need of restoration.

This trend toward the rhetoric of restorative nostalgia is not incidental, but rather, as a number of scholars have shown, fundamental to the ideologies that span the American right wing. Corey Robin has argued, for instance, that "Conservatism requires defeat" and that "failure is its most potent source of inspiration" (247–248), and neoconservativism, more specifically, is founded in Straussian appeals to Western traditionalism. Both schools of thought, as their monikers suggest, are framed as defenses against a changing status quo (which, as society inevitably progresses in one direction or another, provides these groups with an unending supply of grievances). This notion is echoed by Jean Hardisty's still-prescient diagnosis of the 1990s "New Right" coalition (which now comprises much of the Republican party's base) as a "reactionary protest movement," which, she explains, "seeks to restore a previous period, one that is usually seen as a better, more peaceful, and more secure time" (9). In contrast to liberals during the same period, who generally campaigned on progress (even if that progress rarely came to pass), the overwhelming majority of right-wing electoral politics in the twentieth and twenty-first century has been galvanized by reaction to unwanted changes and explicit calls for reversion. Fascism and neofascism, which have grown in visibility (if not outright popularity) in the past decade or so, are also "a matter of returns and repetitions" best understood as efforts to protect against social and economic developments (Toscano x).

In some cases, right-wing resentment has been mobilized against genuine changes: Civil rights legislation, for instance, *did* take place, and its existence was not imagined by the Birchers and Reaganites who rallied against it; so too for the waning influence of Christianity in American society that evangelicals decry. In other cases, such as QAnon or the infamous Great Replacement theory, right-wing resentments are organized around fantasy more than reality (even as the targets can be loosely traced to real developments, like changing demographics and corporate diversity efforts). In the twenty-first century, the latter has begun to play an outsized role in right-wing rhetoric. This chapter, as such, is especially interested in these instances where right-wing revanchism produces a nostalgia directed toward imagined pasts based on imagined losses.

The prevalence of aestheticized nostalgia, with its roots in fantasy and powerful attachment to style, described in the previous chapters is particularly useful for right-wing stories of loss and displacement that do not actually conform to reality (whether because the so-called erasure is not taking place or because the prior state never existed). In a basic sense, these narratives benefit from being deployed in the context of an already backwards-glancing culture that has lost much of its historical grounding. Right-wing stories about the need to return to the glory of an ill-defined past are not out of place at the end of history, in other words, and they often share features found in works like *Stranger Things* and *Ready Player One*: reaction to genuine posthistorical decline and pessimistic futurity, attachments to the styles and aesthetics of a bygone era, reluctance (or refusal) to imagine beyond the confines of capitalist hegemony. The period is also characterized by a lack of popular alternative visions that categorically push back against nostalgia; rather than encountering a relatively forward-thinking cultural milieu—as it often did in, say, the youth culture of the 1960s or the tech futurism of the 1990s—today's right-wing nostalgia arrives in the midst of an era that is already sympathetic to such thinking. Instead of convincing audiences that we need to return to the past, right-wing narratives only need to redirect nostalgic energies to the *right* kind of past.

To do so, right-wing narratives often rely on the language of melodrama, framing nostalgic visions of Edenic pasts as part of a broader Manichaean struggle between virtuous victims and omnipresent oppressors. Goodness, embodied in the traditional values represented by the prelapsarian pasts, must be restored in order to overcome the evils of modern society. Though exceedingly common today, this reliance on the conventions of melodrama within political discourse is itself not a novel development. As Linda Williams and Elisabeth Anker have both shown, melodrama has been central to the construction of American cultural and political identity for much of its history: Melodrama, Anker explains, "is more than a film, literary, or cultural genre; it is also a political genre, more precisely a genre of national political discourse. Melodramatic genre conventions are found in political rhetoric, governing processes, citizenship practices, and formations of national identity. Melodrama shapes the legitimation strategies of national politics, and the very operations of state power" (2). Indeed, despite its origins as a distinctly literary genre, Williams has convincingly argued in *Playing the Race Card* that melodrama is better understood as a "mode" that can be deployed in a variety of discursive registers, from artistic genres to political speech. Though she opts to retain the term "genre," Anker's book *Orgies of Feeling* exemplifies a similar expansion beyond the conventional confines of literary and dramaturgical "melodrama," and likewise beyond the gendered, pejorative sense of the term that is so often deployed today. "Melodrama" in this sense describes a discursive framework organized around the identification of victimization featuring heightened affects that seeks to produce sympathy in an effort to protect or restore moral good. Put simply, "If emotional and moral registers are sounded, if a work invites us to feel sympathy for the virtues of beset victims, if the narrative trajectory is ultimately concerned with a retrieval and staging of virtue through adversity and suffering, then the operative mode is melodrama" (Williams 15). In short, a work can engage in melodrama without being generically melodramatic. For the purposes of this chapter, understanding melodrama in this way enables us to better identify the rhetorical function of these appeals, especially as they come outside the familiar constraints of literary form.

Melodrama and nostalgia, it is worth emphasizing, are also fundamentally compatible modes, as each emerges as a response to loss or absence. Where conventional nostalgia laments loss and emphasizes emotional connection with the lost object, melodrama is primarily a plea for the recognition of loss that emphasizes the suffering it has caused. Melodrama, in other words, is generally an external appeal, a rhetorical form deployed to convince audiences to accept, and subsequently act upon, the victimization it identifies, while nostalgia is focalized around a relationship to the loss itself rather than its effects. In this context, nostalgia becomes an especially useful tool for political projects that seek to convince audiences that they have been directly harmed by the losses that melodrama urges them to recognize. These nostalgic melodramas, as we might call them, often promote a different relationship between their audiences and loss than we see in more conventional, nonnostalgic forms. *Uncle Tom's Cabin*, for instance, seeks to produce *white* sympathy for *Black* suffering, urging readers to change how they view slavery rather than to change how they understand their status vis-à-vis the suffering the novel describes. Whites are not, in other words, encouraged to view themselves as the narrative's victims. *The Birth of a Nation*, on the other hand, depicts a nostalgic past in order to convince its white audiences that *they* are being victimized. Unlike Harriet Beecher Stowe's novel, the melodramatic suffering detailed in D. W. Griffith's film is not meant to induce sympathy for others, but to direct inwards the feelings of loss produced by its antebellum nostalgia, constructing the audience as pitiable victims rather than pitying spectators.

Melodrama is, of course, not a new feature of right-wing narratives in the United States, and the form has also proved particularly useful for attempts to reframe unequal social relations through emotional appeals. In addition to its nostalgic framing, for instance, *The Birth of a Nation* relies on a number of melodramatic conventions—especially the violation of "virginal bodily purity"—in its attempts to invert American racial dynamics by "turn[ing] black victims of white racism in to oppressors of white goodness" (Anker 86). Reagan's invocation of "welfare queens" and related attempts to rally the nation against public services similarly evoked a producer/parasite frame that depicted middle-class Americans as victims of a paradoxically downtrodden Black oppressor. More recently, as Anker has shown, responses to 9/11 depicted a wounded nation beset by unfathomable external evil, in turn justifying not just a military response, but a campaign of total eradication through the War on Terror that resulted in widespread bigotry against the nation's Muslim minority. In recent years, these relatively cohesive melodramatic narratives have largely given way to a proliferation of atomized narratives of conspiracy and victimization. Whether as part of a

Democratic plot to disarm and ultimately disenfranchise conservatives, a global effort to replace the white race, or a pedophilic push to groom children into abandoning the lodestar of biological sex and "traditional" gender roles, these narratives represent an increasingly large and increasingly visible segment of right-wing politics today, particularly online. Broadly speaking, however, these narratives are linked in that, like their predecessors, they rely on melodramatic appeals to give shape to a familiar right-wing paradigm of cultural inversion, in which people with majoritarian identities (white, cisgender, straight) cast themselves as victims oppressed by minority groups.

Much has been written, in the years following the Tea Party's gains in the 2010 elections and, to an even greater extent, Trump's victory in 2016, about this resurgence of conspiracy-inflected right-wing populism and its inciting rationale. The specifics of this debate need not be rehashed here, though it is worth noting the striking degree to which these discussions return to claims of victimization. This is not coincidental, of course: As previous chapters have outlined, the end of history itself is marked by sentiments of loss, decline, and stagnation, and these developments (or lack thereof) have real, material consequences that provide fertile ground for melodramatic framing. The period, put simply, has produced a significant number of genuine victims, making the recognition of suffering one of the central political issues of the day. Melodrama, with its emphasis on the identification of victims, thus emerges as an appealing form. Posthistorical politics, however, with its reluctance to provide real resolutions or remuneration, is, in a deeper sense, at odds with the narrative arc of traditional melodrama, which typically concludes with the victims overcoming their oppression. The end of history, in contrast, is largely incapable of easing (much less ending) suffering on a broad scale, particularly the hardships that have directly resulted from its neoliberal economic agenda. With its need for winners and losers and disavowal of government protections, the end of history can only abide the management and rearrangement of suffering—encouraging the kind of seesawing, zero-sum politics we see later in this chapter. This lack of substantial resolution has resulted in a form of recognition politics whose engine is the public display of misery, and an attention economy has emerged wherein various interests compete to be seen as the *true* victims and thus worthy of the fleeting relief available—or else the cause of ending their suffering becomes the exigence for a political movement. Posthistorical culture, therefore, is simultaneously deeply invested in suffering but also unable to work toward its end; instead, the end of history holds up the recognition of suffering as an ideal—"We see you and we hear you" as a political end.

This is not to suggest, however, that contemporary right-wing melodramatic narratives are unremarkable. Though they follow a long rhetorical tradition and appear in the context of a broader cultural moment that is amenable to the form regardless of political valence, the melodramatic appeals that proliferate on the right nonetheless warrant further attention for the ways that they respond to the conditions out of which they arose. This is especially evident in the way that nostalgic appeals figure within the right's broader melodramatic framework. A deeper study of this tendency, therefore, helps illuminate an outgrowth of reflective-age nostalgia that has, thus far, not been fully articulated.

To understand the contemporary right's investment in melodrama, as well as its implications for nostalgia, it is worth looking more deeply into a few prominent examples. Perhaps the most cogent articulation of the centrality of melodrama in right-wing politics today can be found in Arlie Russell Hochschild's 2016 *Strangers in Their Own Land*. Most famously, the book, which attempts to explain the rise and beliefs of the Tea Party movement based on interviews and observations of party members in Louisiana, identifies what the Berkeley sociologist terms the group's "deep story," essentially an extended narrative that, by way of analogy, purports to represent the subjects' feelings and motivations. In it, Hochschild narrates their feeling of standing in line for access to the American Dream only to be unfairly held back while others (minorities or others deemed undeserving) cut in line. There are numerous issues with Hochschild's "deep story"—not least that it confers narrative coherence and a sense of noble struggle to a heterogeneous array of feelings that, though they are sometimes be founded in legitimate grievance (insufficient government response to environmental disasters in the Gulf, for instance), have manifested in misplaced scapegoating of minorities, open bigotry, and logical inconsistencies—but it remains instructive because it captures the way many on the right *want* their narrative to be understood by the public. In other words, despite Hochschild's belief that her rendering captures some essential truth about the conditions that led these individuals to their beliefs, her subjects' enthusiastic endorsement of Hochschild's framing is more productively understood not as confirmation of its objective veracity, but of its success in justifying their resentments and, perhaps even more deeply, framing them in a way that appeals to their desires: that is, as real victims worthy of sympathy. Given that it is based almost entirely on direct interviews with the subjects—How many of us objectively know ourselves and our motivations? How many would be willing to share parts of ourselves that we know appear damning?—the book is less insightful about how these people actually feel than it is about how they want to be seen and how they want their "feelings" to be understood. In this way, though it does not convincingly articulate the "deep" reasons for the issues it raises,[1] *Strangers in Their Own Land* does tell us something useful about melodramatic identification on the right.

Consider, for instance, one section of the deep story where Hochschild describes her subjects' response to affirmative action:

> Look! You see people cutting in line ahead of you! You're following the rules. They aren't. As they cut in, it feels like you are being moved back. How can

> they just do that? Who are they? Some are black. Through affirmative action plans, pushed by the federal government, they are being given preference for places in colleges and universities, apprenticeships, jobs, welfare payments, and free lunches, and they hold a certain secret place in people's minds, as we see below. Women, immigrants, refugees, public sector workers—where will it end? Your money is running through a liberal sympathy sieve you don't control or agree with. These are opportunities you'd have loved to have had in your day—and either you should have had them when you were young or the young shouldn't be getting them now. It's not fair. (137)

The story of disadvantaged groups gaining access to resources they were previously denied is here depicted through a distinctly melodramatic lens, complete with heightened emotional appeals characteristic of the mode ("How can they just do that? Who are they?" it asks with palpable urgency), which paints those who have benefited as transgressors and the "you" of the story as unjustly victimized. "You," in this formulation, are a rule-following moral agent, a paragon of virtue patiently waiting your turn in a world stacked against you, increasingly kept from the modest rewards you not only deserve but were promised. In fact, the entire premise of Hochschild's line-cutting narrative encourages melodramatic readings in its acceptance of a zero-sum frame. The story of twentieth- and twenty-first-century social progress can, of course, be told without identifying those who did not directly benefit as "victims," yet the right, as exemplified in Hochschild's depiction, treats social progress like Newton's Third Law of Motion: For every instance of progress, there is an equal and opposite regression; for every person's success someone else is made a victim by virtue of not receiving the same. This framework allows the social progress the right wishes to undo to be critiqued on the same terms on which it was founded: sympathy for victims.

Even beyond its broader structure, the deep story is rife with melodramatic appeals. Hochschild's decision to write this story in the second person, for instance, illustrates (perhaps inadvertently) the rhetoric of melodramatic identification that animates these narratives, establishing a sense of immediacy and heightened feeling to the stories by implicitly asking readers to imagine themselves in these situations and to investigate how it might make them *feel*. These are not stories about facts, in other words, they are about feelings, and the desire for those feelings to be justified through expressions of public sympathy. "*Wouldn't you be upset if this happened to you*?" the narrative asks. Indeed, if we take this story to be "true"—that is, reflective of how these individuals feel, or, at least, how they want their feelings to be perceived—there is an even deeper revelation in this seesaw construction. Given that the Tea Party platform is not organized around offering better access to welfare regardless of identity, nor any kind of economic remuneration for the loss of manufacturing jobs or environmental disaster—that is, it offers little in the way of concrete material support for the crises referenced in the deep story—the turn to the right that these individuals articulate seems motivated by something else: namely, a desire for sympathy, recognition of suffering, and the cultural benefits afforded thereof. The right has long complained about the left's "oppression Olympics," but it is also deeply invested in the posthistorical sympathy economy, and, as Hochschild's account illustrates, much of the right's resentment is organized around claims of supposedly unrecognized suffering.

In one part of the deep story, for instance, she writes of "white, Christian, working and middle class" Tea Partiers, "You have the impulse to call out, 'I'm part of a minority too!' . . . You feel stuck between a strong desire to be recognized for who you really are and all you've really done, and dread at joining the parade of 'poor me's'" (145). Setting aside the irony that the minority claim requires the same sort of intersectional identification that the right typically rallies against, this appeal is significant because it illustrates the centrality of sympathetic recognition in right-wing rhetoric that makes melodrama such an appealing mode. Melodrama works by, first and foremost, establishing victimization through emotional, rather than logical, appeals. Audiences need not interrogate more deeply the logic underpinning these feelings—we are not asked to question the analogies Hochschild offers—or the justness of the actions these feelings have manifest; we only need to understand that they *feel* persecuted because, in melodrama, the mere act of suffering—imagined or otherwise—confers sympathy and goodness. We see this play out toward the end of *Strangers*, where Hochschild explains their supposed reluctance to identify as victims despite, in her view, the aptness of this identification: "'Victim' is the last word my Louisiana Tea Party friends would apply to themselves. They didn't want to be 'poor me's' As Team Loyalists, Worshippers, and Cowboys, they are proud to endure the difficulties they face. But in the loss of their homes, their drinking water, and even their jobs in non-oil sectors of the economy, there is no other word for it: they are victims" (232). In true melodramatic fashion, the victims become especially worthy of sympathy by refusing to accept their victimization (if only in name, as their entire "deep story" is founded on notions of victimization), marking their moral virtue and making their suffering all the more compelling. As such, the right-wing beliefs they adopt appear as misguided acts of noble resistance, the desperate maneuvers of a proud people with nothing left to turn to. What is especially notable, in this light, is that the victimization depicted in the deep story—the line-cutting analogy—is largely unrelated to the victimization Hochschild attributes to them here. This slippage is enabled by the strength of the melodramatic identification at work throughout the book, and it illustrates the way that the establishment of victimhood can serve as a cover for more nefarious activity. If we enshrine these individuals as victims in a melodramatic plot, we develop sympathy and it becomes harder for us to scrutinize their beliefs and easier to accept a range of actions taken in response to even unrelated, if not outright imagined, victimization. Sympathy overpowers logic, legitimizing—if not directly authorizing—a range of attitudes and policies that, in isolation, would likely be rejected by nonadherents. This facilitates the same kind of melodramatic reversal, outlined earlier in the chapter, that has characterized right-wing rhetoric from *Birth of a Nation* to Reagan and beyond—can a victim really be a bigot?

Melodrama is also deeply appealing to the right because, as Williams has argued, it is often fundamentally conservative, emphasizing the nostalgic restoration of a lost past instead of movement toward a new future (36). As it was for much of the twentieth century, nostalgia for a supposedly lost past is itself central to right-wing projects today. This is especially true in the context of the right's melodramatic appeals, a relationship that is also spelled out in Hochschild's book. At one point, she describes Trump supporters as being "in mourning for a lost way of life," adding that "their land no longer feels their own" (225). Curiously, at this stage of the book, Hochschild does not elaborate on the contours that define this lost way of life: what has been lost, how it was lost, and so on. Though in one sense indicative of the author's growing sympathy for those she comes to identify as "friends," the ambiguity here is also reflective of the construction of MAGA nostalgia. As I explained earlier, "Make America Great Again" is compelling in part *because* it is vague, enabling audiences to place any time period or cultural formation they choose as the goal of the slogan's restoration. However, despite its amorphousness, we can nonetheless identify many of the traits that have led to this feeling of cultural alienation, from changing demographics and supposed antiwhite cultural hostility to an economic regime that no longer provides sufficient protections (or, we might say, *advantages*) for the so-called white working class and the consequences thereof.

That Hochschild follows this articulation of nostalgia with a comment about ownership of the land provides two insights into the nature of the feeling she describes. First, the two claims reframe the complaints of the Tea Partiers she's ventriloquizing in romantic terms, as though their expressed concerns about the country being overrun by Muslims or the "politically correct" taboo on racist humor are the same as the concerns an elder might have for the generational abandonment of cherished local customs. This framing hollows the complaint of its specificity, sympathetically reimagining a rejection of multiculturalism as connected with a melodramatic loss of traditional folkways (thus priming it for nostalgic return). In turn, this passage also reveals a deeper association with ownership and a rhetoric of dispossession that animates right-wing narratives of victimization—a notion that, in material terms, is a fiction founded more in racial affiliation than actual property relations for many poor and disadvantaged Tea Partiers who never really *owned* the land in the way the narrative imagines. As well as illuminating the complaint's foundation in an imagined nostalgia, the latter claim's emphasis on dispossession also highlights the reactionary aspects of the former claim's rhetoric of loss: The "lost way of life" actually describes an unequal social relation that privileged one group over another, granting it a *feeling* of control. *The Land*, in other words, was *for Them* because it wasn't *for Others*. Thus, yet again, we see the language of melodrama deployed in an effort to invert historical social relations, where the benefactors of previously unequal dynamics have been supposedly dispossessed of their rightful inheritance by those at the bottom; to augment this revision, the right invests in a rhetoric of noble traditionalism and nostalgia for a stolen home—framing utterly emptied of its actual content.

In this way, *Strangers in Their Own Land* illuminates how, at a fundamental level, right-wing discourse relies on melodrama and nostalgia in its attempts to conjure sympathy for imagined losses—losses whose construction also works to obscure the deeper resentments that often motivate the political project. This story is incomplete, however, without a deeper consideration of another right-wing fiction, the "white working class," and how these narratives of victimhood, forged from the conditions of the end of history and filtered through the dual frames of melodrama and nostalgia, serve the right's racial project and its attempts to reorient the economy following neoliberalism's neglect of "the wages of whiteness."

Hochschild's melodrama, in large part, reflects a sentiment of white decline that has become the fundamental animating principle behind much of the post–Tea Party resurgence of right-wing populism. As Wendy Brown illustrates, this is, in one sense, a symptom of the losses and displacement wrought by forty years of neoliberal economics, against which historically dominant social categories, such as whiteness and masculinity, now only provide limited cover (175). To an extent, this idea has grounding in material reality. As Daniel HoSang and Joseph E. Lowndes explain, "The continued upward redistribution of wealth that has accelerated since the Great Recession has greatly reduced the economic guarantees and privileges that many white Americans once took for granted" (47). In other words, the neoliberal economy, whose core tendencies were laid bare in the aftermath of the 2008 financial crisis as well as the manufacturing decline that preceded it, marks a shift in that many ostensibly comfortable middle-class whites, who previously would have felt protected from economic instability thanks to prolabor New Deal politics, were now facing the dangers of downward mobility and general precarity without an adequate safety net—a situation once thought confined to minorities and poor whites. "This period," HoSang and Lowndes continue,

> marks the longest span since the New Deal that many white households have experienced sustained economic abandonment—facing levels of debt, impoverishment, and vulnerability that historically only existed in particular regions or economic sectors. Even since the recovery began in 2009, some

> 95 percent of the country's income gains went to households in the top 1 percent. To be clear, Black workers, low-wage immigrants, and other low-income households of color fared far worse in this era. Median household wealth for white families in 2015 remained twelve times higher than for Black families, and wealth accumulation in Black and Latino/a households has declined steadily in the last thirty years; households headed by women of color face even sharper disparities. But due to enormous income and wealth expansion among the top 5 percent of white households, these median figures also mask the stagnation and decline in wealth and wages for white households in the bottom 50 percent of earners. For many whites, their racial positioning and privilege has not indemnified them from these transformations. (47)

The result, Thuy Linh Tu and Nikhil Pal Singh have argued, is *not* that whites no longer remain "political, economic, and psychic beneficiaries" of their racial identity, but that many of them are witnessing "the stagnation of wages of whiteness." Whiteness, put bluntly, is often not worth what it once was, as many of the economic imperatives (domestic manufacturing, housing policy, wage growth, etc.) that once benefited white (especially blue-collar) laborers have vanished. The politics we find in things like *Strangers in Their Own Land* must be understood, then, as reactions specific to *decline* rather than precarity itself—they are animated by a sense of loss more than a sense of absence. If, as Hochschild put it, Trump supporters are in mourning, it is because they no longer feel in possession of something they once had, their status fundamentally marked by feelings of *dis*possession instead of lack: *no longer have* instead of *never had*. In this sense, insofar as the period has seen a number of very real changes, there is a material (if no less reactionary) basis to the nostalgic melodramas of the right.

However, the material basis of the idea that the right's politics are merely symptoms of white decline or the infamous "economic anxiety" begins to collapse upon closer inspection of the historical notions underpinning it. To begin, the claim that right-wing electoral success is actually motivated primarily by these real losses relies on two key fictions: first, that whites are particularly victimized by neoliberal decline compared to other races (which, as the statistics above show, is not the case unless we create a special emphasis on amorphous sentiments of "dispossession"); second, that the plurality of those on the right who espouse these beliefs do so because they have been directly victimized—that they, like Hochschild's *Strangers*, are genuine victims and their politics is a reaction to very personal grievances. In the latter case, there is ample evidence to suggest that this is not actually true for many on the right (even setting aside billionaire donors like the Kochs and Waltons, who prop up these supposedly grassroots movements). The electoral base for Trump's victory in 2016, for instance, was made up of many comfortably middle- and upper-class voters who earn well above the poverty line. In fact, as *FiveThirtyEight* pointed out, exit polling from the 2016 primaries showed that the makeup of the Trump electorate was not as universally impoverished as it was often made out to be: "The median household income of a Trump voter so far in the primaries is about $72,000, [which is] well above the national median household income of about $56,000. It's also higher than the median income for Hillary Clinton and Bernie Sanders supporters, which is around $61,000 for both" (Silver). As Matthew Karp has pointed out, this trend continued in 2024, when exit polling showed that "the great bulk of the American working class is almost perfectly divided between the two parties," and that Trump's electoral victory resulted more from a collapse in Democratic turnout than a substantial working-class realignment (7–11). Thus, though many point to economic distress as the rationale for the growth in right-wing political affiliation in the wake of the Tea Party and Trump, the reality is considerably more muddled. No doubt there were many white people from disadvantaged and working-class backgrounds who did support the former reality TV star, but they were far from the only group to do so, and there is little evidence to support the idea that they made up the majority to the degree that the conventional narrative emphasizes. Therefore, though this reality does not preclude these genuine material shifts from having mobilized many voters, it does undercut the homogeneity that the right-wing melodrama suggests.

Relatedly, it is also worth noting that the white decline thesis falls apart because it rests on a notion of a singular white working-class history—that working-class whites collectively experienced a fall from security to precarity—when the historical reality is much more complicated. As HoSang and Lowndes have pointed out, geography played a particularly significant role in securing the historical "wages of whiteness" whose loss the right laments today: "the security and indemnification from vulnerability conferred by whiteness [in the years following the New Deal] was uneven and never universal. Particularly in rural areas where economies were predicated on resource extraction necessary for the growth and development of cities, the material privileges of whiteness were far less dependable" (50). There have, in other words, always been whites who received a lesser share of the "wages of whiteness," particularly those who live in rural locales like Hochschild's Louisiana *Strangers*, and the feeling of "loss" (as opposed to lack) that animates much of the "working-class" right is often imagined more than material or historical. These factors complicate the economic struggles typically used to substantiate the nostalgic appeals and melodramas of loss that are so often used to explain the politics of the right.

The most important fiction underwriting right-wing nostalgic melodrama is that of the "white working class" itself, a supposedly homogeneous group of underappreciated, uneducated blue-collar workers who, due to the decline in domestic manufacturing or cultural alienation (depending on who you ask), have turned en masse to the right. Their struggles and resentments, the conventional narrative suggests, are the foundation of right-wing politics today. This notion still undergirds a considerable portion of both the mainstream and academic discourse on the subject, resulting in numerous publications each year seeking to explain this supposedly new phenomenon, but it was especially prominent following the rise of Trump in 2015 and his election in 2016. These events produced great interest among liberals in particular, who sought to understand a political reality for which they were psychologically and ideologically unprepared. At this time, as Christian Ravela notes, "Concern over this white working class [became] ubiquitous, ranging from the public prominence of economists Ann Case and Angus Deaton's 2015 study of the growing number of 'deaths of despair' among middle-aged, working-class white men to academic monographs like Arlie Hochschild's *Strangers in Their Own Land* and Nancy Isenberg's *White Trash*, to countless cover stories on the opiate/heroin crisis in magazines like *Time* and *The New Yorker* . . . to the television reboot of *Roseanne* (2018), and even to the immensely popular podcast *S-Town* (2017)" (181). Identifying and understanding "the white working class," in short, became the exigence for a body of work that rarely, if ever, interrogated its own foundational premises—a victory for the right-wing melodramas that it thrust to the forefront of political discourse.

In the context of this urgent push to understand how the struggles of the white working class led to Trump's election in 2016, one book stands out above the rest due to its popularity, the force of its efforts to enshrine the white working class as a coherent category worthy of unique sympathy, and, especially, its author's recent political ascendancy. Like Hochschild's *Strangers*, J. D. Vance's *Hillbilly Elegy: A Memoir of a Family and Culture in Crisis* was published in 2016 to rave reviews, earning a spot on the *New York Times*' best-seller list for nearly seventy consecutive weeks and featuring in numerous articles outlining "the most important books of the year." Vance subsequently became a regular guest on *CNN*, *NPR*, and other news outlets from across the political spectrum, who identified him as *the* voice of working-class whites. An adaptation of the book, directed by Ron Howard and starring Glenn Close and Amy Adams, was released in 2020. This fame helped fuel Vance's meteoric rise in American politics, as he first secured a seat in the U.S. Senate in 2022 before being elected as Trump's vice president in 2024. Written when Vance worked for tech billionaire and early Trump backer Peter Thiel's venture capital firm, the book traces the author's life from his early struggles as the child of a drug addict in the Ohio rust belt to his graduation from Yale Law School. Marketed as a memoir, *Hillbilly Elegy* is a mixture of family history, personal anecdotes, observations about community, and "commonsense" political polemic. Above all, Vance positions his family story as symptomatic of a larger struggle faced throughout the white working class, which he analyzes through the conservative lens of cultural failure. The broad story, as readers are meant to understand it, is that a complex combination of social and economic factors have led to a cultural crisis for working-class whites, pushing them away from tradition, family, and prosperity, toward isolation, drug abuse, and misery. Much like *Strangers in Their Own Land*, *Elegy's* diagnosis is that, as a cohort, the white working class are victims and they deserve sympathy rather than scorn.

For the purposes of this chapter, *Hillbilly Elegy* should be understood primarily within this larger matrix of right-wing nostalgic melodrama. The book, in this context, played an important role in spreading the right's narrative of the unique plight of the white working class. Less a memoir about poverty and family struggle, the book is therefore more productively seen as a work of political evangelism—a reading supported in part by Vance's political trajectory following *Elegy*'s publication. Though he initially positioned himself as a "sensible" #NeverTrump conservative—he notes in the afterword to the 2018 edition of *Elegy* (included in the 2020 edition) that he voted for a third party in 2016 (262)—who, despite whatever policy disagreements they may have had, was nonetheless palatable to the liberal audiences who helped propel him into the spotlight, Vance's 2022 Senate campaign coincided with a more fulsome embrace of hard-right anti-immigrant, populist, and nationalist rhetoric, followed by an endorsement of (and from) Trump himself. Although, as this chapter shows, their ideologies were never really incompatible to begin with, Vance's public "conversion" to Trumpist politics was cemented in July 2024 when Trump named Vance as his running mate.

Of particular note in the context of this chapter, candidate- and politician-Vance, as Gabriel Winant has shown, has consistently (if indirectly) embraced the white supremacist "great replacement" conspiracy, which posits that declining birthrates are part of a global effort to eradicate white people, a development that was initially met with denials from the same liberal institutions he railed against:

> "Our people aren't having enough children to replace themselves. That should bother us," [Vance] admonished at the 2019 National Conservatism Conference, integrating a semi-tacit white nationalism with the right's antiabortion program. When Ari M. Brostoff pointed out this connection at the time, the far-right and the center-right Never Trump types forced the *Washington Post* to issue a correction and delete Brostoff's lines linking his pronatalism to white supremacy—one of many instances of the contemptible complaisance with which the political establishment received Vance during the long rightward shift he took over the course of the 2010s. Were we really to believe that years of enthusiastic fraternizing with neofascists like Thiel and Curtis Yarvin left him uninfluenced by the concerns that preoccupy those circles, such as the comparative IQ scores of various demographic groups or their relative propensity for crime? That Vance's zest for high birth rates is unrelated to the eugenics increasingly prevalent on the tech industry's far-right wing? That when he used the words "replace" and "our people," he did so innocently—only to repeat the argument more forcefully on the campaign trail?

Winant's criticism of the dismay with which Vance's outward turn to the far right was met with in the liberal media is broadly correct, but this passage also relies on the notion that Vance's adoption of this position was wholly new, the result of his time spent with neofascist ideologues. However, reading *Hillbilly Elegy* in the context of right-wing racial melodrama, as this chapter suggests, reveals that Vance's supposed "turn" was less sharp than often described. The shift, such that it exists, was actually more about "saying the quiet part loud" than adopting new principles; *Hillbilly Elegy*, in fact, is a work that is completely aligned with the same far-right claims of whiteness under siege that Vance peddles today, and suggestions to the contrary—which posit that politician Vance is somehow ideologically distinct from memoirist Vance—mistakes superficial rhetoric aimed at laundering the broader message of white melodrama into liberal popular discourse for sincere political expression. *Hillbilly Elegy* and the Great Replacement conspiracy are two sides of the same coin, distinguished not by their fundamental message but by the way that the message is packaged for its intended audience (liberals for the former, conservatives for the latter). Therefore, instead of seeing the book as it is superficially presented, it is more productive to see it as an effort, from an avowed partisan, to produce the sympathy necessary to make the case for white victimhood that the right's political and economic agenda relies upon (which is, not coincidentally, a cause he explicitly took up once he become an active political agent). Closer inspection of *Hillbilly Elegy* reveals not only the consistency of Vance's ideological project but, more importantly, how melodrama and nostalgia are deployed to construct the right wing's notion of "white working class" suffering, and how this effort is shaped by the political and economic context of the end of history.

As the title suggests, Vance's memoir is fundamentally framed around his identification as a "hillbilly." In fact, the book is filled with passages where the author confirms the centrality of this pseudoheritage to his sense of self. This process begins early: On the third page, for instance, he writes, "To understand me, you must understand that I am a Scots-Irish hillbilly at heart." For attentive readers unfamiliar with the book, the "at heart" part of this passage may seem strange—why would anyone need to attach "at heart" to an essential element of their identity? Shouldn't core ethnic identity reside outside of "the heart?" The reason for this rhetorical flourish is that, though the book is often framed as a study of hillbillies and Appalachia, Vance himself is not actually from the region, nor has he ever lived there. In fact, Vance is two generations removed from permanent residence in the eastern Kentucky town his grandparents emigrated from in the 1940s (nearly forty years before his birth). Instead, Vance, like his mother, was born and raised in Middletown, Ohio, a manufacturing town centered around the then-thriving Armco steel plant, which lured his grandparents north with the promise of a steady job and wages well beyond what the coal mines of Jackson could offer. Vance's connection to the "hillbilly" angle of his title, and the place that term evokes, is, in short, more indirect than it initially appears, and the overwhelming majority of the story takes place in Middletown (which is not, it must be emphasized, *in* Appalachia).

It is worth asking, in this context, why Vance's book is so adamant about its "hillbilly" framing. It is one thing to self-identify as a hillbilly; it is quite another to use that identification as the title of your memoir and to refer to it throughout the book as the frame that best illuminates your experiences and the experiences of the community your story is meant to represent despite the story not taking place within the geographic confines that conventionally define that community. Though Vance may well identify as a "hillbilly," his insistence on using it as a frame for the book is better understood as a reflection of his desire to reframe rust belt decline in sympathetic identitarian terms. Vance explains early in the book that "I may be white, but I do not identify with the WASPs of the Northeast. Instead, I identify with the millions of working-class white Americans of Scots-Irish descent who have no college degree. To these folks, poverty is the family tradition—their ancestors were day laborers in the Southern slave economy, sharecroppers after that, coal miners after that, and machinists and millworkers during more recent times. Americans call them hillbillies, rednecks, or white trash. I call them neighbors, friends, and family" (3). Setting aside the inherent absurdity of Vance "identifying" with an education status that does not apply to him (Vance graduated from Yale with a Juris Doctor degree three years before the book was released), this passage is striking in several ways. Notably, Vance begins by disavowing the centrality of whiteness to his identity by describing his alienation from another white compound ethnicity—one that, not coincidentally, usually reads as "elite," conjuring images of people luxuriating on sailboats off Martha's Vineyard—in stark contrast to the misery of the coal miners in the following sentence. Vance prefers affiliation with a different compound formula of whiteness, which, he implies, is defined as much by its genetic heritage as its historical poverty. The addition of "Southern slave economy" is especially remarkable in this regard, as it suggests a parallel between the struggles faced by Black slaves and those faced by white "day laborers"—that both were grist for the mill of the exploitative Southern economy, thereby establishing a racial parallel that Vance will return to throughout the book. Defined this way, Vance's life's struggles, and those of the dubiously designated "culture" in the book's title, therefore, represent yet another example in a long line of struggles faced by ethnicized whites.

Rhetorically, this early effort to define Vance and his "hillbilly community" as something other than strictly white serves one key purpose: It compels its predominantly liberal readership to forget whatever preconceptions about white people they may have, and to allow for the possibility that, despite the advantages normally accorded the race, some of them have been unfairly marginalized in a manner that is directly tied to their identity. It primes them as subjects worthy of sympathy, and subtly indicts readers who would have argued otherwise. These people are not to be understood purely as white, the book suggests, because they have not been afforded the white privilege that many ascribe to them. Like other recognized minorities in this country, who are subjected to prejudice by the culture at large, these whites are looked down upon by much of the country—they even have their own slurs.

And yet, though these people are not to be seen *only* as white, they are, the book makes clear in its dozens of references to "the white working class," still white, which enables their struggles to serve as a symbol of a broader racialized crisis. Though seemingly contradictory—the book wants hillbillies to be both white and not-quite-white—the purpose behind the paradox is clear: They are not white insofar as minority status is needed to confer sympathy; they are white insofar as this sympathy can be used to indict a culture that has allowed whites to fall so far. This notion brings to light perhaps the central theme of *Hillbilly Elegy*: the debasement of white people. As the book's subtitle makes clear, *Elegy* is not only meant to be read as memoir, but also as a pseudosociological investigation into a "culture in crisis." Given the aforementioned geographic issues with the "hillbilly" appellation, the utter lack of scenes actually staged in Appalachia, the prominence of issues specific to the rust belt (namely, the decline in manufacturing that gives the region its name), and the volume of references to the broadly construed "white working class," the "culture" that emerges from the book cannot be understood as "hillbilly" specifically. Though partially obscured, the real "culture in crisis" of *Hillbilly Elegy* is "white culture," and the struggles faced by the "hillbillies" in the book are merely an extension of the struggles supposedly facing the race more broadly.

The most elegant articulation of the book's racial thesis comes midway through the book, when Vance explains that "bad neighborhoods no longer plague only urban ghettos; the bad neighborhoods have spread to the suburbs" (52).[2] The book's central tragedy, as Vance implies here, is that whites are no longer immune from the kind of decay previously understood to be the province of people of color. It is no coincidence that the book contains reference to the work of Charles Murray, the notorious co-author of *The Bell Curve*, whose analyses of the socioeconomics of welfare condemn its supposedly harmful influence on the Black communities that rely on it, arguing instead that Black people disproportionately find themselves in poverty in America due to a combination of genetic shortcomings and parasitical government policies. Much has been written about *Hillbilly Elegy*'s arguments against the welfare state, critiques that need not be rehashed here, but what is notable about this angle for our purposes is the way that Vance's references to famous critiques of welfare and the plight of "the inner city" are largely used to support this narrative of the blackening of working-class whites. At one point in the book, Vance writes glowingly of William Julius Williams's *The Truly Disadvantaged*, a study of race and poverty in Black communities. He adds that the book appealed to him so much because "[Williams] had described my home perfectly." Vance follows this passage with a reference to Murray's "seminal" *Losing Ground*, which he describes as "another book about black folks that could have been written about hillbillies" (144). As a number of scholars have pointed out, much of *Hillbilly Elegy* also bears a striking resemblance to the infamous Moynihan Report, which proposed that a cultural crisis was at the heart of Black poverty.

This is not a connection specific to *Hillbilly Elegy*, however; as HoSang and Lowndes have noted, "The anti-Black tropes of cultural and familial degradation proposed by Moynihan's 1965 *The Negro Family* now circulate in explanations of white poverty" (58). Discursively, at least, this tendency resembles what they refer to as "racial transposition," which describes "a process through which the meaning, valence, and signification of race can be transferred from one context, group, or setting to another, shaping the ways in which racial categories structure broad fields of social meaning" (12). Within the right, they argue,

> explanations of dependency, behavioral pathos, family breakdown, and cultural dysfunction that have long been used to contrast Black failure with white success are now summoned and deployed to discipline white workers around privatized market logics. As some of the central conditions in the postwar economic, political, and social settlement have changed, the (economic) wages of whiteness are no longer guaranteed. The legibility of efforts to explain these new forms of privation as effects of cultural degeneracy and dependence is premised upon an enduring racialized logic and domination that has long naturalized white supremacy. They are rooted in a social vision based on categories of worth and unworthiness that ignores structural explanations of inequality and invites scrutiny into the failures or successes of the individual body and family. (65)

Though their explanation of the coercive function of this rhetorical shift is undoubtedly correct, and this certainly factors into *Hillbilly Elegy*'s more overt calls for cultural reform, this passage also misses another function of racial transposition within right-wing politics. More than simply disciplining workers under a decaying economic regime, racial transposition—specifically, the depiction of white culture's degradation using the terms originally deployed against Blacks—enables the right to create an equivalence between white and Black suffering. This depiction serves two important functions. First, it enables the right to argue against race-based remuneration by pointing out cases of white suffering that are unfairly overlooked by such policies, which serves their broader goal of "entitlement reform" based on the wholesale removal of the social safety net. Second, and more important for the context of this chapter, it feeds into the larger narrative of right-wing melodrama that is central to its electoral appeals. This is especially advantageous for a book like *Hillbilly Elegy*, which targets a distinctly liberal audience rather than a conservative one—much less the hillbillies whose "culture" the book directly indicts. These stories of Black cultural crisis are familiar to liberal audiences, who are sympathetically attuned to this rhetoric of suffering and lament, and *Hillbilly Elegy*'s invocation of this language and these connections therefore works to redirect the liberal sympathy economy toward forgotten, underprivileged whites. Likewise, the narrative of white decline, a fall from status marked by the rise of "Black" cultural problems, animates racist right-wing narratives of white supremacy—how can the white race be supreme if its people are so debased? Remuneration for white suffering becomes part of the broader enforcement of white supremacy. Thus, in both cases, the racial transposition depicted in *Hillbilly Elegy* casts "working-class whites" as victims whose status must be restored—the starting point of all melodrama.

And yet, it must be noted that this reading of the racial dynamics of *Hillbilly Elegy* contradicts Vance's framing early in the book, where he insists that readers consider his study of "the white working class" and its constant cross-racial comparisons as a study of "class and family" rather than race:

> Although I focus on the group of people I know—working-class whites with ties to Appalachia—I'm not arguing that we deserve *more* sympathy than other folks. This is not a story about why white people have *more* to complain about than black people or any other group. That said, I do hope that readers of this book will be able to take from it an appreciation of how class and family affect the poor without filtering their views through a racial prism. To many analysts, terms like "welfare queen" conjure unfair images of the lazy black mom living on the dole. Readers of this book will realize quickly that there is little relationship between that specter and my argument: I have known many welfare queens; some were my neighbors, and all were white. (7–8; emphasis added)

At best, this attempt to delimit the book's interpretation is, as this chapter attests, a clumsy misrepresentation of its actual content; at worst, it's an intentional obfuscation that flies in the face not only of its content, but of the entire marketing campaign—from its title and the blurbs that consistently reference the racial component of the narrative, to Vance's own appearances promoting the book where he consistently speaks to the struggles of "whites" rather than the struggles of the deracialized "poor" he evokes here. Setting aside the obvious issues with this overt "race-blind" posturing, it is worth pointing out that, even amid these disavowals of the centrality of racial politics to his project, Vance still invokes race and the book's fundamentally comparative function by transposing the raced trope of the welfare queen onto whites. Like the book's larger narrative arc, this specific instance of racial transposition speaks differently across the political spectrum: To liberals, who in 2016 largely understood the inherent racism of the "welfare queen" trope and saw the "lazy black mom living on the dole" as an object of sympathy rather than scorn and resentment, the reference transposes the sympathy onto similarly afflicted whites; for the right, particularly the white supremacists who largely retain the same resentments that animated the moniker's initial adoption, Vance's claim that he has "known many welfare queens . . . and all were white" serves as a shock to their racial pride, identifying the depth of the crisis that has befallen the "white working class."

As a whole, the passage cited above may seem internally contradictory thanks to its seeming rejection of comparison in its first two sentences; however, as the added emphasis shows, Vance's complaint is not against comparison itself, but comparison that directly claims that poor whites deserve *more* sympathy than poor Blacks. The paragraph, more than anything, serves to ward off notions of white supremacy, which obscures its deeper truth: The book is not trying to directly claim that whites deserve *more*, only that they deserve *the same*, in effect erasing race as a factor in the story of poverty (again, undoing the logic of race-based policies like affirmative action) while simultaneously reifying it in terms of public and political sympathy ({"whites deserve sympathy too" is, whether Vance wants to admit it or not, obviously a claim about race). Nonetheless, *Hillbilly Elegy*, its author insists, is not a book about race; it is merely a book about how a culturally homogeneous, pseudoethnic subset of white people finds themselves suffering from a unique cultural crisis that, as long as we ignore the impact of structural and historical racism, also perfectly mirrors the one facing Black people.

On a rhetorical level, this effort to center white suffering through the erasure of "race" is also reflected in Vance's broader depiction of rust-belt decline as an ethnic rather than geographic crisis. In the introduction, Vance first invokes these circumstances in broad terms before immediately shifting focus to race (under the guise of "culture"): "This book is about . . . what goes on in the lives of real people when the industrial economy goes south. It's about reacting to bad circumstances in the worst way possible. It's about a culture that increasingly encourages social decay instead of counteracting it" (7). Thus, to read *Hillbilly Elegy* as its author requests, one is asked to see Middletown's economic downturn and the issues that result from it as reflective of the struggles faced by many former manufacturing towns across the country, while also seeing the struggles faced by the Vance family in Middletown, many of which Vance ties to the city's decline, as issues relating to "culture." This effort suggests, yet again, that there is something essentially unique about white suffering in the rust belt, and that the struggles faced by poor Blacks in the region, for instance, are not worth remarking on in Vance's story of "how class and family affect the poor." No attention is paid, therefore, to the conditions facing nonwhites in Middletown (over 15% of the population according to the 2010 census), nor to the fact that its white residents are also disproportionately better off than their nonwhite counterparts.

The reality, of course, is that rust-belt decline is not a white-specific issue, and *Elegy*'s depiction of problems like drug abuse and familial instability faced by many groups who inhabit places like Middletown as a problem specifically faced by a pseudoethnicity mainly serves to flatten the issue. Ironically, despite Vance's "preference" for avoiding race-based analysis, this approach only serves to narrowly racialize an economic crisis that is felt across racial boundaries. In this way, the book takes for granted minority suffering, suggesting that what makes the plight of rust-belt decline unique is its effects on whites.

To return to the broader point: *Hillbilly Elegy*, with its focus on suffering and its narrative arc organized around the identification of victimization and the heroism of a protagonist who manages to overcome the obstacles laid before him, is consistently engaged in the melodramatic mode Williams describes. The book is replete with conventionally melodramatic appeals, and most of the scenes Vance actually stages—that is, scenes he doesn't just briefly summarize, which, along with sections of "sociological" investigation, are actually the majority of the book—are centered around the heightened emotions of his mother's drug abuse and its consequences: We see her fight with a revolving succession of boyfriends and husbands; we see Vance run to a stranger's house for help as his mother tries to drag him out in a fit of rage; we see her ask him for clean urine for a drug test that would result in the loss of her nursing license. The core of the narrative is this family melodrama. Ron Howard's adaptation is a testament to this fact, as the film jettisons Vance's musings on "culture" and politics in favor of telling a more straightforward story of familial struggle. These emotional appeals represent the most memorable parts of the book for most readers and reviewers, who consistently describe the book as "moving," "heartbreaking," and "unflinching," which is particularly vital for the book's efforts to construct sympathy for the white working class.

To take this analysis of the book's adoption of melodrama a step further, in the context of its emphasis on racialized decline, Vance's triumph—his success in leaving behind the repressive "hillbilly" culture of his family and his integration into the "elite" culture of Yale—is not only about his overcoming barriers to the American Dream; it is also about how he managed to triumph over the *minority* struggles that have come to plague the white working class. In other words, the book can be read as a story whose victory is that the hero overcomes his debased status by becoming white. The book's depiction of "hillbilly" struggle is regularly communicated through Vance's alienation from "elite culture" and its supposedly arcane customs, like wearing a suit to a job interview (which Vance insists is a practice he was unfamiliar with until his early twenties). This is especially evident in the sections detailing his time at Yale, where Vance continually identifies himself as an outsider whose experiences are more in line with those of minorities. In one part, he describes a group of friends that emerged from a constitutional law course: "We called ourselves the island of misfit toys," he explains, made up of "a conservative hillbilly from Appalachia, the supersmart daughter of Indian immigrants, a black Canadian with decades' worth of street smarts, a neuroscientist from Phoenix, an aspiring civil rights attorney born a few minutes from Yale's campus, and an extremely progressive lesbian with a fantastic sense of humor, among others" (200–201). Reading this passage closely, a pattern appears in which "outsiders" are depicted through reference to something fundamental to their identity (Indian, Black, lesbian), while the others, who are presumably white (and straight) given the absence of description, are identified by their profession. It should come as no surprise that Vance racializes himself with the redundant (and inaccurate) "hillbilly from Appalachia" moniker. Though somewhat indirect, the message here is clear: Vance is a minority in the context of elite white institutions.[3] In fact, he argues at one point that he may have been the most isolated minority there: "Very few people at Yale Law School are like me. They may look like me, but for all of the Ivy League's obsession with diversity, virtually everyone—black, white, Jewish, Muslim, whatever—comes from intact families who never worry about money" (203). In this, as Winant points out, Vance depicts "an institution that gave rise to the CIA and the Bush family, which holds the looted bones of Indigenous heroes and employs the country's oldest university police force to maintain its segregated frontiers, as uniquely cruel to him." Vance takes this imagined victimization even further when he recounts a networking event where he is confronted with dining rituals that expose his ignorance of elite white culture. In one scene, he describes his anxiety at being asked, after choosing white wine over red, if he would like chardonnay or sauvignon blanc, because, he claims, he did not realize there were multiple types of white wine (211). Moments later, he describes comically spitting out water that he believed to have gone bad because he was unaware of the difference between sparkling and tap. The comedy of errors concludes when he is confronted with the restaurant's place setting, which features "an absurd number of utensils" (212). Panicking, Vance excuses himself from the table and calls his girlfriend (now-wife) Usha, the aforementioned "supersmart Indian," who explains the procedure to him. These scenes, especially the concluding note that he was taught the proper course of action by a minority, highlight Vance's alienation from white culture, which confirms his minority status and essential victimization. Readers are invited to simultaneously sympathize with his confusion while also recognizing the depth of his distance from his racial heritage.

If *Hillbilly Elegy*'s central thesis relates to the racial transposition of the white working class, his experiences at Yale serve the crucial function of identifying the depth of his alienation from whiteness and the struggles he faced becoming fully white. Vance's victory, then, is not just about "making it" by securing stable economic status (which he had essentially already accomplished by joining the Marines and then graduating with a bachelor's degree from Ohio State), but rather in his ability to *restore* the whiteness that was rightfully his by making it to the most exclusive echelons of white society. In this light, it is significant that the Yale incidents have little in common with the victimization outlined elsewhere in the book—that is, not knowing about chardonnay has nothing to do with having a mother addicted to opiates. The issue is cultural, a matter of belonging and alienation, rather than socioeconomic—in the afterword to the 2020 edition, Vance says that when he decided to write the book, he wanted to answer the question, "Why does this elite institution seem so culturally foreign" (259). Just as we saw in *Strangers in Their Own Land*, Vance's depiction of his own victimization is often at odds with the genuine struggles he faced. *Hillbilly Elegy* concluding with its author recounting how he overcame these comparatively trivial struggles at Yale identifies the centrality of "cultural" alienation to the entire project. The story, as such, is less about poverty itself, and more about how poverty made it tougher for him to enjoy the privileges his race provides. In telling his life story, Vance therefore casts himself as the star of a cultural melodrama, triumphant against the forces that sought to limit his potential—a white working-class übermensch. *Elegy*, in other words, is the right-wing restorative impulse in microcosm.

Because *Hillbilly Elegy* is fundamentally a melodrama of nostalgic restoration, it bears considering what, specifically, the book seeks to restore. While, in one sense, Vance's book is about his struggle to reinstate his own wages of whiteness, the book also seeks to detail a "culture in crisis" and spends considerable time lamenting its loss of "tradition"; therefore, having explored the essentially melodramatic nature of this "crisis," it is now worth turning our attention to the "culture" in question and Vance's nostalgic depiction of its losses.

Explicitly framed as a lament for the dead, Vance's *elegy* evinces a conventionally nostalgic sense of loss and irreconcilable distance, founded in acute feelings of alienation and disconnect from what he construes as "home." There is a sense throughout the book that Vance is out of place, whether in Middletown or New Haven—a stranger in his own land, if you will. As he explains in the book's first chapter, "My address was where I spent most of my time with my mother and sister, wherever that might be. But my home never changed: my great-grandmother's house, in the holler, in Jackson, Kentucky" (11). In contrast to Middletown, where most of the book takes place, Vance repeatedly emphasizes the sense of wholeness he felt in the summers he spent in Jackson as a kid: "The surrounding mountains were paradise to a child. . . . I'd run around with my cousins, unaware of the ever-present poverty or Mamaw Blanton's deteriorating health. At a deep level, Jackson was the one place that belonged to me, my sister, and Mamaw" (13). Jackson, Vance explains, is also defined by its fundamental goodness: "Jacksonians say hello to everyone," he explains at one point, "willingly skip their favorite pastimes to dig a stranger's car out of the snow, and—without exception—stop their cars, get out, and stand at attention every time a funeral motorcade drives past" (12). Yet, despite its Edenic nature, and the apparent significance of the holler to Vance's life (especially its centrality to his sense of self), scenes in the book hardly ever actually take place in Jackson—the location exists mainly as the setting for unadorned references to family history, brief mentions of time spent there as a child, and anecdotes showing contemporary socioeconomic decay. There is virtually no dialogue staged in Jackson; it is not a place where people talk, or laugh, or do anything in detail. It is a place where good things *happened* in the past and where bad things *happen* in the present. In the book, therefore, Jackson is depicted less as a real, living place and more as an inert container for the losses the book laments.

Hillbilly Elegy also depicts Jackson as a doubly absent "home": first, as a physical space that is a great distance from Vance's *actual* home in Middletown; and second, as a place that no longer exists due to the passage of time (death of family, migration, growing up, etc.) and its own supposedly fallen status. The absence of the home, which Vance can never *truly* return to (in part because it only existed as an idea to begin with), therefore forms the foundation of his elegy, and its status becomes a metaphor for the loss of tradition and cultural decline that the book seeks to overturn. In this, Vance invokes the trope of the prelapsarian past and the apocalyptic, postlapsarian present so common in the nostalgic media at the end of history. Crucially, as much as the book depicts the Edenic holler as an omnipresent absence that structures his sense of alienation, it also depicts Middletown and New Haven as places where Vance does not feel at home despite his race suggesting that he should. In this sense, Vance's nostalgia for the sense of belonging the holler gave him also serves as an indictment of its lack in other "white" spaces.

The afterword to the 2020 edition takes these restorative nostalgic impulses a step further, as Vance recounts his recent purchase of a plot of land in Jackson, Kentucky, "that has been in our family for around one hundred years (and maybe longer)" (264). Vance describes this attempt to "rebuild the lost home" (as Boym would put it) as a kind of nostalgic pastoral futurity, an opportunity for his newborn son to visit "the place that formed such a large piece of my childhood." "I want Ewan to explore those hills," he explains, "search for crawdads in those creeks, and feel at home there like I did" (265). Here, for one of the only times in the book, Vance suggests a deep connection to the land itself, emphasizing, much like Hochschild's deep story, the romantic nobility at the heart of the desire for restoration. And yet, given that in 2023 Vance purchased a million-dollar home in Alexandria, Virginia, there seems to be a limit on the now–vice president's desire to *actually* return to his lost home, and, for now at least, the call to restore remains more of an ideal than an actual undertaking.[4] Though somewhat ironic, this is not actually a contradiction of the broader goals laid out in the book. *Hillbilly Elegy*'s project, in other words, is not really focused on rebuilding the literal home, but is instead an effort to restore the conditions that characterized the idealized "home" and the lost cultural traditions that, he claims, defined it. The book's notion of a lost "home," therefore, is more intrinsically tied to this abstract notion of "cultural" loss and racial debasement than its attention to geography may suggest, and Vance's call for restoration of the homeland should be understood not as a call to revitalize Appalachia or Middletown but more as a call for the (imagined) restoration of the nation as a space that privileges *all* whites, not just the elites.

Though he sometimes frames the crisis in geographic terms, Vance's elegy, we should remember, is for the "hillbilly," not for "Appalachia" or "the rust belt." The book, in other words, is fundamentally about a lost people and the way of life the people supposedly represent. The broad effect of this focus, as I pointed out earlier, is that it enables Vance to reframe socioeconomic issues affecting the populations of the regions in question through the same narrowly racialized lens he explicitly disavows—to mark rust belt and Appalachian suffering as a white phenomenon. Regional decline, as a result, becomes instead the story of "cultural" decline, which Vance organizes around a hyperspecific ethnic simulacrum that is constructed to contain precisely the elements that, he contends, have been lost. Put another way, *Elegy* grounds its analysis of cultural loss in a nostalgia for white working-class virtues that he embeds into this specter of the ancestral hillbilly.

Vance's notion of "hillbilly culture," therefore, is largely imagined, resulting from his rendering of traits specific to his family and life experiences, and the erasure of experiences to the contrary, as categorically endemic—not only within "hill people" but also within the white working class more broadly. At its core, the book is premised on the idea that the post–financial crisis economic downturn and, more specifically (though unspoken), the loss of the wages of whiteness heralded by neoliberalism have led "his" people to abandon their traditional values (strength, resilience, and a fierce commitment to family chief among them) and turned them into ignorant, lazy, often drug-addled parasites. *Hillbilly Elegy*, in this way, is a nostalgic lament for the supposed loss of the hillbilly way of life set within a melodrama that centers white victimization resulting from the abandonment of traditional values in the face of posthistorical decline—a trajectory that, Vance suggests throughout, exemplifies the tribulations of the white working class more generally. Vance's elegy, therefore, is as much an elegy for the "white working class" as it is for the "hillbilly" of its title, and his nostalgia for their "culture" is fundamentally bound in notions of virtue that supposedly extend to working-class whites regardless of geography.

In light of this nostalgic framing, it would be easy for Vance to depict the past as purely Edenic in contrast with the fallen present. However, despite the instances cited above where Vance speaks of the region in romantic terms, the book does not attempt to depict the past as a time without struggle. In fact, *Hillbilly Elegy* is careful to note that the Appalachia from which his grandparents fled has faced tough times throughout much of its history. "As Papaw once told me," he explains, "the sole option for many of his friends was to work 'in the mines'—mining coal not far from Jackson. Those who stayed in Jackson spent their lives on the edge of poverty, if not submerged in it" (25–26). "Jackson taught me that 'hill people' and 'poor people' usually meant the same thing," he laments (18). Although in one sense this avoidance of easy historical revisionism is commendable, it should be noted that this depiction also feeds into Vance's nostalgic vision of the virtuous hillbilly and the culture that produced him. What emerges from these sketches of historical struggle is a culture of resilience that responds to strife with vigor, where people are unwilling to accept their lower lot in life and deeply motivated by the pursuit of the good life: "Both of my grandparents had an almost religious faith in hard work and the American Dream. Neither was under any illusions that wealth or privilege didn't matter in America. . . . Still, Mamaw and Papaw believed that hard work mattered more. They knew that life was a struggle, and though the odds were a bit longer for people like them, that fact didn't excuse failure. 'Never be like these fucking losers who think the deck is stacked against them,' my grandma often told me. 'You can do anything you want to'" (35–36). This depiction forms a stark parallel with the defeatism that, he argues, abounds today: "Jackson," he explains, "is undoubtedly full of the nicest people in the world; it is also full of drug addicts and at least one man who can find the time to make eight children but can't find the time to support them. . . . Its people are hardworking, except of course for the many food stamp recipients who show little interest in hard work" (21). Stories of cultural decline proliferate throughout the book, from the "thin man, no older than thirty-five" in Jackson who Vance sees standing on his front porch surrounded by "several ferocious, malnourished, chained-up dogs protect[ing] the furniture strewn about the barren front yard" who, Vance's cousin Rick claims, "had no job and was proud of it" (19), to the tile warehouse worker with a pregnant girlfriend in Middletown who, despite "miss[ing] work about once a week" and taking "three or four daily bathroom breaks, each over half an hour," was dismayed when he was fired (7). Vance responds to these incidents by saying that "Nobel-winning economists worry about the decline of the industrial Midwest and the hollowing out of the economic core of working whites. . . . Fair enough—I worry about these things, too. But this book is about something else: what goes on in the lives of real people when the industrial economy goes south. It's about reacting to bad circumstances in the worst way possible. It's about a culture that increasingly encourages social decay instead of counteracting it" (7). This shift from economic to "cultural" causation is enabled by Vance's recognition of the historical pervasiveness of poverty in Appalachia. In effect, passages like these work to create a logical equivalence between the poverty of the past and the poverty of the present, whereby the telling distinction is not the degree of poverty or the availability of opportunity but a change in cultural response to hardship. To accept the losses that *Hillbilly Elegy* describes, one must believe that the problems that truly plague the "culture" today are wholly new, that the holler never used to have people who didn't like to work, that no one dawdled at work in the mines, that no one had a debilitating addiction that led to familial crisis—that, in other words, the cultural crisis he describes is a recent development. We must also, as Winant has argued, ignore the obvious parallels between the lazy warehouse worker and Vance's supposedly virtuous grandfather (who fled the holler after impregnating his thirteen-year-old girlfriend, drank, stayed out late, and cheated on his young wife so frequently that she once attempted to burn him alive). Charting this contrast requires Vance to construct two fictional hillbillies: the virtuous hillbilly of the past and the parasitical hillbilly of the present.

Much work has been done to counter Vance's depiction of the region and its supposed decline in passages like these—particularly in the collection *Appalachian Reckoning*, which, among other things, provides a thorough account of how *Elegy*'s framing of the region relies on harmful stereotypes that serve to support Vance's conventionally conservative political aims, especially his party's assault on entitlement programs (Harkins and McCarroll). What is nonetheless notable in this discussion, and has been subject to less emphasis in these critiques, is the way these myths operate within the larger context of right-wing appeals to tradition. It is here that *Hillbilly Elegy*'s nostalgic melodrama fully takes shape, as stories of traditional hillbilly culture, wisdom, and virtue are nearly omnipresent in the book, conjuring lament for their losses as well as the suffering supposedly brought on in their absence. The nostalgic sensations this lament provokes are particularly notable in the context of the reflective age because they are based on generalized reconstructions—drawn almost exclusively from anecdotes about Vance's immediate family—of a prior state that did not truly exist and whose loss is subsequently also imagined. The book's elegy, in other words, requires looking backwards at *what once was*, but the image Vance conjures is false, founded especially in, as Douglas Dowland has shown, narrow synecdoche that takes often-idiosyncratic family anecdotes as representative of an entire culture and class. "Vance's lever for understanding the world," Winant explains, "is to compare others against his grandparents and find them wanting." As Vance tells it, the virtuous hillbillies of generations past like Mamaw and Papaw possessed a host of ennobling traits, such as "an intense sense of loyalty, a fierce dedication to family and country" (3), and "a robust sense of honor" (41). Even their vices, like a distrust of outsiders or their distinct penchant for violence—examples of "hillbilly justice" (17), which, like when his grandfather busted down the door to a rest stop women's bathroom holding a loaded pistol out of worry that his daughter, who had taken longer than expected, "was being raped by some pervert" (108); or when his grandparents trashed a pharmacy after finding out the clerk had asked their unaccompanied child to leave the store (34), Vance gleefully enumerates throughout—serve as evidence of a libidinal passion that he argues is simultaneously so widespread, and so essential to their cultural heritage, that it borders on genetic ("I believe we hillbillies are the toughest goddamned people on this earth" [255]). However, this passion, as evidenced by their turn to drug abuse and their unwillingness to fight for a better life, is sorely lacking in younger generations. Perhaps if welfare hadn't made them so lazy, *Elegy* implies, they might not have turned to drugs and could have led a productive life of pulling guns on strangers and feeding dogs antifreeze for threatening their children as Vance's papaw did (108)—or, as his Uncle Pet had done, "beat [a man] unconscious, and [run] an electric saw up and down his body" for insulting Pet's mother (14–15). While, in one sense, these scenes and the centrality of violence they suggest correspond to centuries-old stereotypes of "hillbilly culture" that take exceptional events and turn them into the essence of a people, Vance's continual deployment of the "violent hillbilly" trope is especially noteworthy for the aforementioned contrast it helps establish between the virtuous hillbilly of the past and the degraded hillbilly of the present. This penchant for violence, Vance notes again and again, was not wielded without cause—hillbillies are, in effect, depicted as noble savages, who deploy violence in service of a moral code (violent acts are almost always tied to some notion of protecting family or honor). Vance's mother, the epitome of the fallen hillbilly, stands out in this regard because her violent acts are *against* her family (mostly J. D.). This indicates how "cultural" decline has taken a supposedly genetic penchant for violence and warped it into something sinister, a violation of a more noble tradition. This notion, of course, requires a nostalgic view of the violence of the past, including the whitewashing of earlier examples of familial violence (like, again, his grandmother setting his "violent drunk" grandfather on fire while he slept [43]) and the redesignation of a malignant social behavior as "traditional culture" grounded in virtue ("that's what Scots-Irish Appalachians do when people mess with your kid," Vance says of the pharmacy-trashing incident [40]). For all his efforts later in the book to point out that these acts of violence are harmful to the children who witness them, *Hillbilly Elegy* remains deeply reverent of these figures and their actions, and, despite his discussion of the psychological concept of "adverse childhood experiences" (ACEs) in the book's penultimate chapter and its prevalence among those in the working class regardless of race,[5] Vance nonetheless treats violence as a culturally endemic tradition.

Vance's insistence on "culture" as the locus of white working-class crisis as opposed to "economics" or even "society" more broadly is, as has been pointed out by many (including Vance himself in the 2018 afterword), reflective of a common conservative tendency that centers the amorphous notion of "culture" in political debates. However, this preference also mirrors the broader tendency in the reflective age to understand political, social, and economic problems under the rubric of culture. As the preceding chapters often illustrate, posthistorical society emphasizes the primacy of culture—especially in the construction of political problems and solutions—marking everything else as downstream or subordinate. Unlike *Ready Player One*, however, this is not (as Travis Linnemann and Corina Medley have argued) an expression of capitalist realism, where the author struggles to imagine solutions beyond the confines of the present, but rather the arguments of a political agent whose ideology is tied to the broader economic system that produced the crisis. Vance's issue, it bears repeating, lies not with capitalism broadly—or even, we can assume given his work as a venture capitalist, with neoliberalism—but with the more specific scaling back of the wages of whiteness that has taken place since the civil rights era. *Hillbilly Elegy* engages in nostalgic melodrama, therefore, as part of an effort to recover the losses incurred by whites resulting from decades of neoliberalism. Vance's goal, and the goal of the party whose ideology he represents, isn't to abandon capitalism entirely, but to reorder it so that whiteness is better protected from its ravages—an essentially fascist project focused on "repair[ing] the infrastructure of the racial state" (Toscano 72). Thus, rather than serving as another example of how the end of history has captured the imagination, *Hillbilly Elegy* instead illuminates the reactionary character of the reflective age, showing how its nostalgic impulses, coupled with the posthistorical narrowing of the horizon of possibility, serves to maintain—and, indeed, strengthen—a fundamentally right-wing status quo.

Hillbilly Elegy, in this way, reveals a tension at the heart of the right's political program: In order to advance its project, the right must depict itself as having incurred losses even as its economic and political vision still largely drives the nation's policies. Its gains, in other words, must be understood as recovery in the face of losses, a return to *something that once was* instead of a continuation or intensification of present trends. This, again, is where melodrama and nostalgia play a crucial role, offering aesthetic forms and emotional appeals that help popularize and/or obscure the logic underpinning the project. Likewise, the deployment of these modes enables the right to better target the cultural sphere, where the left—or at least liberalism—still remains more influential.

The most overt attempts to target culture directly, specifically younger audiences distinct from those who were the primary readers of *Hillbilly Elegy*, can be found in online spaces, where the kind of hyperaestheticized nostalgia typical of the reflective age is regularly deployed in service of right-wing, often openly fascist, racial and gender melodrama. If we understand *Elegy* as the story of how melodrama and nostalgia are deployed to construct the "white working class" whose imagined victimization is the narrative foundation of the right's political aims, this online tendency takes the project a step further by depicting whiteness itself—and social constructs framed as elements thereof, like traditional gender roles and "historical" notions of masculinity—under siege through appeals fashioned for an era of posthistorical alienation and aestheticized nostalgia. Grounded in the same sentiments of loss and restoration, *Elegy* and *Strangers*, then, may be understood as offering mainstream variations on the fascist revanchism found online, as their melodramatic accounts of white suffering support the case for ethnonationalist renewal that many popular right-wing social media accounts (and an increasingly large segment of the right, in general) more openly advocate.

This tendency is best exemplified by the "trad" or "retvrn"[6] movement online, a loose, unofficial collection of social media accounts, podcasts, and blogs lamenting the supposed erasure of Western (read: white) Culture. Though not organizationally unified (as far as has been made public, at least), these accounts are nonetheless united by both their manner of appeals and their broader political aims. They should also not be understood as *discrete from*, but rather fundamentally *embedded within* the broader online presence of the New Right, Alt-Right, Neofascist—or whatever label one prefers[7]—movement, which represents the overwhelming majority of its base and is the primary driver in its spread. Though this emergent online tendency is expressed in a variety of ways, from "Tradwives" on TikTok posting baking videos while discussing the advantages of traditional domesticity and Twitter accounts with Greek statue avatars interrogating the disappearance of textured walls[8] to explicitly racist, xenophobic, misogynistic, or otherwise nakedly fascist diatribes about the Fall of the West, they are nonetheless united by the fundamental notion that the America has lost its way by abandoning the traditions and customs of the past, and that resolution to the ills of society today—whether caused by multiculturalism, cultural Marxism, postmodernity, wokeness, feminism, the Deep State, liberals, Jews, or any combination thereof—can therefore only be found by embracing nostalgia as a political project, by looking backwards and modeling one's life—and society more broadly—on the virtuous lives led by the Great People and Cultures of History. What constitutes a "Great Culture"—the point to which we must retvrn, in other words—may change, as may the primary sentiment underpinning the retvrn—the social ills the turn to the past is meant to counter, in other words. But the melodramatic foundations are, essentially, the same: White culture is under attack as part of a conspiracy to "take things away from you (straight, cisgender, white people)." Taken together, this "movement" tells a powerful story about how the right has weaponized reflective-age nostalgia in their efforts to establish white victimhood and mobilize the resulting resentment in order to "restore" the historical benefits of whiteness and traditional gender norms that, they contend, have been unjustly taken away. The horrors of modernity, and posthistorical decline most specifically, are, in this paradigm, the result of deviation from this natural order—an order whose restoration is authorized by appeals to imagined histories.

While the lost objects may change, and the causes (named or implied) may shift, these complaints usually revolve around the same laments for losses incurred by traditional white culture, and feature conventional narratives of nostalgia and right-wing melodrama that have been merged with the stylistics of contemporary nostalgia that this book has described. However, though not as deeply invested in the same form of hyperaesthetic nostalgia that, as we will see later in this chapter, is particularly notable in the context of this study, the most fulsome, and most influential, account of the philosophy underpinning this tendency can be found in the writing of Costin Alamariu, a Yale political science PhD[9] better known through his online persona Bronze Age Pervert (BAP). To understand the New Right broadly, and the retvrn "movement" specifically, as well as their similarity to, and deviation from, more conventional right-wing politics, a brief look at BAP's work and its influence is necessary.

In the years following the self-publication of his 2018 manifesto *Bronze Age Mindset*, and its subsequent popularization among the "Alt-Right" (a label that, like many similar figures, he disavows), Bronze Age Pervert has garnered considerable media attention even outside of the online right, receiving mention in reporting by *The New York Times* and *The Washington Post* and serving as the subject of articles in widely read publications like *Politico*, *Mother Jones*, and *The Atlantic*. While BAP's writing is predominantly structured around a relatively anodyne claim that modern decline is the result of Western abandonment of Classical virtues—an argument whose logic is not dissimilar to the claims the right has made concerning the abandonment of midcentury traditional values since Reagan's first campaign—his notoriety comes from his less conventional rejection of Enlightenment rationality; his general distaste for Christianity (which is essentially just a rehashing of Nietzsche's critique of Christianity's slave morality); his explicit disdain for democracy; his veneration of the aestheticized Greek male body; and, most of all, the unambiguous endorsement of misogyny and white supremacy that not only accompanies these claims, but is inextricable from the philosophy underpinning them. Unlike many popular right-wing treatises, *Bronze Age Mindset* does not hide its belief that some people (non-whites, women, homosexuals, weak men, and so on) are less than others, and his popularity no doubt stems, at least partially, from this lack of sugarcoating, offering right-wingers the thrill of reading "what we all think but aren't allowed to say." "Suffice it to say," John Ganz writes, "'BAPism' is simply fascism, repackaged and re-marketed."

As a result, BAP has become a rather infamous name on the right, a polarizing figure whose popularity is either a harbinger of doom or a welcome sign of the ascendancy of a new brand of right-wing politics. It is difficult to truly measure his popularity: he boasts 150,000 followers on Twitter, including (at the time of his selection as Trump's vice president) J. D. Vance, though many of them are journalists and those who identify themselves with the left, and, as with many Twitter accounts, it is hard to say how many are bots. Similarly, his book was, at one time, one of the top sellers on Amazon, though it's unclear how many copies were actually sold and to whom; BAP himself also urges his readers to stay in the shadows (though this may be less for the strategic reasons he cites and more a matter of promoting a sense of allure within his acolytes—this book is too dangerous for people to know you're reading it!—while also covering for its relative obscurity outside of its immediate readership). The media attention BAP has received can largely be traced to his reported popularity among those in the orbit of the Trump administration, most notably Michael Anton, who was one of the president's national security officials and the author of a review of *Bronze Age Mindset* published by the conservative *Claremont Review of Books*; Darren Beattie, an aide who was fired for speaking at a white nationalist conference; and Curtis Yarvin (aka Mencius Moldbug), the "neo-monarchist" who gave first Anton a copy of *BAM*, and who was reportedly an informal advisor to former Trump strategist Steve Bannon (Gray). According to an interview with a former Ron DeSantis staffer in *The New York Times Magazine*, "every junior staffer in the Trump administration read *Bronze Age Mindset*" (Zerofsky). While there is reason to remain skeptical about how far his reach actually is, BAP's work is still broadly reflective of key emergent tendencies in right-wing political melodrama, and, whether their popularity can be traced to him or he is simply giving voice to an extant formation (or, most likely, some combination thereof), his work provides a useful platform for understanding them.

As many critics have noted, *Bronze Age Mindset* is difficult to analyze, not least because of its author's evasive tactics, which include ungrammatical sentence structures, misspelled words, and other hallmarks of internet lingo that, based on his other work (including a successfully defended dissertation about Nietzsche and Plato advised by renowned political philosopher Steven Smith), are a matter of affect rather than a testament to a lack of proficiency in English,[10] as well as a host of explicitly racist, misogynist, and homophobic diatribes. Though the book identifies itself as an "exhortation" (2) and a "manifesto" (150), BAP claimed, in a response to Anton's aforementioned *Claremont* review, that "it is a book written primarily for fun and entertainment: it's not a philosophical treatise, and it's not a political manifesto. I wrote it in a mood of revelry and laughter. . . . The media adopts humorlessness as a strategy and pretends to see policy proposals when we engage in fun and trolling—you have doubtless seen this many times when they misrepresent Trump's humor. They distort what is primarily a movement of irreverence and satire, and if there's anything I wish to add to Anton's review of my book proper, it is this: it is a book of laughter." Thus, as Nathan J. Robinson puts it, "To articulate Alamariu's philosophy is not easy, because he does the classic alt-right thing of 'maybe I'm a fascist or maybe it's just a joke, and if you earnestly treat it as fascist I'll laugh at you for not getting the humor.'" This posturing, as Graeme Wood has shown, serves a couple of important functions: "A BAPist can take pleasure in having entered an exclusive cognitive club. One of his supporters wrote to me that BAP's character was layered with irony, and that the ability to see the truth in BAP, and separate it from the hilarious megalomania, is a kind of Straussian test, to determine who can read and think, and who is so offended by the racism, misogyny, and anti-Semitism that he is incapacitated and unable to focus on anything else, even to criticize it." In other words, like his insistence on his readers remaining secret, BAP's style serves to create a feeling of in-group affiliation and, indeed, a sense of superiority that is crucial to the text's broader project. Likewise, the book's strategy seems geared toward creating an interpretive minefield, a way of simultaneously sorting out "unworthy" interlocutors who cannot see past its explicit misdeeds and leading those who do persist in reading it down a series of paths resulting in the wasted effort of uncovering and countering claims that were either "a joke" or whose conclusions were already obvious (what use is close reading for evidence of racism in a book written by an author who would not refute the label to begin with?). The result is often analysis that critiques BAP's overt heresies in lieu of a deeper refutation of his philosophy, which he and his readers seem to count as a win: "There is, among BAP's fans, perverse pleasure in watching their critics passionately denounce their hero, to no discernible effect" (Wood). For this reason, it is not particularly useful to analyze passages in great detail—such efforts offer little interpretive insight—and, arguably, *Bronze Age Mindset*'s rather shallow depths have already been sufficiently plumbed by other critics.[11] Instead, for the purposes of this chapter, the book is better understood in broad strokes, through reference to ideas that recur throughout its many chapters as well as in its author's later, more straightforward writing, which together acquire significance not because BAP wrote them, but because they express ideas that proliferate within the movement he represents. In other words, within the larger story of right-wing nostalgic melodrama that this chapter tracks, Bronze Age Pervert justifies specific attention because his writing provides philosophical justification for emergent revanchist tendencies online. The overwhelming majority of the explicit "retvrn" content found on social media, in other words, encodes and implies but doesn't often explicitly state the political aims that, BAP illustrates, are actually central to the project. A look at this ecosystem, with BAP serving as a central node, illuminates a few key themes that form the bedrock of the movement.

Above all else, the most important insight *Bronze Age Mindset* provides for this study is that, just as I have argued throughout this chapter regarding contemporary right-wing politics more broadly, nostalgia and melodrama are also central to the New Right's overt appeals and, indeed, its entire project. Thus, though there are notable distinctions between the philosophies of this younger, predominantly online sect and its establishment counterpart, the chasm separating them is not as wide as it may initially appear—nor as wide as many on the right pretend—and they are fundamentally united by this melodramatic posturing and a program organized around the nostalgic reestablishment of supposedly lost privileges. It is in part due to this fundamental compatibility that otherwise discrete segments of the right, from 4Chan to the Heritage Foundation, have rather seamlessly coalesced behind Trump's candidacy and the Make America Great Again platform. Nonetheless, this newer movement often positions itself in contrast to the conventional Republican party platform, and there are important divergences in their rhetoric. Therefore, despite the fundamental similarities, it is worth considering some of the differences between the two camps as a way of identifying what *is* new about the New Right, and how this novelty shapes their use of nostalgia and melodrama as well as their response to the conditions of the reflective age.

The most obvious point of divergence is how the two camps position themselves in relation to the white supremacy inherent in their projects. Where the narratives found in *Strangers in Their Own Land* and *Hillbilly Elegy* work to disavow racism even as they promote white supremacy and traffic in racist frameworks, *Bronze Age Mindset* and its ilk largely drop this pretense. Instead of working to convince the public that racism plays no role in its melodrama of white victimization and calls for nostalgic returns to times characterized by white supremacy and minority subjugation, as the right has largely done for years, the New Right allows its racist and white supremacist exigence to remain visible. Instead of working to occlude its white supremacy, in other words, the New Right prefers to justify it forthrightly, framed as a rational response to the conditions of modernity. *Bronze Age Mindset*, for instance, narrates a fascist, explicitly antidemocratic vision of a world in which power has been seized by the weak (Jews, liberals and leftists, women, people of color, etc.) in an effort to suppress the powerful: "The world [according to BAP]," as Murtaza Hussain summarizes, "is sunk in a form of decentralised tyranny, ruled over by 'bugmen' . . . as well as matriarchal tyrants empowered by feminism and democracy. Beauty has been effaced from human society and the natural world is being despoiled. The hypocritical supporter of liberalism, a physical weakling with a bad conscience, 'pretends to be motivated by compassion, but is instead motivated by a titanic hatred of the well-turned out and beautiful.'" Though *BAM* does not name white supremacy itself as its goal, the construction of the crisis to which the New Right responds is deeply founded in the belief—it is not so much that whites *ought* to be seen as superior, it's that History tells us it is true, and the crisis of modernity coinciding with the era of civil rights and "wokeness" confirms the same conclusion. The centrality of white melodrama within the New Right's project is especially evident in BAP's response to Anton's *Claremont* review, where he echoes the "white genocide" claims that have begun to proliferate on the right, which takes the familiar claims of white victimization found in *Strangers* and *Elegy* to its logical end: "The anti-male and anti-White rhetoric of the new left is extreme. The racial attacks on whites in particular approaches exterminationist propaganda seen only in, e.g., the Hutu against the Tutsi in

1990's Rwanda," he explains. "The left has been saying exactly what they plan to do for decades. They want to destroy your country, instill a death wish in the white population, set majorities against market-dominant minorities, atomize everyone." Here and elsewhere in his writing, BAP treats racial domination and white supremacy not as a political goal in and of itself, but as a natural fact whose Truth, and modernity's rejection thereof, animate this vision of a fallen world. In this extension of the rhetoric of white victimization, the New Right offers a framework for understanding the same supposedly antiwhite policies that the conventional right has been lamenting for years without offering a compelling, coherent explanation of its cause. Hochschild's deep story in *Strangers*, for instance, does not provide a cogent explanation for why whites are being cut in line. It gestures toward a programmatic justification—feminism, affirmative action, and other vague gestures toward "equality"—but it does not explain the rationale underpinning the policy. The result is a host of people who feel as though they have been victimized without a compelling explanation for why. The New Right offers an explanation, insisting that whites are not simply being disenfranchised by a political elite seeking to "level the playing field" or even take power for itself, but, echoing Nazi propaganda, that these changes are all part of a broader conspiracy in which malignant forces are actually seeking to erase whites from existence. White victimization is not a by-product, in other words, it is the goal: Things have not simply been lost, "they" took them away from you—and they are planning to take more.

If we understand *Hillbilly Elegy* and *Strangers in Their Own Land* as expressions of a right-wing desire to convince people that the claims of victimization made by the right are legitimate, *Bronze Age Mindset* here presents another point of divergence. The New Right is largely a movement about directing the energies of those who are already broadly on the right, or at least sympathetic to its resentments, toward a specific framework for understanding the world and the feelings it generates. It is not, in other words, an effort to convince outsiders or convert nonbelievers—"I hardly have anything to say to most who aren't like me, still less do I care about convincing," BAP explains in the opening paragraph of *Bronze Age Mindset* (2)—it is about legitimizing the beliefs of those who already identify as victims, saying that they not only *are* victims, but actually the targets of a deep conspiracy seeking to keep at bay their natural greatness. It lends credence, in other words, to more conventional right-wing resentments; provides a compelling, flatteringly pseudointellectual, and heroic explanation for those resentments; and urges readers to overcome the tyrannies that have led to their suffering by adopting its principles.

There is also a palpable hypermasculine appeal to this framing, and *BAM* serves as a libidinal exhortation calling its (presumed-to-be male) readers to rehabilitate "traditional" masculine virtue, laden with appeals to vigor, strength, and the aestheticized beauty of the ideal male form found in Classical art and, especially, Greek statuary. This is significant for two reasons. First, it highlights another distinction with conventional right-wing thought: *BAM* is a project oriented around explicit claims of male supremacy and misogyny, whereas the establishment right opts for "traditional gender roles" as the framing for its project—suggesting not that women are inherently lesser, just inherently *different* and therefore suited to certain tasks in society and unsuited to others. BAP, on the other hand, argues that women actually *are* lesser beings, and that the feminist push for women's liberation and gender equality has caused much of the crisis we face today by thrusting them into roles that they are not only ill equipped for, but psychogenetically hostile to. Vague notions of Classical prosperity, nostalgically rendered as a promasculine, structurally patriarchal paradise, become evidence of the cause of the present's condition.

Second, the New Right's call for a form of masculinity defined by its capacity for violence, coupled with the framing of sociopolitical change as theft (they *took* this from you), takes the conventional depiction of white victimization a step further by urging that its acknowledgment be followed by reaction (only the weak stand idly by, and you, dear reader, are not weak, are you?). Thus, rather than settling for claims of victimization and appeals to political and economic reform, the New Right reconfigures right-wing melodramatic revanchist rhetoric as an active, violent existential struggle. As the story shifts from "whites are unfairly disadvantaged" to "there is a global conspiracy to prevent white people from taking their rightful place as the rulers of society," white supremacist nostalgia acquires a kind of historically authorized moral legitimacy, and a near-religious call to restore natural order emerges. Retvrning is not just a matter of racial justice—though that is central to the project's appeal—but a mythical effort to restore order to a world of chaos.

BAP's restorative vision relies on a nostalgic account of history for support, gesturing toward a supposedly deeper truth about how the world used to work in order to justify its claims of loss. The establishment right has, of course, long relied on nostalgic visions of the recent past (Reagan's appeals to the utopia of the 1950s, for instance), which depicts it as free from the ills of the present, in order to promote the idea that social progress has caused the problems of the present, and that a return to those times will promote a better society for all. In contrast, the "retvrn" movement, as BAP articulates it, depicts the present as a perversion of this deeper historical reality, which positions the past as not merely a time of prosperity, but a time when human flourishing was directly tied to the establishment of specific (though largely imagined) racial and gender paradigms. Most notably, in BAP's philosophy, "the present" is constructed to include the entire twentieth century and much of life before it. He does not locate the prelapsarian Eden in the Reaganesque nostalgic '50s, instead preferring a much earlier point of divergence. Rejecting naturalist, pastoral appeals to rural premodern communal life, BAP argues that "life appears at its peak not in the grass hut village ruled by nutso mammies, but in the military state. In Archaic Greece, in Renaissance Italy and in the vast expanse of the heroic Old Stone Age, at the middle of the Bronze Age of high chariotry, lived men of power and magnificence in great numbers" (87). As Wood summarizes,

> The "great ugliness" is the liberal bureaucratic state. Democracy, he writes, destroys "personal freedom and initiative" by elevating an unworthy caste of subhuman creatures he calls "bugmen," who flourish only under these debased conditions, like roaches in a pit latrine. On his podcast, BAP praises the philosopher James Burnham, who wrote that the heroic age of capitalism had passed, and that a "managerial revolution" had elevated to power bean counters and bureaucrats . . . over noble intellects and creators. Any person of talent or intelligence is ground down by this system, by "life under the thumb of the empowered old matriarchs and the conceptual dildoes they use to clobber the heads of young men." In response to these conditions, BAP tells his reader that "Above all you must reach for the great aim, physical and military independence. Only the warrior is a free man. The only right government is military government, and every other form is both hypocritical and destructive of true freedom."

BAPs melodramatic victims, therefore, do not strive for justice founded in the reestablishment of a supposedly lost equality; they're fighting for justice founded in a natural order defined by *in*equality—a process that is notably not tied to the reorganization of present systems (though that may be the result, particularly if this logic only results in the election of Republican politicians who, for all their radical posturing, remain loath to overthrow capitalism), but to the wholesale contravention of the structural status quo. This distinction marks a shift in the rhetoric of political agency on the right: For the New Right "retvrn" crowd, the project is the reconstruction of a deeper tradition that transcends the political inventions of the modern world—indeed, in many cases, abandoning the logic and systems that characterize modernity is the goal—instead of the Republican establishment's "democratic equality" under capitalism that can be enacted through electoral politics. This tendency is best understood as a reflection of the growing sense, on both the right and the left, that liberal democratic capitalism is more central to the problems faced by American society today than conventional political discourse previously allowed, and that progress (even if founded in regression, as the right typically frames it) may involve more than just reforms—including the establishment of something entirely different. BAP, in this sense, is a distinctly posthistorical phenomenon, a figure whose ideology is positioned in direct response to the conditions outlined throughout this book.

If we strip away some of its hyperbole and the specific attachment to antiquity as a real point of return, and read instead for the points of emphasis that underpin these ideas, *Bronze Age Mindset* lays bare the philosophy that guides much of the "retvrn" sentiment online. It revolves around a few central ideas: naturally ordained inegalitarianism, antiwhite and antimasculine conspiracy as the cause of the crises of modernity, and a notion of progress founded in restoration of the Truths of the past. We should take BAP seriously when he says that his book is not a policy proposal—there is little evidence that he is seriously advocating for the reestablishment of the Greek military state (which he surely realizes never actually existed as he describes it anyway). *Bronze Age Mindset* is, rather, an attempt to produce a philosophical ideal that invigorates its readers, gives structure and coherence to their resentments, and creates attachments to beliefs that, together, can be used to support the right's broader revanchist aims.

This effort is bolstered by "retvrn" content online, composed largely of videos or images of things imbued with a sense of pastness—British Pathé footage of London in the 1930s, a painting of a white family's homestead, a photograph of children on bikes in the suburbs—usually captioned with commentary asking an open question about its disappearance ("How did this happen?") or explicitly identifying its current absence as theft ("This is what they took from you").[12] Though they often appear inoffensive, or even outright absurd, these posts, which proliferate in right-wing circles, are founded in the same essential New Right nostalgic melodrama BAP gives voice to, connecting resentments in the present, including attachments to nostalgic objects, to the broader abandonment of the ways of the past. In true reflective-age fashion, there is a notable subtendency within this push whereby posts identify the past with explicitly aesthetic objects like art and architecture, linking shifts in style and taste to cultural decay. These posts commonly feature a side-by-side comparison of a beautiful "past" object and an ugly "contemporary" one, like Michelangelo's *Creation of Adam* and Jackson Pollock's *Convergence*.[13] In essence, these nostalgic attachments are not unlike those found in works like *Stranger Things* and *Ready Player One*: Styles and artifacts, divorced from the historical realities in which they were initially embedded, form the basis of the appeal. As with *Bronze Age Mindset*, the desire here is not to truly *retvrn* to the periods in question—which, in the case of a post about Gothic castles, for instance, would also entail the loss of a host of modern conveniences like medicine, industrial food production, and the internet that these individuals rely on—but to produce nostalgic aesthetic attachments that are inextricably tied to racial and gender melodrama: The capitalist prioritization of strip malls over Renaissance churches is to be understood not merely as an effect of the system, but as part of a plot to undo European cultural and racial superiority, to take away the social hegemony that was once theirs. Configured this way, these "losses" can only then be countered by a hard right turn away from the liberal pluralism and "race-blindness" of neoliberalism that produced them. In this light, the turn to nostalgia for lost aesthetics that we see in much of this "movement" serves as a way to connect popular reflective-age tendencies to right-wing political aims. It takes the reflective age's attachments to empty style and fills those attachments with meaning—"Don't you think these old churches are beautiful? Isn't it a shame modern society abandoned the principles that led to their creation? Wouldn't it be nice to go back to a time when beauty was valued?" This, in essence, is the same appeal found in *Bronze Age Mindset*'s complaints about the modern rejection of Classical aesthetics, as both tie stylistic shifts to sociopolitical conspiracy—changes didn't just happen, they were *made* to happen for the purpose of erasing the creations that white civilization holds dear. Aesthetic ugliness exists in this context to demoralize you both through the depression you feel at its drab appearance and through its contrast with the Beauty that Was Once Yours But No Longer Is.

In these appeals, the New Right poses a problem for the establishment: It is difficult to lament these aesthetic losses on these terms and not see capitalism itself, with its abandonment of traditional virtue and Classical beauty in favor of the financial bottom line, as a major factor in their disappearance. Even if the root cause is understood as a genocidal global conspiracy, capitalism nonetheless appears as a mechanism for enacting it. This reflects a growing schism in the Republican party, which still largely remains captured by the principles of "cultural" conservatism within a capitalist economy: As *Hillbilly Elegy* illustrates, much of the right's current project seeks a reordering of capitalism, and a reinvestment in the logic of racial capitalism, rather than its abandonment—but it is now dealing with a New Right movement that is often characterized by its lack of reverence for, if not outright hostility to, capitalism itself. In this way, Bronze Age Pervert and the New Right represent a threatening rejection of conservative orthodoxies, even as they rely on the same nostalgic and melodramatic appeals.

This schism is also reflected within the world of "retvrn" posting, where the same nostalgic appeals and melodramatic framing of the passage of time as "theft" are sometimes applied to more recent, decidedly non-Classical objects like video games and even the decor of fast food chains—like one @Culture_Crit post that features an image of a vibrant red 1960s McDonald's alongside a contemporary gray one captioned, "Why did we allow this?"—in an apparent bid to redirect nostalgic energies of the online New Right to more recent, explicitly capitalist pasts. Another post, from @LindyTasteful, includes a 1980s or early-1990s Pizza Hut training video with a caption that reads, "Imagine being a boomer growing up. Every massive chain restaurant was new and exciting, instead of depressing. You could go to Pizza Hut and celebrate the dream of capitalism with your community." The function of these posts is not the rejection of the New Right's foundation in nostalgia or melodrama, but to associate these tendencies with aesthetic fixations that are more in line with conventional conservative aims than BAP's anticapitalist rhetoric.[14]

The content of one Twitter account, @wokal_distance, is especially notable in this regard. In 2022, the account (which, as of May 2025, boasts over

150,000 followers) gained notoriety after it began posting a series of digital art images depicting conventionally nostalgic moments from the '80s and '90s—like a pair of kids playing Mario Kart in front of a wall of classic video game posters or a half-eaten plate of spaghetti flanked by Pokémon cards, Tamagotchi, green army men, and a Game Boy Color—accompanied by somewhat subtler appeals to right-wing grievances. In one series of posts, the account laments the collapse of the modern world by repeating the evocative phrase "The world you were raised to survive in no longer exists." In some cases, this phrase is deployed alongside conventionally nostalgic images—one such post, for example, adds the caption "We can't ever go back but we can go through the postmodern world and on the other side create a world where Nostalgia dissipates as we find ourselves in a world built from the memories of . . . Home" along with an image of a young boy marveling at the shelves of a Toys "R" Us—but other times the phrase is bizarrely superimposed over an image of a young blonde girl[15] in a park with the World Trade Center Towers standing prominently in the background. Finally, as if to make the project's procapitalist goals as clear as possible, one post shows a Christmas morning scene with a child triumphantly holding a Nintendo 64 box above his head, simply captioned, "This is not consumerism." Eschewing BAP's nostalgia for the Greek military state and the Reaganite obsession with the 1950s, and in spite of its stated animus toward postmodernity, this is, superficially at least, nostalgia for Reagan-, Bush-, and even Clinton-era postmodern neoliberalism. Unlike their traditionalist cousins, though, the nostalgic longing expressed in these posts is tied less explicitly to prior social conditions and more toward childhood and an attachment to products—in other words, the objects of nostalgia on display here are the same as those found throughout the previous chapters of this book, framed by right-wing melodramatic accounts of their disappearance.

The example of @wokal_distance is especially important because of its proximity to the Republican party establishment. The account, as Miles Klee reported in 2022 in *Rolling Stone*, is run by Michael Young, "a visiting fellow at the Center for Renewing America, a conservative think tank that exists to combat supposed threats to the nation like vaccine mandates and Critical Race Theory." "Apart from his work with CRA," Klee continues, "Young has written for right-wing publications like *The Federalist* and co-authored an anti-LGBTQ pamphlet titled *A Parent's Guide to Radical Gender Theory* with conservative agitator Christopher Rufo."[16] Young's bio on the CRA website describes him as "a leading writer and researcher focused on culture, political philosophy, and the rise of postmodernism . . . [whose work has] been key in shaping the debate on the pushback against cultural Marxism, as well as postmodernism, education, and Critical Social Justice." Although it is obviously ironic for a writer who otherwise rails against the evils of postmodernity to wax nostalgic about a vision of childhood that is firmly rooted in the period, this apparent paradox is actually an illuminating reflection of the writer's attempts to resolve a fundamental contradiction within right-wing nostalgic appeals: The easiest target for nostalgia is childhood experience, but the right's politics are increasingly framed in opposition to the same period in which these experiences, for the young adults they target online, took place. Thus, they must simultaneously depict the '90s as a nostalgic Eden founded in memories of childhood innocence *and* as a time of great evil based on its "postmodern" rejection of the tenets of cultural conservatism. Like *Stranger Things*, the past must be seen as both fallen and utopic, which requires isolating the positive, often heavily mediated elements, while ignoring, reconfiguring, or railing against everything else. The abandonment of culturally conservative lodestars like traditional family life, in other words, is to be understood as *bad*, but sitting in your room all day playing video games is *good*. Moreover, the right must also invest in the notion that these things have disappeared, marking those who enjoyed them as victims of social change. The reality, of course, is that wokeness, cultural Marxism, feminism, and all of the other boogeymen the right usually identifies have not prevented anyone from playing video games and buying toys. Children would, in fact, still shop at Toys "R" Us had private equity firms—including Mitt Romney's Bain Capital—not purchased the company in a leveraged buyout and subsequently forced it to declare bankruptcy. The primary shifts that have occurred with regard to the images reflected in @wokal_distance's posts actually resulted more from aging and changing cultural tastes than a broader social decline or cultural conspiracy. This project, however, works to redirect the kind of nostalgic attachments, and the desperation—even resentment—that we see expressed in works like *Ready Player One* as a response to their losses, toward right-wing explanations. Thus, in light of his deep institutional affiliation—unlike Alamariu, for instance, there is nothing fringe about Young's status within the conservative political establishment—and this obvious rhetorical intent, @wokal_distance's posts read less like the genuine yearning of a '90s kid nostalgiac they are positioned as, and more like a kind of conservative outreach program. In other words, these posts are a pointed effort to capture millennial and Gen-Z nostalgia within the context of conventional right-wing politics, while also redirecting the young men who predominantly make up the New Right toward Home and away from Greek statues—that is, towards a more comfortable, capitalist past instead of a comparatively more radical anticapitalist one (even as both are founded in mediated fantasy to begin with).

If, as I have argued throughout this book, we understand contemporary nostalgia in part as an attachment to an imagined, mediated loss, there is one final phenomenon in the story of right-wing nostalgic melodrama that deserves mention. The recent popularization of GenAI software, especially image generators, has been something of a boon for the online right, allowing the rapid creation of imagery that removes the hindrances of talent and time. Propaganda, in other words, no longer requires the same amount of effort, nor, especially, does it require any correspondence to reality—if one can imagine it, an AI image can be made to represent it. In one sense, this decoupling from reality has been possible for much of the past couple of decades with the advent of Photoshop and other digital art tools. The relative speed of AI processes, however, changes the situation considerably, allowing more people the ability to produce more images and thereby enabling a greater volume overall. This has resulted in a proliferation of images depicting present or near-future conditions that correspond to right-wing melodramas of white victimhood. One (now-deleted) image, for instance, posted on Twitter by @EuropeInvasionn [*sic*], captioned "Your future child returning from school," showed a crying blonde girl in a Union Jack T-shirt standing in the middle of a bus surrounded by laughing women in hijabs. As of July 2024, the post showed fifty million views and 120,000 likes. It almost goes without saying, but images like this are notable because they attempt to represent a reality that does not exist: The use of AI is necessary, in fact, because there is no way to visually represent these claims using real images. Unsurprisingly, this technology has also been deployed to produce images of "history" that never existed in order to play into the right's nostalgic fixations. These images depict simulacra of the past in an effort to make it seem as though something has been lost, which, ironically, cannot be represented neatly in real images. As this chapter attests, the aim of the right is to depict a group (typically white people or some specific subset thereof) as having suffered the most significant losses at the hands of modernity, neoliberalism, and so forth. In this way, AI and reflective-age nostalgia share a fundamental essence: Each is an act of creation based in loose signifiers—blonde hair, laughing immigrants, and white misery, or synthesizers, suburban bicycles, and Pokémon cards—that coalesce to produce something that is truly novel despite being framed as a reflection of a pervasive reality.

In light of this, I would like to close this chapter by describing one final image, which was posted in December 2023 by a Twitter account named @sovereignbrah. The post, which has since been deleted, features a quote from C. S. Lewis: "The homemaker has the ultimate career. All other careers exist for one purpose only—and that is to support the ultimate career." Below the quote is an AI-generated image of a rural homestead, featuring a shimmering stream, a pack of elk, and the exterior of a log cabin, all framed before a grand, mountainous backdrop. In the foreground stands a tall, thin, large-breasted blonde woman with eleven toes holding a baby while wearing a form-fitting sheer lace nightgown. The baby is held tightly to the woman's chest like it is breastfeeding, though there is an unidentifiable white object—it does not have the dimensions of a conventional bottle—in her hand from which the baby is apparently suckling. In a woven basket to her right is a pile of deformed woodland critters—possibly bunnies or beavers or groundhogs, but not clearly identifiable as any. To her left is a man in overalls with square, blocky hands, sitting on a stump at a table with an unrecognizable pile of white before him. The window of the cabin behind her does not reveal its interior, as one might expect; instead, it shows an impossible continuation of the natural backdrop. The home, in other words, is nothing more than a facade.

In the distance flies what appears to be a pterodactyl.

Conclusion

NOSTALGIA *AFTER* THE END OF HISTORY?

The end of history may be ending.

Though at times throughout this book I have argued to the contrary—that, despite the emergence of a variety of challenges to the neoliberal, posthistorical status quo, we still remain firmly within its grasp—it is worth closing this study by remarking more fully on the growing belief that we are entering, or else have already entered, a new era, and to consider the ramifications of the end of the end of history as well as the role nostalgia may play, or has played, in this shift.

Contrary to Fukuyama's diagnosis of the End of History, which frames the post–Cold War liberal democratic consensus as the emergence of a final ordering of human society—surpassable only by the establishment and widespread adoption of a wholly different political system—this book understands the end of history more narrowly, as the social and political conditions that developed alongside the liberal democratic neoliberal consensus in the late twentieth century. The end of history, in this conception of the term, is defined less by the *literal* finality Fukuyama supposes, and more by the consequences of its political pursuit. If, in this light, a major economic or political shift takes hold, then this notion of the end of history would likely wither away.

Arguments that we are in the midst of such a shift have, in recent years, begun to circulate widely. These claims take many forms: Adam Tooze highlights the destabilizing effects of "polycrisis"; Wendy Brown locates us "in the ruins of neoliberalism;" Anna Kornbluh describes the cultural style of "too late capitalism;" Gary Gerstle narrates "the rise and fall of the neoliberal order;" Alex Hochuli, George Hoare, and Philip Cunliffe proclaim "the end of the end of history" and the rise of "anti-politics;" political scientists, sociologists, and historians revive debates about "liberalism in crisis" and "the interregnum"; articles in *The New Yorker*, *The Nation*, *The Atlantic*, *The New York Times*, and *The Washington Post* (among many more) develop these arguments for popular audiences; and Fukuyama himself is compelled to appear every few months to reassure everyone that, despite any evidence to the contrary, whatever new, potentially world-shaping event taking place (Brexit, Trump, Covid, Ukraine, etc.) does *not* mean the end of history is over. The evidence for these claims varies as widely as the diagnoses themselves, ranging from social, (geo)political, and economic trends to cultural and aesthetic ones. What remains consistent, however, is the sense that the structures and tendencies that have characterized much of the twenty-first century are under significant strain. If the collapse has not already taken place, these writers seem to agree, the stress will prove too much for the system to bear. For many, then, the end of the end is nigh—a sentiment seemingly validated by Trump's reelection in 2024 and the slew of executive orders aimed at dismantling the nation's regulatory infrastructure that he issued shortly after taking office.

If, for the sake of argument, we grant that something like the end of the end is taking place, then the texts, narratives, and tendencies described in this book mark not just the nadir of posthistorical American culture, but also the moments just before its collapse. The end of history, in this context, entails more than just a politics founded in stasis and an attachment to formulas of the past that no longer work; it also signifies, more broadly, an attachment to a liberal fantasy of consensus whose foundational inflexibility—even in the face of crisis—led to its own demise.

Recent developments, particularly the ascendancy of the populist right, the conservative capture of the judicial branch, and Trump's reelection, highlight this frailty within the end of history's fundamental premises: In addition to suggesting a teleological end, the end of history also relies on a notion of universality—that, for better or worse, there is broad popular and political agreement about the shape of history—that was perhaps never the case to begin with (see, for instance, the contrast between Fukuyama's Hegel-inflected teleology and the apocalyptic teleology of evangelicals, which posit, and work toward, radically different—if not diametrically oppositional—visions of *the end*). What was commonly depicted, in the 1990s and the first decade of the 2000s especially, as a general consensus among liberals and conservatives about the core principles of Western liberal democracy and its historical contours often obscured a deeper, growing discontent on the American right that went beyond mere policy disagreement. Initially positioned as fringe populism within the Republican Party, the political projects that eventually coalesced into movements like the Tea Party and MAGA ultimately became its center. In part spurred on by the decline and alienation produced by neoliberal politics, which provided the impetus for an increasingly coherent political project, these "fringe" movements worked tirelessly to seize institutional power while their liberal counterparts, still gripped by the posthistorical end of politics, outsourced much of theirs to the private sector and pursued neoliberal policy solutions organized around corporate appeasement.[1] Thus, it appears that the same circumstances and beliefs that gave rise to nostalgia at the end of history, particularly the liberal embrace of a politics of reactive crisis management, have also produced the institutional vacuum upon which the right has seized (a seizure that, as chapter 4 shows, is founded in nostalgic appeals). After slowly building organizational and structural power over several decades, this antineoliberal[2] right is exercising its power at the state, judicial, and federal level at a time when many of its opponents seem more invested in maintaining a rarely functional notion of bipartisanship than in political countermaneuvers that might upset the already dwindling status quo. Thus, in a somewhat ironic turn, while Fukuyama's End of History began as neoconservative triumphalism, its remaining proponents now reside almost exclusively on the other side of the aisle. American liberal politicians, it often appears, are gripped by nostalgia for an order that may be in the process of disappearing. In an ironic twist, this very fidelity to a false sense of closure has, perhaps more than anything else, produced the conditions that may lead to the end of the end.

As the chapters in this book attest, this conflict is particularly evident in discourse surrounding the period's pseudoapocalyptic teleology. *Ready Player One*, *Stranger Things*, and *Twin Peaks: The Return* each deal, in one way or another, with the loss of futurity endemic to the end of history and, in doing so, showcase the continual failures of mainstream liberal responses to it: *Ready Player One* simply invokes this crisis only to shrug at it, and hope that someone, somewhere, will conceive of a magical technocratic solution, while *Ready Player Two* attempts to address inequality through canonical representation; *Stranger Things* hides its concerns about the future behind metaphor and trope, seemingly fearful of direct confrontation and resolution; and in *The Return*, we see the failed pursuit of these metaphysical solutions to material problems, resulting only in a pattern of rearticulation where the same structural issues persist, only to be framed in a new way. In each of these works, the problems of the end of history are met with an inability even to imagine coherent alternatives, much less solutions. Meanwhile, the right is actively working to stave off (their conception of) the end—or, at least, to be the ones piloting the ship into oblivion, ensuring that their enemies are the first ones cast off.

The works discussed in chapters 1, 2, and 3, therefore, not only illuminate the relationship between nostalgia and the end of history; they also reflect the conditions that may lead to its downfall. In reproducing the posthistorical ambivalence that has enabled the right's ascendancy, these texts highlight the fundamental asymmetry between liberal and right-wing approaches to the various ends wrought by the end of history. The emphasis on aesthetics and other metaphysical responses to the material conditions of the end of history found in both the liberal politics and media of the period provide an especially stark contrast with a right wing that is laser-focused on enacting tangible legislative, executive, and judicial solutions: *Ready Player One* and *Stranger Things* make the '80s cool again while the conservative Supreme Court nullifies *Roe v. Wade* in an effort to reestablish the social conditions of mid-century America. Nostalgia, in this light, appears not just as a response to the conditions of the end of history but also serves as an active force in both its maintenance and its possible dissolution.

The nostalgic past, in other words, has become something of a battleground in the fight over the shape of the present and the future. It is sometimes conventional to conclude books like this one with a turn toward utopian possibility or, at least, a gesture toward works that present radical alternatives to the problems described therein. This is especially common in scholarship that takes a critical position on nostalgia and its role in society today, as writers attempt to provide a road map for the concept's rehabilitation. Often, these works seek to illustrate how we can recapture nostalgia's radical potential. Summarizing this view, Michael Pickering and Emily Keightley have argued that scholars who treat nostalgia solely as an object of cultural critique ignore the ways in which it can produce positive contributions to historical imagination, suggesting instead that "we should perhaps reconfigure [nostalgia] in terms of a distinction between the desire to return to an earlier state or idealized past, and the desire not to return but to recognize aspects of the past as the basis for renewal and satisfaction in the future. Nostalgia can then be seen as not only a search for ontological security in the past but also as a means of taking one's bearings for the road ahead in the uncertainties of the present" (921). Here, nostalgia functions not solely as uncritical yearning, but also as a potential way of interacting with history in the move toward positive social change. Grafton Tanner also echoes these perspectives in the conclusion of *The Hours Have Lost Their Clock*, writing that "the past is teeming with lost realities, some of which may be helpful in working towards a present that can 'breed futures,' as Audre Lorde wrote. . . . If we're already looking back, we owe it to the future to scan beyond the horizon, to search the remote regions of the past where the visionaries huddled in the margins, whispering dreams of a better world, drawing plans to make it happen. Deep in those hidden spaces is where you'll find the future" (251). Tanner, in other words, goes a step further than Pickering and Keightley, urging the left to enter more forcefully into the nostalgia battleground by redirecting extant sentiments toward sites of radical potential that lay dormant in the past. Setting aside the immediate question of how this proposal could move from abstraction to practice in the current hypermediated cultural climate—making leftist TV reboots? vaporwave remixes of "Which Side Are You On?"—what is notable in these critical approaches is the degree to which this line of thinking relies on accepting "nostalgia" as a useful frame for reviving historical thinking and promoting a renewed investment in the future. In these perspectives, nostalgia itself becomes something of a utopian object.

This logic, however, seems tenuous. For one, this notion—that the lack the nostalgiac finds wanting in the present but finds in abundance in the past can be used to emphasize the need for renewal in the present and future—is at odds with the fact that, as this book has shown, the nostalgic attachments that proliferate today are often not really about the past at all, but about style, mediation, and consumption. The "lack" at the center of this "nostalgia" is therefore not a particularly fertile site for renewing historical consciousness. Even when the historical past is itself an object of longing—the "life used to be so much simpler" angle—these sentiments today are overwhelmingly premised on an incomplete version of the past at best, or a complete fabrication of it at worst (usually drawn from media rather than memory, in either case). Suggestions that nostalgia provides untapped potential for radical politics also lose sight of the central functions of nostalgia in contemporary culture. Chapters 1 and 2, for instance, both end with discussions of nostalgia as responses to the feelings of impending death and disaster that proliferate at the end of history, providing the illusion of having delayed or overcome the end. Chapter 3 extends this, illustrating how these fantasies of recuperative repetition support comforting notions of progress and stability, which only further bind the nostalgiac to the conditions of the present. As chapter 4 shows, nostalgia is politically powerful because it naturalizes preexisting fantasies and resentments, offering a flattering view of the world and the conditions the nostalgiac finds themselves in. Claims that nostalgia should be reconfigured to promote radical futures misunderstand the role these valences play in nostalgia's popularity today, misrecognizing what makes nostalgia a mobilizing force. This is to say that nostalgia prevails precisely because it provides comfort where history does not. Attempting to redirect nostalgic sentiments toward historical reality, which offers none of the affective pleasures that drive individuals to the nostalgic past in the first place, thus appears like a losing battle. If the nostalgiac flees from the horrors of the present into the paradise of the past, what use to them is a project that centralizes recognition that the past, too, was a site of horrors with only small pockets of utopian thinking "huddled in the margins"? For some, breaking the spell of nostalgia may be radicalizing; for many more, the premise will be rejected outright because it fails to remediate the sentiments that animate the nostalgic impulse in the first place (solidarity and class struggle is unlikely to be a compelling substitute for synthesizers and *Fuller House*).

For these reasons, I find it difficult to recognize any radical potential in nostalgia beyond the abstract. In the current cultural climate, these suggestions appear more as nostalgia for an earlier conception of nostalgia than the foundations of an actionable social or political project. Indeed, unless recovery of nostalgia itself is part of the goal, visions of a better present and future need not be anchored to the past to begin with.

It remains to be seen whether we are on the verge of something new, or if the posthistorical, neoliberal consensus will hold. If the end of history *is* to end, however, and it is to be replaced by something other than the vision put forward by the right, it seems more likely that this will come through an evasion of nostalgic thinking altogether than through successfully defeating the neoliberal center and antineoliberal right on their own ground (where, we must remember, they already have a significant head start).

In other words, to exit the reflective age's hall of mirrors and not find oneself stumbling around in a persistent state of disorientation thereafter, the solution is not to attempt to rearrange the mirrors or add new ones, but to find a way to see beyond the illusions they produce.

Acknowledgments

It's difficult for me to fully express my gratitude to everyone who has helped throughout this process, but I will try.

First, I would like to extend my deepest thanks to my doctoral advisor, Alan Nadel, for the countless hours he spent helping me shape these ideas into a coherent whole. There has been no greater influence on my work, and my growth as a writer and thinker, than Alan, and I am so grateful for his ceaseless commitment and kindness. This book would not exist without him.

I am eternally grateful to Jim Ridolfo: for his feedback, for his mentoring, and for providing the institutional support needed to complete this project. I would also like to thank the other members of my dissertation committee, Carol Mason and Michelle Sizemore, for their enthusiastic contributions, as both readers and teachers, to this work and to my development as a scholar. I feel profoundly fortunate to have found myself in the orbit of these wonderful people.

Huge thank yous to my PhD cohort, Katie McClain, Shannon Branfield, and Jenn Murray: Not only did they read, comment on, and debate draft after draft, but their own work consistently pushed me to better my own. I truly could not have asked for more.

I would also like to express my gratitude to my friends Daniel Floyd and Matt Spencer, who always found time to read drafts and provide both generous and generative feedback—or even just listen to my complaints. It really means so much.

It is not an exaggeration to say that this book would not exist without the love and support of my mother, my grandmother, and my late father. I am who I am because of you, and my successes are yours.

I would like to thank my daughter Zoe, who cannot read this yet but will be able to someday, for bringing so much happiness into my life. I hope this makes you proud one day.

Lastly, I want to thank my wife, Cheyenne, for everything: for her robust and relentless belief in my abilities, for reading revision after revision (sometimes of the same sentence), for her unwavering support even in the most challenging times, for her patience, and for everything else that I can't express in words.

An earlier version of chapter 2 was previously published as "*Stranger Things*, Nostalgia, and Aesthetics." *Journal of Film and Video*, vol. 74, no. 1, 2022, pp. 3–18. Used with permission of the University of Illinois Press.

Notes

INTRODUCTION

1. In critical theory, the notion of the "end" of things has an even longer history, which Derrida in particular discusses at length in his critique of Fukuyama in *Specters of Marx*. Nonetheless, few, if any, of these ideas have been incorporated as successfully into the public consciousness as Fukuyama's.

2. This is not to suggest that Fukuyama's theory is without reproach, or that all criticism leveled at it was somehow unfounded; instead, I only wish to note, as the author himself frustratedly pointed out in the book's introduction and again in the afterword to the second edition in 2006, that a great deal of the popular response to his claims mischaracterized them beyond recognition, which is part of what led the idea of the end of history to become widely derided.

3. As Fukuyama himself explains: "We are interested not in Hegel per se but in Hegel-as-interpreted-by-Kojeve, or perhaps a new, synthetic philosopher named Hegel-Kojeve. In subsequent references to Hegel, we will actually be referring to Hegel-Kojeve, and we will be more interested in the ideas themselves than in the philosophers who originally articulated them" (*End of History* 143). This intellectual lineage, Perry Anderson points out, forms the basis of one of the most common critiques of Fukuyama's arguments—namely, that "his construction rests on a basic misinterpretation of Hegel" (284). Anderson also notes that Kojeve is the first thinker to conceive of Hegel's philosophy as containing "a full conception of an end of history, as not just the result of human development but also its halting place" (314).

4. For a more thorough critique of Fukuyama's arguments, see Perry Anderson's *A Zone of Engagement*.

5. See, for example, Fukuyama's 2018 book *Identity: The Demand for Dignity and the Politics of Resentment* and his March 2022 article "Preparing for Defeat" in *American Purpose*.

6. The end of history, framed in this way, suggests that the crises of the twenty-first century are perhaps not a matter of neoliberalism in decline, but neoliberalism *as* decline. Social, political, and cultural decline are not, in this sense, a symptom of a dying system, but rather foundational to the system itself.

7. Even these developments, despite their growing influence, have thus far largely failed to remake the world as they would have liked, and the posthistorical status quo, albeit under significant strain, broadly remains intact. Fukuyama, for his part, has claimed that the election of Joe Biden in 2020 signaled the ability for the system to self-correct, and that Putin's invasion of Ukraine will result in a defeat that gives rise to "a 'new birth of freedom,' and get us out of our funk about the declining state of global democracy. The spirit of 1989 will live on," he concludes, "thanks to a bunch of brave Ukrainians" ("Preparing For Defeat"). Rather than marking "the end of The End of History," in other words, Fukuyama claims that Putin's invasion will instead result in a reawakening of belief in liberal democracy, effectively resolidifying the conclusions of The End of History ("Putin's War on the Liberal Order").

8. A notion Fukuyama directly challenged in a March 2022 article for the *Financial Times*.

9. Kornbluh herself makes a compelling case that both complements and contradicts the account presented in this book.

10. This is, of course, not to suggest that reflective nostalgia is totally absent. As Katherina Niemeyer has shown, there is a considerable amount of scholarship on this kind of constructive nostalgia, illustrating the ways in which contemporary art and artists use nostalgia to produce insightful work. However, while unquestionably present, this more optimistic reading of the power of nostalgia does not represent the dominant mode in American media of the period, and is thus significantly less representative of the cultural moment more broadly.

CHAPTER 1 — *READY PLAYER ONE*, NOSTALGIA, AND RECOGNITION

1. Notably, the novel offers no explanation for why Halliday and the world in 2041 are *exclusively* obsessed with the media of the 1980s, why there seems to be so little reverence for classics from even the 1990s. The only explanation is that, as the time of his adolescence, the 1980s are the primary object of Cline's nostalgia. Spielberg's adaptation recognized the limitations of this approach, and extended references into the 2000s with figures like Master Chief from the *Halo* franchise.

2. Additionally, it's hard to see how "genuine human exchange," as Aronstein and Thompson put it, will solve climate change or the energy crisis, so the novel's supposed insights aren't really up to the task facing the world either.

3. And, arguably, for Cline, whose hometown of Ashland, Ohio, is a three-hour drive from Middletown. This is yet another example of Halliday's biography mirroring his creator's.

4. Middletown is briefly referenced in *Ready Player Two*, when Wade reflects on the OASIS re-creation of the Oklahoma City trailer park in which he grew up: "Those visits made me understand why Halliday had re-created Middletown in such loving detail, when it had been the setting of so many of his own unhappy childhood memories. He wanted to be able to revisit his own past, to get back in touch with the person he used to be, before the world had changed him" (42). While this explanation offers a little more insight, the affordances of visiting a virtual facsimile of one's hometown over simply *remembering* it remain unclear.

5. This is part of a growing trend in Hollywood as major studios seek to consolidate their brands through synergistic content. The first trailer for the 2021 *Space Jam* sequel, for instance, featured a scene where a crowd of characters from Warner Brothers

properties, ranging from *Batman*'s Mr. Freeze and Bette Davis's Baby Jane to the white walkers from *Game of Thrones* and Alex's droogs from *A Clockwork Orange*, watch a basketball game together. This can also be seen to an extent in the 2012 animated film *Wreck-It-Ralph*, and in many of the films from the Marvel Cinematic Universe, particularly the *Avengers* movies. While studios seeking to use new releases as tools for cross-promotion and brand loyalty is not exactly the same as Cline's fanboy exuberance, the formal techniques, and the emphasis on recognition as primary content, fundamentally are.

6. The potential exclusion of the late-millennial or Gen-Z gamer provides further proof that "gamer" is not an adequate description of the novel's ideal reader.

7. This is, of course, not to suggest that race, class, gender, and sexuality are absent from these formulations, or that these categories are somehow discrete. My point here is simply that, in many cases, taste occupies an elevated status in self-definition.

8. This is the animating logic behind a number of recent entries in the culture war—most notably Gamergate, whose spirit has been linked to *Ready Player One* by several commentators (Condis; Grady; Hudson, "If You Want to Know").

9. To be clear, this is not exclusive to Generation X, either. Millennial memes like "only '90s kids remember" similarly showcase a self that is at least partially constituted through nostalgic recognition.

10. This is not to suggest that the opposite is necessarily true, but to pinpoint, yet again, the retro simplicity of the novel's conception of these issues.

CHAPTER 2 — *STRANGER THINGS*, NOSTALGIA, AND AESTHETICS

1. To justify this rhetorical flourish by way of clarification: for *Stranger Things*, I use "exterior" here as a synonym for "form," referring to its stylistics, including, most notably, its emphasis on nostalgic mimicry and pastiche. Interior, in this case, refers to the series' narrative content and meaning. I recognize that such a distinction is, in some ways, problematic, and that the line between content and form in narrative is not as stark as that between box and Eggo; however, I believe that the explanatory value of the analogy overrides whatever clumsiness it may produce.

2. "Artificially" because, in both cases, the form—to the extent that it can be considered discrete from content—creates the perception (or the environment for the perception) that the content is more than it is. It infuses, in other words, a product with an air of novelty and complexity that isn't present in the content alone. This is in contrast to texts where the relationship between content and form is more evenly symbiotic.

3. It's worth noting, too, that *Carrie*'s 1976 release puts it somewhat outside of the 1980s that the overwhelming majority of *Stranger Things*' nostalgic objects are confined to. Further, it would be, to my knowledge, the only example with no direct connection to the show's conception of the '80s through either directorial style (Spielberg's 1977 *Close Encounters of the Third Kind*) or sequelization (*Star Wars: A New Hope*, 1977). This slippage provides further evidence of the malleability of the series' referential core in critical appraisals.

4. This is not to suggest that no one can provide an accurate rendition of a past they did not experience, but rather to illustrate, once again, how distanced the series' nostalgia is from experience, further pinpointing media rather than memory as the defining frame of reference.

5. While studies have since suggested that this "rise" and its coverage in the news were based on statistics that misleadingly included runaways and family abductions, the

moral panic that ensued was nonetheless a historical reality that impacted the cultural landscape.

6. This is most apparent in the contrast between the two predator stand-ins: Pennywise, who appears in the form of a clown—an icon rich in signification—and the Demogorgon, a vaguely humanoid form with a nightmarish visage that symbolically doesn't resonate in any particular direction.

7. Although the resurgence of Russia as a geopolitical villain following the 2016 U.S. presidential election and its 2022 invasion of Ukraine, as well as the subsequent conflation of the USSR (especially hammer and sickle imagery) with the contemporary Russian state across various social media platforms, shows that earlier tensions still remain in the minds of many Americans.

8. While labeling anything from the *Grand Theft Auto* series "rosy" might at first seem like a stretch, the series is clearly meant to present a vision of the past that is fun and alluring, and that pays little serious attention to the negative realities its gameplay corresponds to. The '80s Miami and '90s California of these games are merely theme parks for players to explore, not spaces for serious interaction. These games are instead, much like *Stranger Things*, attempts to mimic the zeitgeist of the era but only as it exists in pop mythology drawn from films, television, and music.

9. Here, the disconnect between mediated and experiential nostalgia is especially important. While those who lived through the 1980s might retain positive memories of, or associations with, the period and its media, and thus the primary version of the decade they hold in their minds may not include unseemly historical realities, the two are not mutually exclusive: a soldier's nostalgia for the camaraderie of war, for instance, does not preclude the recognition of its damage. It is, in short, the distinction between personal memory and history. On the other hand, mediated constructions of the 1980s, particularly those consumed largely by audiences without mnemonic connection to it (or whose memory is already filtered due to age), produce visions of the period that, in the absence of memory and lived experience, compete directly with historical narratives for cultural supremacy.

10. *Stranger Things*' cast of protagonists includes several adult allies who fight alongside the children, destabilizing any age-based boundary. Further, the emphasis on childlike wonder, imagination, and goodness emblematized in Elliot's treatment of *E.T.*, which forms one side of the metaphorical opposition with the cynical adult world represented by the government, is also notably absent in *Stranger Things*.

11. Despite championing them in speeches, Reaganite austerity programs and trickle-down economics only exacerbated the decline of towns like Hawkins across the nation.

CHAPTER 3 — *TWIN PEAKS: THE RETURN*, NOSTALGIA, AND FANTASIES OF REPETITION

1. *Girl Meets World*, a Disney Channel reboot of a *Boy Meets World*—a show whose original run was similar to *Full House*'s—premiered two years earlier in 2014, but was much less nostalgically driven, focusing less on the lives of the few holdover characters and more on their offspring. Moreover, the show played out stylistically like a conventional Disney Channel sitcom tailored for children and preteens. Unlike *Fuller House*, which, as the pilot attests, was explicitly geared toward fans of the original show, the target audience for *Girl Meets World* seemed to be the *children* of the fans of the original.

2. See Nochimson, Boulegue.

3. In this, the neoconservative foundations of the posthistorical turn to nostalgia again rear their head. As imagined by Leo Strauss (and later expounded by Fukuyama, among others), and vocalized most forcefully by President Reagan, the neoconservative project relied on the creation of an explicitly mythical American past around which a new polity could subsequently be (re)fashioned.

4. In this, there is a procedural parallel between *The Return* and the inclusion efforts of recent televisual revivals and reboots, which seek to bring into the fold groups who, in the original, were excluded or whose presence was minimized—even if the past they're being brought into wasn't desirable for them in the first place. Would low-income people of color or members of the LGBTQ+ community really feel at home in the wealthy, conservative, overwhelmingly white world of *Saved by the Bell*? Furthermore, aside from enabling the show's return, what is the point of dramatizing this false reunion to begin with?

5. In addition to Coulson, Miguel Ferrer, who played FBI agent Albert Rosenfeld, died before *The Return* premiered; David Bowie was too ill to reprise his role as Phillip Jeffries (his parts in the new episodes were either reused from *Fire Walk with Me* or dubbed) and died a few months before filming concluded; Harry Dean Stanton, like Coulson, was able to reprise his role from *Fire Walk with Me*, but passed away only weeks after the finale aired; cocreator Mark Frost's father Warren, who played Doctor Hayward, appeared briefly in the Showtime series, but passed away before it aired in 2017; Don Sinclair Davis, who played Major Briggs, died in 2008; and Jack Nance, who played Pete Martell, died in 1996. Frank Silva, who played BOB, died in 1995. *The Return* is haunted by these absences, which cast a noticeably, unmistakably real, shadow on the nostalgia of *Twin Peaks*' return.

6. See, for instance, the anecdote in *Lynch on Lynch* in which the director follows up a recollection of his idyllic '50s childhood by noting, "Little did we know we were laying the groundwork then for a disastrous future. All the problems were there, but it was somehow glossed over. And then the gloss broke, or rotted, and it all came oozing out" (Rodley 5). He later describes coming closer to a seemingly idyllic cherry tree only to find "pitch oozing out—some black, some yellow, and millions of red ants crawling all over it. I discovered that if one looks a little closer at this beautiful world, there are *always* red ants underneath" (10–11). This inseparability of light and dark, idyllic and horrific, is mirrored in otherwise "nostalgic" works like *Blue Velvet*, which insists upon the embeddedness of the two fantasies within the same world—light and dark always coincide, as shown in the opening dive into the seemingly perfect suburban lawn that reveals a chaotic hoard of bugs just below the surface.

CHAPTER 4 — *HILLBILLY ELEGY*, NOSTALGIA, AND RIGHT-WING MELODRAMA

1. Hochschild offers no explanation for the leap from legitimate grievance to scapegoating aside from gesturing to Fox News propaganda. *Strangers in Their Own Land* also offers no explanation for why millions of people who find themselves facing the same conditions don't turn to right-wing politics, bigotry, racism, and so forth—why, in other words, they are not taken in by the Fox News propaganda that she suggests radicalized Tea Partiers. Lastly, the book also treats these narratives as causal, suggesting that the ideological affiliation followed the deep story; given that the book offers no account either way, however, it is just as likely that these individuals held these beliefs to begin with, and the story is merely post hoc justification for preexisting tendencies. Louisiana, it should be noted, voted

Republican in eight of the thirteen presidential elections from 1960 to 2008 (a period bookended by the start of the Republican Party's Southern Strategy on one end and Barack Obama's first election, to which the Tea Party is conventionally framed as a reaction, on the other). If we grant that the Tea Party is a novel phenomenon, the decision to base a study of the conditions that gave rise to it in a state that has only voted Democratic four times in nearly fifty years (one of the non-Republican results cited above was for George Wallace, the Alabama segregationist who ran for the American Independent party) is odd.

2. Note not only Vance's use of racially coded geographic markers—the Black ghetto and the white suburb—but also the absence of the one marker most typically used throughout the book to refer to Appalachia: the holler. That the book opts not for the ethnically coded holler but for the racially coded suburb is evidence of the book's attempts to invoke a broader racial crisis than the book's "hillbilly" framing suggests.

3. This despite the fact that, as Gabriel Winant has pointed out, "elite universities love promising young conservative men like him. Institutions often seek them out and do them favors: doing so makes faculty and administrators feel broad-minded." Rather than the hindrance he depicts it as, Vance's "hillbilly" background has actually been a great boon to his professional career—he quite literally made his name on the back of it. Indeed, Vance does not indicate anywhere in the book that he was faced with prejudice or particular hardship based on this "minority" status, aside from these apparent *feelings* of alienation. Thus, the endpoint of these stories is not the assertion that Vance was materially impacted by structures rigged against him, but that he *felt* bad. Emotional suffering, like in *Strangers*, overrides the logical foundation of the claim to injury.

4. As Nathan J. Robinson reported following Vance's nomination at the 2024 Republican National Convention, Vance had also promised in 2016 to "use his newfound fame and fortune to return home to Ohio and make a difference," later founding a nonprofit called Our Ohio Renewal. Rather than make good on this promise, however, as *The New York Times* reported, the group only raised about $220,000 before folding in 2021 (Fahrenthold). Researchers later found that it had "spent more than 95 percent of its 2017 fundraising on staff salaries and overhead, and $0 on charitable activities or grants" (Lizza and Bade). This serves as further evidence that Vance's interest in renewing the homeland is more discursive than material.

5. It must be noted that Vance's analysis is reliant on "A report by the Wisconsin Children's Trust Fund," a citation for which the book does not provide, and whose findings he summarizes in dubious terms. In the context of this report, Vance describes "those with a college degree or more" as "the non-working class" (227), which, again, works to blur the boundaries of the concept of "the working class." The suggestion that those with college degrees cannot be working class and, in the inverse, that those without college degrees are automatically working class is a falsification of American class stratification based on tortuous logic. This effort makes "working class" less an identification of economic class and more a matter of "cultural" affiliation that sees all college graduates as "elite" whether they make $30,000 a year as a teacher or $30 million at a hedge fund, and all non–college graduates as "nonelite" whether they own a factory or mop its floors. This deceptive framing is necessary for Vance to pursue his project of upholding the narrative that right-wing political resentments are founded in the legitimate concerns of the "white working class." Under this rubric, complaints about tax rates felt by the non–college educated owner of a chain of regional car dealerships earning $300,000 per year is legitimized as "working class economic anxiety" just as those of the foreman of a factory whose production moved over-

seas, while a Brooklyn barista with a humanities degree earning minimum wage is part of the non–working class "elite."

6. Stylized as such—with an imitation-Latin "V" in place of a "U"—in order to invoke a connection to Classical aesthetics. While the two terms can be used somewhat interchangeably given the informal nature of the "movement," I prefer to use "retvrn" for its more evocative connection to the content of this book, especially its emphasis on aesthetic primacy.

7. For this chapter, I will generally use the term New Right. "Alt-Right," though popular for a period, appears to have lost cogency on the right with many figures, including Bronze Age Pervert himself and Richard Spencer (who is generally credited with coining the term), distancing themselves from it. "Neofascist," though certainly an apt description in a lot of cases, suggests a degree of philosophical cohesion that I'm not sure exists in this grouping, and the moniker also sparks debates about the meaning of "fascism" that are outside the purview of this chapter. "The New Right," however, provides a way of contextualizing the movement, which is notable largely because, in its rejection of many tenets of traditional Republican policy, it signals a paradigm shift (even if the shift is not as great as many make it out to be). It also enables a variety of micro-"movements" distinguished by small differences—do they want to return to Ancient Greece or 1950s America?—to be understood under the same broader rubric. I am also drawn to the irony that the "New" right's platform is largely founded on nostalgia and other appeals to *old* ideas.

8. On November 8, 2023, @culturaltutor, whose avatar is a bust of Plato, posted "What happened to walls with texture?" accompanied by photos of walls with popcorn, comb, and slap brush textures.

9. According to Graeme Wood, Alamariu also briefly held a postdoctoral fellowship at Emory University in 2015, which was not renewed the following year for reasons related to his performance and behavior (though nothing explicitly political has been cited, and Alamariu was reportedly suffering from "a vague but apparently real physical infirmity" according to Wood). He has not held an academic position since, and his professional life is something of a mystery—it is unclear, aside from book sales and blog subscriptions, how he makes money.

10. I also suspect that, like the discussion of the "Straussian test" in the following paragraph, BAP's feigned struggles with grammar and spelling function as a trap meant to highlight the illiberalism of any critics who would mock or otherwise disregard him for it: "Though they pretend to care about other people," he might retort, "they're actually just as bigoted as I am."

11. There is little academic writing on the subject of Bronze Age Pervert, but, for those who are interested in a deeper look at his work, thoughtful analysis and critique can be found in several nonacademic sources: Nathan J. Robinson's "Beware Ideologies That Tell You You're Better Than Everyone Else" in *Current Affairs*, John Ganz's "The Super-Duper-Men: Reading the 'Bronze Age Pervert' Phenomenon" in *Unpopular Front*, and Graeme Wood's "How the Bronze Age Pervert Charmed the Far Right" in *The Atlantic* are especially insightful. Vassar College's online *Pharos* project, "a website where classical scholars, students, and the public more broadly, can learn about appropriations of Greco-Roman antiquity by hate groups," also features multiple helpful articles about this element in BAP's writing.

12. It should be noted that these posts have been met with considerable mockery online and many of the posts you see today use this language ironically. Even on the

right, this has become something of a meme, and posts are often imbued with layers of ironic detachment, whether they agree with the fundamental sentiment or not.

13. Of course, the irony that both objects are from "the past" is not acknowledged.

14. This attempt to reject Bronze Age Pervert and the New Right on the grounds of its violation of conservative principles can be seen outside of retvrn posting as well, in articles like Jack Butler's "How 'Bronze Age Pervert' Seduced Right-Wing Thought Leader" in the *Daily Beast*, which repeatedly emphasizes how "there is nothing conservative about Alamariu's views of women" and "Alamariu's (at best) ambivalence toward Christianity isn't exactly conservative either."

15. All of the children in these posts, it should be noted, are white. In all but the World Trade Center photograph, the subjects are boys.

16. Following this reporting, produced in response to the considerable mockery he faced following these posts—which led him to lock his account—Young's focus appears to have shifted, and very few of his posts in the years since feature such explicitly nostalgic content. Though likely a reaction to this negative reception, the turn may also be due to the fact that he had used an artist's work without permission. As Klee reported, the digital paintings Young posted, though they could easily have come from the concept art for *Ready Player One*, were actually the work of Rachid Lotf, a Moroccan-born Londoner who, upon finding out about the posts, posted on Twitter that Young did not have his permission and requested that his art not be used for political purposes. "My artworks are made just to immortalize some moments of our childhoods," the artist explained. "There is no political or critical message towards anyone."

CONCLUSION

1. This Democratic fidelity to posthistorical politics is neatly reflected in the party's response to the candidacy of Bernie Sanders, which saw a remarkably choreographed effort within the establishment to close ranks around Joe Biden as a means of blunting the Vermont senator's electoral momentum early in the 2020 primaries. This response to the Sanders campaign, which urged a break with neoliberal economics via a return to the prolabor New Deal politics of the 1930s and '40s, shows the fundamental distinction between Republican and Democratic reactions to the challenges to the end of history that have emerged in recent years. The Biden administration's refusal to address the right's capture of the Supreme Court for fear of eroding institutional norms likewise illustrates the party's commitment to the status quo, as well as the foundational asymmetry between the two parties.

2. "Anti-" insofar as their politics are founded, implicitly or explicitly, in reaction to many of the outcomes of neoliberalism—especially, as chapter 4 shows, its neglect of the wages of whiteness and relative indifference to nonredistributionary social change (as long as such change takes place within—or at least does not threaten—the market). This, of course, should not be understood as necessarily indicative of a comprehensive ideological break with many of the founding principles of neoliberalism, and it is, instead, better understood as a rhetorical appeal that seeks to direct a wide range of energies toward the right's racial and social project. It is, in other words, less about revising the economics of neoliberal capitalism and more about remediating the social outcomes it has allowed. Whether this amounts to a radical break with the end of history or merely represents a comparatively minor shift within a posthistorical frame that remains broadly intact is a debate that is beyond the scope of this book. What seems clear, for now, is that the emergence of the New Right does pose a challenge to the posthistorical status quo.

Works Cited

Alexander, Jonathan. "The Uses and Abuses of Pop Culture in *Ready Player One* and *Grandmother's Gold*." *The Journal of Popular Culture*, vol. 53, no. 3, 2020, pp. 524–546.

Anderson, Perry. *A Zone of Engagement*. Verso, 1992.

Anker, Elisabeth R. *Orgies of Feeling: Melodrama and the Politics of Freedom*. Duke UP, 2014.

Anton, Michael. "Are the Kids Al(t)right?" *Claremont Review of Books*, Summer 2019, claremontreviewofbooks.com/are-the-kids-altright/.

Arcade Fire. "Reflektor." *Reflektor*, Merge, 2013.

Armbruster, Stefanie. *Watching Nostalgia: An Analysis of Nostalgic Television Fiction and Its Reception*. Transcript, 2016.

Aronstein, Susan, and Jason Thompson. "Coding the Grail: Ready Player One's Arthurian Mash-Up." *Arthuriana*, vol. 25, no. 4, 2015, pp. 51–65.

Austin, Linda M. *Nostalgia in Transition: 1780–1917*. U of Virginia P, 2007.

Baudrillard, Jean. *The Illusion of the End*. Stanford UP, 1994.

———. *Simulacra and Simulation*. U of Michigan P, 1994.

Bauman, Zygmunt. *Liquid Modernity*. Polity, 2000.

———. *Retrotopia*. Polity, 2017.

Bering-Porter, David. "White Nostalgia." *Post45*, 4 July 2019, post45.org/2019/07/white-nostalgia/.

Berlant, Lauren. *Cruel Optimism*. Duke UP, 2011.

Berlatsky, Noah. "In Season 3, Stranger Things' Celebration of '80s Pop Culture Becomes a Political Ideology." *The Verge*, 8 July 2019, www.theverge.com/2019/7/8/206 86502/stranger-things-season-3-80s-pop-culture-mind-flayer-cold-war-russia-analysis.

Berns, Fernando Gabriel Pagnoni, et al. "The Monstrous Queer Child: Mobbing, Bullying, and Bad Parenting in the 1980s." *Uncovering Stranger Things: Essays on Eighties Nostalgia, Cynicism, and Innocence in the Series*, edited by Kevin J. Wetmore, Jr., McFarland, 2018, pp. 146–155.

Boulegue, Franck. *The Return of* Twin Peaks: *Squaring the Circle*. Intellect Ltd, 2021.

Boym, Svetlana. *The Future of Nostalgia*. Basic Books, 2001.

Brew, Simon, and Nick Harley. "121 Movie Remakes and Reboots Currently in the Works." *Den of Geek*, 10 Nov. 2018, www.denofgeek.com/movies/movie-remakes-reboots-in-development/.

Breznican, Anthony. "*Ready Player One*, by Ernest Cline: EW Review." *Entertainment Weekly*, 24 Aug. 2011, ew.com/article/2011/08/24/ready-player-one-review-ernest-cline/.

Briefel, Aviva. "Familiar Things: Snow Ball '84 and Straight Nostalgia." *Post45*, 4 July 2019, post45.org/2019/07/familiar-things-snow-ball-84-and-straight-nostalgia/.

Brogan, Jacob. "Imagining the Future Is Dangerous." *Slate*, 14 July 2015, slate.com/technology/2015/07/an-interview-with-ernest-cline-author-of-ready-player-one-and-armada.html.

Bronze Age Pervert. "America's Delusional Elite is Done." *The American Mind*, 22 Oct. 2019, americanmind.org/salvo/americas-delusional-elite-is-done/.

———. *Bronze Age Mindset*. 2018.

Brown, Wendy. *In the Ruins of Neoliberalism*. Columbia UP, 2019.

Burges, Joel. "The Violence of Nostalgia, or, the Crisis of Middle-Class Modernity." *Post45*, 4 July 2019, post45.org/2019/07/the-violence-of-nostalgia-or-the-crisis-of-middle-class-modernity/.

Burges, Joel, and Jason Middleton. "Boys Fractured: *Stranger Things* and Nostalgia Now." *Post45*, 4 July 2019, post45.org/2019/07/boys-fractured-stranger-things-and-nostalgia-now/.

Butler, Jack. "How 'Bronze Age Pervert' Seduced Right-Wing Thought Leaders." *Daily Beast*, 10 Feb. 2023, www.thedailybeast.com/how-bronze-age-pervert-seduced-right-wing-thought-leaders.

Butler, Rose. "The Eaten-for-Breakfast Club: Teenage Nightmares in *Stranger Things*." *Uncovering Stranger Things: Essays on Eighties Nostalgia, Cynicism, and Innocence in the Series*, edited by Kevin J. Wetmore, Jr., McFarland, 2018, pp. 72–83.

Chaney, Jen. "Stranger Things Is a Throwback to '80s Chills and Spielbergian Thrills." *Vulture*, 13 July 2016, www.vulture.com/2016/07/stranger-things-a-throwback-to-80s-terror.html.

Charli XCX and Troye Sivan. "1999." *Charli*, Asylum, 2018.

Cline, Ernest. *Ready Player One*. Broadway, 2011.

———. *Ready Player Two*. Random House Large Print, 2020

Condis, Megan Amber. "Playing the Game of Literature: *Ready Player One*, the Ludic Novel, and the Geeky 'Canon' of White Masculinity." *Journal of Modern Literature*, vol. 39, no. 2, 2016, pp. 1–19.

@culturaltutor. "What happened to walls with texture?" *Twitter*, 8 Nov. 2023, 2:53 P.M., x.com/culturaltutor/status/1722341640273092991.

@culture_crit. "Why did we allow this?" *Twitter*, 27 Mar. 2023, 5:29 P.M., x.com/Culture_Crit/status/1640466062046289920?lang=en.

Curtis, Adam, director. *Hypernormalisation*. BBC Films, 2016.

Davis, Mike. "Thanatos Triumphant." *New Left Review: Sidecar*, 7 Mar. 2022, newleftreview.org/sidecar/posts/thanatos-triumphant.

Derrida, Jacques. *Specters of Marx*. Translated by Peggy Kamuf, Routledge, 2006.

Dowland, Douglas. "The Politics of Resentment in J. D. Vance's *Hillbilly Elegy*." *Texas Studies in Literature and Language*, vol. 61, no. 2, 2019, pp. 116–140.

The Duffer Brothers, creators. *Stranger Things*. 21 Laps Entertainment and Monkey Massacre Productions, 2025.

Egan, Elisabeth. "Ernest Cline Was 'Raised by Screens.' Look How Well He Turned Out!" *The New York Times*, 7 Jan. 2021, www.nytimes.com/2021/01/07/books/review/ready-player-two-ernest-cline.html.

Fahrenthold, David A. "The Future of J. D. Vance's Charity in Ohio Is Unclear." *The New York Times*, 6 Sept. 2024, www.nytimes.com/2024/09/06/us/politics/jd-vance-charity-ohio.html.

Fienberg, Daniel. "The Duffer Brothers Talk 'Stranger Things' Influences, 'It' Dreams and Netflix Phase 2." *The Hollywood Reporter*, 1 Aug. 2016, www.hollywoodreporter.com/tv/tv-news/duffer-brothers-talk-stranger-things-916180/

Fisher, Mark. *Capitalist Realism*. Zero Books, 2009.

———. *Ghosts of My Life: Writings on Depression, Hauntology, and Lost Futures*. Zero Books, 2014.

Franklin, Jeff, creator. *Full House*. Jeff Franklin Productions and Miller-Boyett Productions, 1995.

———. *Fuller House*. Warner Bros. Television Group, 2020.

Fraser, Nancy. "Rethinking Recognition." *New Left Review*, vol. 3, no. 1, 2000, pp. 107–120.

Fukuyama, Francis. "The End of History?" *The National Interest*, vol. 16, 1989, pp. 3–18.

———. *The End of History and the Last Man*. Free Press, 2006.

———. *Identity: The Demand for Dignity and the Politics of Resentment*. Picador, 2019.

———. "Preparing for Defeat." *American Purpose*, 10 Mar. 2022, www.americanpurpose.com/blog/fukuyama/preparing-for-defeat/.

———. "Putin's War on the Liberal Order." *Financial Times*, 4 Mar. 2022, www.ft.com/content/d0331b51-5d0e-4132-9f97-c3f41c7d75b3.

Gallow, Timothy William. "From *Lost Highway* to *Twin Peaks*: Representations of Trauma and Transformation in Lynch's Late Works." *Critical Essays on Twin Peaks: The Return*, edited by Antonio Sanna, Palgrave Macmillan, 2019, pp. 201–220.

Ganz, John. "The Super-Duper Men: Reading the 'Bronze Age Pervert' Phenomenon." *Unpopular Front*, 20 Feb. 2023, www.unpopularfront.news/p/the-super-duper-men.

Genzlinger, Neil. "With 'Stranger Things' Netflix Delivers an Eerie Nostalgia Fix." *The New York Times*, 14 July 2016, www.nytimes.com/2016/07/15/arts/television/review-with-stranger-things-netflix-delivers-an-eerie-nostalgia-fix.html.

Gerstle, Gary. *The Rise and Fall of the Neoliberal Order: America and the World in the Free Market Era*. Oxford UP, 2022.

Giovannone, Aaron. "'Stranger Things 2' Relies on Nostalgic Race Politics." *Salon*, 7 Jan. 2018, www.salon.com/2018/01/06/stranger-things-2-relies-on-nostalgic-race-politics_partner/.

Grady, Constance. "The Ready Player One Backlash, Explained." *Vox*, 26 Mar. 2018, www.vox.com/culture/2018/3/26/17148350/ready-player-one-book-backlash-controversy-gamergate-explained.

Grainge, Paul. *Monochrome Memories: Nostalgia and Style in Retro America*. Praeger, 2002.

Gray, Rosie. "How Bronze Age Pervert Built an Online Following and Injected Anti-Democracy, Pro-Men Ideas Into the GOP." *Politico*, 16 July 2023, www.politico.com/news/magazine/2023/07/16/bronze-age-pervert-masculinity-00105427.

Hardisty, Jean. *Mobilizing Resentment: Conservative Resurgence from the John Birch Society to the Promise Keepers*. Beacon Press, 2000.

Harkins, Anthony, and Meredith McCarroll, editors. *Appalachian Reckoning: A Region Responds to* Hillbilly Elegy. West Virginia UP, 2019.

Hibberd, James. "Ready Player Two Author Ernest Cline on Returning to the Oasis." *Entertainment Weekly*, 11 Nov. 2020, ew.com/books/author-interviews/ready-player-two-one-interview/.

Hochschild, Arlie Russell. *Strangers in Their Own Land: Anger and Mourning on the American Right*. The New Press, 2016.

Hochuli, Alex et al. *The End of the End of History: Politics in the Twenty-First Century*. Zero Books, 2021.

HoSang, Daniel Martinez, and Joseph E. Lowndes. *Producers, Parasites, Patriots: Race and the New Right-Wing Politics of Precarity*. U of Minnesota P, 2019.

Howard, Ron, director. *Hillbilly Elegy*. Netflix, 2020.

Hudson, Laura. "If You Want to Know How We Ended Up in a Cyber Dystopia, Read *Ready Player One*." *The Verge*, 19 April 2018, www.theverge.com/2018/4/19/17250892/ready-player-one-book-facebook-internet-dystopia.

———. "*Ready Player Two* Is a Horror Story but Doesn't Know It." *Slate*, 1 Dec. 2020, slate.com/culture/2020/12/ready-player-two-review-ernest-cline-sequel.html.

———. "Serious Bill-Paying Skillage." *Slate*, 7 July 2015, slate.com/culture/2015/07/armada-by-ernest-cline-follow-up-to-ready-player-one-reviewed.html.

Hussain, Martaza. "The Importance of Bronze Age Pervert." *Unherd*, 26 Jan. 2023, unherd.com/2022/01/the-importance-of-bronze-age-pervert/.

Hutcheon, Linda. "Irony, Nostalgia, and the Postmodern." *Methods for the Study of Literature as Cultural Memory*, edited by Raymond Vervilet and Annemarie Estor, Rodopi, 2000, pp. 189–207.

Jameson, Fredric. "The End of Temporality." *Critical Inquiry*, vol. 29, no. 4, 2003, pp. 695–718.

———. *The Political Unconscious*. Cornell UP, 1982.

———. "Postmodernism and Consumer Society." *Postmodern Culture*, edited by Hal Foster, Pluto Press, 1985, pp. 111–125.

———. *Postmodernism, or, The Cultural Logic of Late Capitalism*. Verso, 1993.

———. *The Seeds of Time*. Columbia UP, 1994.

Karp, Matthew. "Trump Redux: From 2016 to 2024." *New Left Review*, no. 150, 2024, pp. 5–17.

Khan, Dara. "The Real Demogorgon: Stranger Things' Bold Allegory for Overcoming Childhood Trauma." *Medium*, 3 Aug. 2016, medium.com/@palakchaval/the-real-demogorgon-stranger-things-bold-allegory-of-childhood-trauma-239b8b1d4872.

Kimmel, Jimmy, creator. *Live in Front of a Studio Audience*. Sony Pictures Television Studios, 2019–2021.

Klee, Miles. "Anti-Woke Crusader Is Trying a New Recruitment Tool: 1990s Nostalgia." *Rolling Stone*, 21 Oct. 2022, www.rollingstone.com/culture/culture-news/anti-woke-1990s-video-nostalgia-art-1234613774/.

Kornbluh, Anna. *Immediacy: or, The Style of Too Late Capitalism*. Verso, 2024.

Landrum, Jason. "Nostalgia, Fantasy, and Loss: *Stranger Things* and the Digital Gothic." *Intertexts* vol. 21, no. 1–2, 2017, pp. 136–158.

LCD Soundsystem. "Losing My Edge." *LCD Soundsystem*, DFI and Capitol Records, 2005.

@LindyTasteful. "Imagine being a boomer growing up. Every massive chain restaurant was new and exciting, instead of depressing. You could go to Pizza Hut and celebrate the dream of capitalism with your community." *Twitter*, 24 Jan. 2024, 6:19 P.M., x.com/LindyTasteful/status/1750297179506286668.

Linklater, Richard, director. *Dazed and Confused*, Gramercy Pictures, 1993.

Linnemann, Travis, and Corina Medley. "Down and Out in Middletown and Jackson: Drugs, Dependency, and Decline in J. D. Vance's Capitalist Realism." *Appalachian Reckoning: A Region Responds to* Hillbilly Elegy, edited by Anthony Harkins and Meredith McCarroll, West Virginia UP, 2019, pp. 136–154.

Lizardi, Ryan. *Mediated Nostalgia*. Lexington Books, 2015.

Lizza, Ryan, and Rachel Bade. "Politico Playbook: The Book J. D. Vance Doesn't Want You to Read." *Politico*, 5 May 2022, www.politico.com/newsletters/playbook/2022/05/05/the-book-j-d-vance-doesnt-want-you-to-read-00030287.

Lucas, George, director. *American Graffiti*. Universal Pictures, 1973.

Lynch, David, director. *Blue Velvet*. De Laurentiis Entertainment Group, 1986.

———. *Twin Peaks: Fire Walk with Me*. CIBY Pictures, 1992.

Lynch, David, and Mark Frost, creators. *Twin Peaks*. ABC and Showtime, 1989.

McCaffrey, Matthew. "*Stranger Things* and the Monstrous State." *InfoWars*, 12 Sept. 2016, www.infowars.com/stranger-things-and-the-monstrous-state/.

McCarthy, Kayla. "Remember Things: Consumerism, Nostalgia, and Geek Culture in *Stranger Things*." *The Journal of Popular Culture*, vol. 52, no. 3, 2019, pp. 663–677, https://doi.org/10.1111/jpcu.12800.

McGowan, Todd. *The Impossible David Lynch*, Columbia UP, 2007.

———. "Waiting for Agent Cooper: The End of Fantasy in *Twin Peaks: The Return*." *Freud/Lynch: Behind the Curtain*, edited by Jamie Ruers and Stefan Marianski, Phoenix, 2023, pp. 119–138.

Menand, Louis. "Francis Fukuyama Postpones the End of History." *The New Yorker*, 27 Aug. 2018, www.newyorker.com/magazine/2018/09/03/francis-fukuyama-postpones-the-end-of-history.

"Michael Young." *The Center for Renewing America*, americarenewing.com/team/michael-young/.

Nadel, Alan. *Flatlining on the Field of Dreams*. Rutgers UP, 1997.

Nelson, Samantha. "*Ready Player Two* Tries but Fails to Make Up for the Problems of the Original." *The A.V. Club*, 30 Nov. 2020, www.avclub.com/ready-player-two-tries-but-fails-to-make-up-for-the-pro-1845775704.

Niemeyer, Katharina, editor. *Media and Nostalgia: Yearning for the Past, Present and Future*. Palgrave Macmillan, 2017.

Nochimson, Martha P. *Television Rewired: The Rise of the Auteur Series*. U of Texas P, 2019.

Nussbaum, Emily. "'Stranger Things' and 'The Get Down.'" *The New Yorker*, 15 Aug. 2016, www.newyorker.com/magazine/2016/08/22/stranger-things-and-the-get-down-reviews.

"Our Very First Show." *Full House*, written by Jeff Franklin, directed by Joel Zwick, ABC, 1987.

"Our Very First Show, Again." *Fuller House*, written by Jeff Franklin, directed by Mark Cendrowski, Netflix, 2016.

Pharos. Vassar College, pharos.vassarspaces.net/. Accessed 19 Aug. 2024.

Pickering, Michael, and Emily Keightley. "The Modalities of Nostalgia." *Current Sociology*, vol. 54, no. 6, 2006, pp. 919–941.

Ravela, Christian. "Becoming White Again: The Bildungsroman, Whiteness, and the Culture of Poverty." *Cultural Critique*, no. 110, 2021, pp. 181–203.

Reich, Elizabeth. "The Ecology of the Upside Down: or, the Possibility of Black Life in *Stranger Things*." *Post45*, 4 July 2019, post45.org/2019/07/the-ecology-of-the-upside-down-or-the-possibility-of-black-life-in-stranger-things/.

Reynolds, Simon. *Retromania: Pop Culture's Addiction to Its Own Past*. Faber and Faber, 2011.

Roach, Emily E. "AIDS, Homophobia, and the Monstrous Upside Down: The Queer Subtext of *Stranger Things*." *Uncovering Stranger Things: Essays on Eighties Nostalgia, Cynicism, and Innocence in the Series*, edited by Kevin J. Wetmore, Jr., McFarland, 2018, pp. 135–145.

Robin, Corey. *The Reactionary Mind: Conservatism from Edmund Burke to Sarah Palin*. Oxford UP, 2013.

Robinson, Nathan J. "Beware Ideologies That Tell You You're Better Than Everyone Else." *Current Affairs*, 2 Oct. 2023, www.currentaffairs.org/news/2023/10/beware-ideologies-that-tell-you-youre-better-than-everyone-else.

Rodley, Chris. *Lynch on Lynch*. Farrar, Straus, and Giroux, 2005.

Rottenberg, Josh. "How the Team Behind 'Ready Player One' Wrangled a Bonanza of Pop Culture References into a Single Film." *The Los Angeles Times*, 1 Apr. 2018, www.latimes.com/entertainment/movies/la-et-mn-ready-player-one-references-20180401-story.html.

Rust, Amy. "Analog Nostalgia and the Promise of Props in the Digital Age." *Post45*, 4 July 2019, post45.org/2019/07/analog-nostalgia-and-the-promise-of-props-in-the-digital-age/.

Schager, Nick. "How Is Steven Spielberg Going to Make a Great Movie Out of This God-Awful Book?" *The Daily Beast*, 31 Dec. 2017, www.thedailybeast.com/how-is-steven-spielberg-going-to-make-a-great-movie-out-of-this-god-awful-book?ref=scroll.

Scott, A. O. "Nerd's Paradise, via Spielberg." *The New York Times*, 29 Mar. 2018, www.nytimes.com/2018/03/28/movies/ready-player-one-review-steven-spielberg.html.

Silver, Nate. "The Mythology of Trump's 'Working-Class' Support." *FiveThirtyEight*, 3 May 2016, fivethirtyeight.com/features/the-mythology-of-trumps-working-class-support/.

Smith, Lacey N. "'A nice home at the end of the cul-de-sac': Hawkins as Infected Postmodern Suburbia." *Uncovering Stranger Things: Essays on Eighties Nostalgia, Cynicism, and Innocence in the Series*, edited by Kevin J. Wetmore, Jr., McFarland, 2018, pp. 215–224.

Smokler, Kevin. "Stranger Things and the Sinister Innocence of Reagan's America." *Salon*, 24 Oct. 2017, www.salon.com/2017/10/24/stranger-things-and-the-dubious-innocence-of-hawkins-indiana/.

"Space Jam: A New Legacy—Trailer 1." *YouTube*, uploaded by Warner Bros. Pictures, 3 Apr. 2021, www.youtube.com/watch?v=olXYZOsXw_o&ab_chan`nel=WarnerBros.Pictures.

Spencer, Samuel. "25 TV Shows Rebooting in 2021." *Newsweek*, 21 Mar. 2021, www.newsweek.com/tv-reboots-2021-frasier-sex-city-icarly-1577311.

Spielberg, Steven, director. *Ready Player One*. Warner Brothers, 2018.

Tanner, Grafton. *The Hours Have Lost Their Clock: The Politics of Nostalgia*. Repeater, 2021.

Tooze, Adam. "Welcome to the World of Polycrisis." *Financial Times*, 28 Oct. 2022, www.ft.com/content/498398e7-11b1-494b-9cd3-6d669dc3de33.

Toscano, Alberto. *Late Fascism: Race, Capitalism, and the Politics of Crisis*. Verso, 2023.

Tu, Thuy Linh, and Nikhil Pal Singh. "Morbid Capitalism." *n+1*, no. 30, 2018, www.nplusonemag.com/issue-30/essays/morbid-capitalism/.

"Units of One." *Can't Get You Out of My Head*, written and directed by Adam Curtis, BBC Films, 2021.

Vance, J. D. *Hillbilly Elegy: A Memoir of a Family and Culture in Crisis*. Harper, 2020.

VanDerWerff, Emily. "A Potentially Frustrating *Twin Peaks* Finale Asks One Big Question: Are We Owed Answers?" *Vox*, 3 Sept. 2017, www.vox.com/culture/2017/9/3/16250822/twin-peaks-finale-recap-part-17-18-the-return.

———. "*Twin Peaks: The Return* Episodes 3 and 4." *Vox*, 28 May 2017, www.vox.com/culture/2017/5/28/15702900/twin-peaks-episode-3-4-recap-the-return-dougie.

Williams, Linda. *Playing the Race Card: Melodramas of Black and White from Uncle Tom to O. J. Simpson*. Princeton UP, 2001.

Winant, Gabriel. "J. D. Vance Changes the Subject." *n+1*, no. 45, 2023, www.nplusonemag.com/issue-45/politics/j-d-vance-changes-the-subject-2/.

@wokal_distance. "Born / Parents / Pre-school / Elementry school / High-school / Girlfriend / College / Graduate / Job / House / Wife / Kids / Family / Community / PTA meetings / Grand Kids . . . This path will not exist in the world I am raising my son to survive in." *Twitter*, 13 Apr. 2022, 7:42 P.M., x.com/wokal_distance/status/1514388624594284545. Accessed 27 July 2024.

———. "This is not consumerism." *Twitter*, 15 Oct. 2022, 11:52 P.M., x.com/wokal_distance/status/1581493312795865089.

Wood, Graeme. "How Bronze Age Pervert Charmed the Far Right." *The Atlantic*, 3 Aug. 2023, www.theatlantic.com/magazine/archive/2023/09/bronze-age-pervert-costin-alamariu/674762/.

Zerofsky, Elisabeth. "How the Claremont Institute Became a Nerve Center of the American Right." *The New York Times*, 3 Aug. 2022, www.nytimes.com/2022/08/03/magazine/claremont-institute-conservative.html.

Žižek, Slavoj. *First as Tragedy, Then as Farce*. Verso, 2009.

———. *Trouble in Paradise*. Melville House, 2014.

Index

Adele, 83
aestheticization, 3, 17, 61, 64–65, 91, 102, 105, 133. *See also* hyper aestheticization
affirmative action, 109–110, 123, 138
AI, generative, 144–146
Alamariu, Costin, 134–135, 137–141, 161n7, 161nn9–11, 162n14. See also *Bronze Age Mindset*
Alexander, Jonathan, 25, 29
alienation, 112, 115, 119, 124–127, 132, 148, 160n3
All in the Family (Norman Lear), 84
Alt-Right movement. *See* New Right movement
American Dream, the, 109, 124, 129
American Graffiti (George Lucas), 15, 67
Americans, The (Joe Weisberg), 67
Anderson, Perry, 5–6, 155n3
Angel of History, 2–3
Angelus Novus (Paul Klee), 2
Anker, Elisabeth, 106–107
anti-Semitism, 136
Anton, Michael, 135, 137
Appalachia, 119, 122, 128–130, 160n2
Appalachian Reckoning (Anthony Harkins and Meredith McCarroll), 130
Arcade Fire, 1–3, 18
Armada (Ernest Cline), 27
Aronstein, Susan, 34, 156n2
artificiality, 157n2
attention economy, 108
Austin, Linda, 11
Back to the Future (Robert Zemeckis), 12, 26, 64, 72
Baudrillard, Jean, 1, 9, 16, 19, 30, 36
Bauman, Zygmunt, 2, 3, 5, 9, 85
Beattie, Darren, 135
Bel-Air (Morgan Cooper, Malcolm Spellman, TJ Brady, and Rasheed Newson), 85
Bell Curve, The (Richard J. Herrnstein and Charles Murray), 120
belonging, 18, 40, 126, 127
Benjamin, Walter, 2–3
Bering-Porter, David, 62, 75–77
Berlant, Lauren, 43, 92
Berlatsky, Noah, 78
Biden, Joe, 9, 156n7, 162n1
bipartisanship, 9, 149
Birth of a Nation, The (D. W. Griffith), 107
blue-collar workers, 114, 115
Blue Velvet (David Lynch), 102, 159n6
Body Heat (Lawrence Kasdan), 15–16
Boulegue, Franck, 94, 97, 103
Bowie, David, 159n5
Boym, Svetlana, 2, 5, 11, 17, 104
Breakfast Club, The (John Hughes), 63
Brexit, 8, 148
Briefel, Aviva, 59–61
Brogan, Jacob, 27–28
Bronze Age Mindset (Costin Alamariu): aesthetics in, 141–142; audience for, 138; hypermasculine appeal of, 138–139; as melodrama, 135–137, 140; nostalgia in, 139–141; popularity of, 134; racism in, 137–138; and the retvrn movement, 140–141; worldview expressed in, 137

Bronze Age Pervert (BAP). *See* Alamariu, Costin
Brostoff, Ari M., 117
Brown, Wendy, 8–9, 113, 147
Burges, Joel, 61–62
Burnham, James, 140
Butler, Jack, 162n14
Butler, Win, 1–3, 18

capitalism: and bureaucracy, 140; and identity, 43; and ideology, 6, 21, 74, 77, 106; neoliberal, 7, 162n2; and nostalgia, 21, 77, 85, 143–144; oligarchic, 31; and politics, 142, 144; and race, 141–142; Vance on, 132
capitalist realism, 4, 132
Carrie (Brian De Palma), 60, 157n3
Case, Ann, 116
Center for Renewing America (CRA), 143
Christianity, 8, 105, 111, 134, 162n14
Christmas Story, A (Bob Clark), 12, 62
Claremont Review of Books, 135, 137
class, 51–52, 115–117, 122, 124–125, 160n5
climate change, 27, 28, 30, 156n2
Cline, Ernest, 23, 26–31, 34, 41, 49–50, 54, 156n1, 156n2, 157n5 (chap. 1). See also *Ready Player One*; *Ready Player Two*
Clinton, Hillary, supporters of, 115
Condis, Megan Amber, 40, 44, 45
conspiracy theories, 104, 107, 117–118, 133, 138–139, 141–142
consumption, 19, 25, 42–43, 49, 74, 151
cruel optimism, 92–93
Cunliff, Philip, 147
Curtis, Adam, 22, 29
cyclical time, 9

Davis, Don Sinclair, 159n5
Davis, Mike, 8
Dazed and Confused (Richard Linklater), 167
Deaton, Angus, 116
democracy, 5–7, 36, 134, 140, 147–148, 156n7
democratic consensus, 8, 147
Democrats, 115, 160n1, 162n1
Diff'rent Strokes (Jeff Harris and Bernie Kukoff), 84
digital spaces, 23
disadvantaged groups, 110
doppelgängers, 88–89, 99–100
Dowland, Douglas, 130
dystopia, 23–28, 35

Eggo, 56–58, 157n1
end of history, the: and depoliticization, 14; Fukuyama on, 5–7, 43, 147–149, 155nn1–3, 156n7, 159n3; and neoliberalism, 17; and nostalgia, 10, 17–19; and postmodernism, 16–17
E. T. (Steven Spielberg), 39, 61, 69–70, 158n10
ethnonationalism, 133
Europe, 8, 104, 141

Facebook, 23
Facts of Life, The (Dick Clair and Jenna McMahon), 84
fascism, 8, 21, 105, 117–118, 132–135, 137, 161n7
fashion, 1, 12–13, 24, 80, 83
feminism, 42, 70, 133, 137–139 passim, 144
Ferrer, Miguel, 159n5
Ferris Bueller's Day Off (John Hughes), 26, 50, 69
Field of Dreams (Phil Alden Robinson), 84
Fire Walk with Me (David Lynch), 88–89, 94–95, 159n5
Fisher, Mark, 4–5, 31, 41
Fox News, 159n1
Fraser, Nancy, 42
Freaks and Geeks (Paul Feig and Judd Apatow), 67
Frost, Mark, 88, 101. See also *Twin Peaks: The Return*
Frost, Warren, 159n5
Fukuyama, Francis, 5–7, 43, 147–149, 155, 156n7, 159n3
Fuller House (Jeff Franklin), 80–82, 84–87, 93, 96–99, 158n1

Gallow, Timothy William, 102–103
Ganz, John, 134
gender: in *Ready Player One*, 44–46; in *Ready Player Two*, 46–49; traditional norms of, 133; in *Twin Peaks: The Return*, 94–95
Gen-X, 43, 157n9
Gen-Z, 12, 68, 144, 157n6
Gerstle, Gary, 147
Ghostbusters (Ivan Reitman), 24, 74–76
Girl Meets World (Michael Jacobs and April Kelly), 158n1
Glow (Liz Flahive and Carly Mensch), 67
Goonies, The (Richard Donner), 58, 74–75
Grady, Constance, 27, 40, 44
Grainge, Paul, 2

Grand Theft Auto (Rockstar Games), 67, 158n8
Great Replacement conspiracy, 105, 117–118

Hardisty, Jean, 105
Harris, Kamala, 9
Hegel, Georg Wilhelm Friedrich, 6, 43, 148, 155n3
hegemony, 7, 106, 141
Hibberd, James, 27
Hillbilly Elegy (J. D. Vance): on culture, 120, 123, 124, 126, 128–132; hillbilly framing of, 119; as melodrama, 124, 126, 128, 130–132; overview of, 116–118; popularity of, 116; and race, 117–120, 122–127, 128, 131–132, 138–139, 142, 160n2; and right-wing politics, 116–118, 126, 130, 132–133; violence in, 130–131
Hillbilly Elegy (Ron Howard), 116, 124
Hives, The, 67
Hoare, George, 147
Hochschild, Arlie Russell, 109–114, 138, 159n1
Hochuli, Alex, 147
Hofer, Johannes, 10–11
HoSang, Daniel, 113–114, 115, 121
Hours Have Lost Their Clock, The (Grafton Tanner), 150
Hudson, Laura, 26, 39, 48
Hughes, John, 49–51
Hussain, Murtaza, 137
Hutcheon, Linda, 12
hyper aestheticization, 19, 57–58, 92, 132. *See also* aestheticization
Hypernormalisation (Adam Curtis), 29

iconography, 12, 69
identity formation, 19
ideology: and the end of history, 7–9, 21; in the fantasy genre, 92; neofascist, 118; in *Ready Player One*, 45–46, 51–52; right-wing, 105, 117–118, 132, 140, 159n1, 159n1; in *Stranger Things*, 69, 73–74, 76
I Love the '80s/'70s/'90s (TV series), 25, 67
InfoWars, 70
Instagram, 23, 68
Isenberg, Nancy, 116
It (Andy Muschietti), 67
It (Stephen King), 64, 75

Jackson, Kentucky, 120, 126–127, 129
Jameson, Fredric, 4–5, 8, 14–17, 36–37, 39, 92
John Birch Society, 104

Karp, Matthew, 115
Keightley, Emily, 11, 150
kitsch, 50, 66
Klee, Miles, 143, 162n16
Klee, Paul, 2
Kojève, Alexandre, 6, 155n3
Kornbluh, Anna, 14–15, 42, 147, 156n9

Lewis, C. S., 145
liberal politics, 149
Lizardi, Ryan, 2, 13
Lorde, Audre, 150
Losing Ground (Charles Murray), 121
Lotf, Rachid, 162n16
Louisiana, 109, 111, 115, 159n1
Lowndes, Joseph E., 113–114, 115, 121
Lynch, David, 88, 102, 159n6. See also *Fire Walk with Me*; *Twin Peaks: The Return*

Mad Men (Matthew Weiner), 67, 84
MAGA. *See* Make American Great Again (MAGA) campaign
Make American Great Again (MAGA) campaign, 8, 104–105, 112, 137
Marxism, 133, 143–144
McCaffrey, Matthew, 70
McGowan, Todd, 92, 94–95
mediation, 3, 10–11, 14, 16, 72, 101, 151
melodrama: of *Bronze Age Mindset*, 135–137, 140; and conservatism, 112; defined, 106–107; and generative AI, 144–146; of *Hillbilly Elegy*, 117–118, 121, 124–126, 130–133; and nostalgia, 107, 109; as political discourse, 106; of the "retvrn" movement, 133, 141–143; of *Strangers in Their Own Land*, 109–113; of the "trad" movement, 133; and victimization, 108, 111; and the white working class, 113, 115–116, 132
Menand, Louis, 5
Meta, 23
Middleton, Jason, 61–62
Middletown, Ohio, 37–38, 118–119, 123–124, 126–127, 156nn3–4
millennials, 13, 64, 144, 157n6, 157n9
misogyny, 134, 136, 139
misrecognition, 99–101, 103
modernity, 11, 17, 64, 82, 133, 137–138, 140, 141, 145
Monty Python and the Holy Grail (Terry Gilliam and Terry Jones), 25, 38
Moynihan Report (Daniel Patrick Moynihan), 121

multiculturalism, 42, 112, 133
Murphy, James, 12
Murray, Charles, 120–121
music, 12, 24, 26, 52, 67–69, 81, 83, 101

Nadel, Alan, 73
Nance, Jack, 159n5
Nelson, Samantha, 40, 48
neofascism. *See* fascism
neoliberalism: Cline and, 49; and economics, 102, 108, 162n1; and the end of history, 7, 17, 21, 42–43, 87, 102, 147–148, 152, 155n6; and identity, 19; in the late twentieth century, 3–4; and politics, 148–149, 152, 162n2; postmodern, 143; in *Ready Player Two*, 4; and white nostalgia, 62, 113–114, 128, 132, 141
New Deal politics, 113, 162n1
New Right movement, 105, 133–134, 136–142, 144, 161n7, 162n2, 162n14
Niemeyer, Katherina, 156n10
9/11, 107
"1999" (Charli XCX), 12
Nochimson, Martha, 97
nostalgia: and alienation, 18; Benjamin on, 2; borrowed, 12–13; cultural impact of, 21; cyclical nature of, 10; etymology of, 10–11; experiential, 2, 158n9; and fantasy, 91–92; Hofer on, 10–11; as impetus for social change, 150–151; Jameson on, 14–17; mediated, 1–3, 11–13, 18, 42, 78, 102, 158n9; and melodrama, 107, 109; posthistorical, 10; reflective-age, 14, 17–18, 58, 79, 93, 109, 133, 145; reflective vs. restorative, 17–18; restorative, 104
nostalgia films, 14–16, 67
nostalgia TV, 10, 85, 91, 95–96, 101, 103

Obama, Barack, 8–9, 160
Our Ohio Renewal, 160n4
outrun (musical genre), 67

parody, 16, 57
pastiche, 14, 16, 31, 58, 69, 74, 87, 157n1
Pickering, Michael, 11, 150
playlist past, 13
political discourse, 8, 106, 116, 140
posthistorical politics, 108, 162n1
postmodernism, 14–17, 39, 143
postmodernity, 14, 17, 133, 143
Pretty in Pink (Howard Deutch), 51, 60
Prince, 52–53
Putin, Vladimir, 8, 156n7

QAnon, 105

race: in *Bel-Air*, 85; in *Bronze Age Mindset*, 137–138, 141; and economics, 114, 124; in *Hillbilly Elegy*, 117–120, 122–127, 128, 131–132, 138–139, 142, 160n2; and melodrama, 21, 106–108, 118–119; and nostalgia, 21; and politics, 20, 112–113; prejudice based on, 6, 49; in *Ready Player One*, 44–46; in *Ready Player Two*, 45–48, 52; and the retvrn movement, 133, 141; in *Stranger Things*, 20, 49, 62, 74–78; and transposition, 121–122, 125–126; in *Twin Peaks: The Return*, 94
racial transposition, 121–123, 125
racism, 107, 123, 136–137, 159n1
Ravela, Christian, 116
Ready Player One (Ernest Cline): and class, 51–52; critical agenda of, 26, 35; cultural objects in, 24–25, 36, 38, 46; as dystopian entertainment, 28; and the end of history, 149; and gender, 44–46; and identity, 42–44; and nostalgic space, 37–38; overview of, 22–26, 30–31; and pastiche, 31; pessimism of, 35; and postmodernism, 37, 39; and race, 44–46; and sexuality, 44–46; technology in, 23, 38; tropes in, 27; view of democracy in, 36
Ready Player Two (Ernest Cline): and class, 51–52; and the end of history, 149; and gender, 46–49; and identity, 44, 46–49, 149; overview of, 33–35; pessimism of, 35; and race, 46, 48–49; and sexuality, 46–49, 53; technology in, 33–34, 46
Reagan, Ronald: economics of, 5, 14, 158n11, 159n3; and nostalgia, 64, 72–73, 139, 143; politics of, 70–71, 105, 107, 134; as symbol, 61, 63
Reaganism, 59
reboots: commentary on, 20; and diversity, 159n4; and idealization, 100; and optimism, 93; and the past, 10, 20, 101; vs. revivals, 91, 95; themes in, 85–87, 96–97; volume of, 1, 84, 87
recognition politics, 42, 108
"Reflektor" (Arcade Fire), 1–3, 18
Reich, Elizabeth, 62
religion, 6, 7, 23, 24
remakes, 1, 15, 67, 83–85, 116
retromania, 1, 22, 26, 83
retrotopia, 2

retvrn movement, 133–136, 139–142, 161n6, 162n14
revivals: commentary on, 20; fashion, 12; and the past, 10, 20, 101; vs. reboots, 91, 95
Reynolds, Simon, 1, 11, 67, 83
right-wing politics: of the 2010s, 19, 21; discourse of, 113; in *Hillbilly Elegy*, 116–118, 126, 130, 132–133; in John Hughes films, 19, 21; and melodrama, 19, 21; and national identity, 17; and populism, 7, 108, 113; as reactionary, 105
Robin, Corey, 105
Robinson, Nathan J., 135, 160n4
Roe v. Wade, 150
Rufo, Christopher, 143
Russia, 7, 158n7
Rust, Amy, 62

Sanders, Bernie, supporters of, 115, 162n1
Saved by the Bell (2020, Tracey Wigfield and Sam Bobrick), 85–86, 159n4
Schager, Nick, 41
Scott, A. O., 30–31
sexuality: in *Ready Player One*, 44–46; in *Ready Player Two*, 46–49
Silva, Frank, 159n5
simulacra, 16, 18, 36–38, 57, 73–74, 128, 145
Singh, Nikhil Pal, 114
slavery, 119
Smith, Lacey N., 73–74
Smith, Steven, 135
social media, 23, 56, 68, 133–134
socioeconomic decline, 104
Soviet Union, 4, 5, 7, 61, 66
Space Jam: A New Legacy (Malcolm D. Lee), 156n5
Spencer, Richard, 161n7
Spielberg, Steven, 39–40, 64, 66, 68, 156n1
Stand by Me (Rob Reiner), 12, 62
Stanton, Harry Dean, 159n5
Star Wars (George Lucas), 15–16, 25, 157n3
Strangers in Their Own Land (Arlie Russell Hochschild), 20, 109–114, 137, 138, 159n1
Stranger Things (Duffer Brothers): aesthetic of, 16, 20, 36, 57–58; conservatism of, 70–72; and the end of history, 149; heteronormativity of, 60–61; interpretations of, 59; marketing for, 56–57; and the past, 10, 12, 16, 20; and race, 20, 49, 62, 74–78; references in, 39, 60; vision of the 1980s in, 61–63
Strauss, Leo, 105, 136, 159n3, 161n10
streaming services, 11, 13, 56, 83–84
Strokes, The, 15, 67, 83
Supreme Court, 150
synthwave (musical genre), 67, 69

Tanner, Grafton, 104, 150
Tea Party (political movement), 20, 104, 108–111, 115, 148, 159–160n1
tech boom, 5
television: and ideology, 73; and nostalgia, 2–3, 10–12, 16, 43, 62–64, 67, 69, 84–85, 91, 95–96, 101, 103, 158n8; remakes on, 1, 83–85, 116. *See also* nostalgia TV
Thompson, Jason, 34, 156n2
TikTok, 23, 68, 133
Tooze, Adam, 147
traditionalism, 105, 113, 133
Tradwives, 133
Truly Disadvantaged, The (William Julius Williams), 120–121
Trump, Donald: elections of, 20, 108, 115–116, 148; humor of, 135; and J.D. Vance, 117; and MAGA, 104–105, 137; and nostalgia, 8–9; supporters of, 112, 114–115
Tu, Thuy Linh, 114
tulpas, 100
Twin Peaks: The Final Dossier (Mark Frost), 101
Twin Peaks: The Return (David Lynch and Mark Frost): as classical epic, 97; cruel optimism of, 102–103; doppelgängers in, 88–89, 99–100; and the end of history, 149; and fantasy, 102; and gender, 94–95; and identity, 101; overview of, 87–91; as posthistorical epic, 98; reconstructive impulse of, 96; sexual violence in, 94; and the televisual past, 96; tulpas in, 100
2008 financial crisis, 7–8, 113, 128
2016 primary elections, 115

Ukraine, 7, 148, 156n7, 158n7
Uncle Tom's Cabin (Harriet Beecher Stowe), 107
Urban Outfitters, 13

Vance, J. D.: on birthrates, 117; early life of, 118–119, 124, 126; grandparents of, 126, 129–131; politics of, 117–118; Senate campaign, 117; as supporter of Bronze Age Pervert, 134; at Yale Law School, 116, 124–126. See also *Hillbilly Elegy* (J. D. Vance)

VanDerWerff, Emily, 97, 101
vaporwave (musical genre), 67, 150
victimization, 20, 106–108, 111–112, 124–126, 128, 137–139

WarGames (John Badham), 24, 38
War on Terror, 107
Washington Post, 117
welfare, 107, 110, 120, 122–123, 131
whiteness: hegemonic, 8; in *Hillbilly Elegy*, 118–119, 125–126, 128, 132–133; in *Strangers in Their Own Land*, 113; in *Stranger Things*, 74–75, 78; "wages of," 113–115, 121, 126, 128, 132, 162n2. *See also* race
white nostalgia, 59, 62, 74, 76–77
White Stripes, The, 67, 83
White Trash (Nancy Isenberg), *116*
Williams, Linda, 106, 112, 124
Williams, William Julius, 120–121
Winant, Gabriel, 117–118, 125, 130, 160n3
@wokal_distance. *See* Young, Michael
Wonder Years, The (Neal Marlens and Carol Black), 12, 62
Wood, Graeme, 135, 140, 161n9

XCX, Charli (Charlotte Aitchison), 12

Yale Law School, 116, 124–126
Yarvin, Curtis, 135
Young, Michael, 142–144, 162n16

Žižek, Slavoj, 7, 36
Zuckerberg, Mark, 23

About the Author

Zachary Griffith teaches in the Department of Writing, Rhetoric, and Digital Studies at the University of Kentucky. His research examines twentieth- and twenty-first-century American literature, television, film, and culture.